THE NEIGHBORHOOD FORAGER

The

NEIGHBORHOOD
FORAGER

A Guide for the Wild Food Gourmet

Robert K. Henderson

CHELSEA GREEN PUBLISHING COMPANY

White River Junction, Vermont

Totnes, Devon

Designed by Suzanne Church.

This book is not intended to be used for identifying plants. Readers should use it in conjunction with at least one, and preferably several, reliable field guides. Important features to look for in a field guide are comprehensive coverage of plants in the region and clear color photos or detailed drawings.

This book is not a medical guide, either. Material contained herein on medicinal herbs is for information only. Medicinal herbs should be used in consultation with a qualified professional.

Finally, neither the author nor the publisher are responsible for allergic reactions or other illnesses readers may experience. Though all the plants described in this book are documented edibles, it is impossible to foresee all complications that may be brought on by individual circumstances. Readers should therefore observe first-try protocol as explained in chapter 1.

Printed in the United States.
First printing, June 2000.
Printed on acid-free, recycled paper.

03 02 01 00   1 2 3 4 5

Library of Congress Cataloging-in-Publication Data

Henderson, Robert K., 1962-
The neighborhood forager: finding and preparing delicious wild foods anywhere / Robert K. Henderson.
p.   cm.
Includes bibliographical references and index.
ISBN 1-890132-35-7 (alk. paper)
1. Cookery (Wild foods) 2. Wild plants, Edible. 3. Wild foods. I. Title.

TX823 .H423 2000
642.6—dc21   00-020327

Green Books Ltd
Foxhole, Dartington
Totnes, Devon TQ9 6EB, United Kingdom
44-1-803-863-843

Chelsea Green Publishing Company
P.O. Box 428
White River Junction, VT 05001
800-639-4099
www.chelseagreen.com

To my family, whose moral and financial support made my eccentric lifestyle possible.

To my wife Nathalie, who gamely tries everything I bring home at least once.

And to the memory of Euell Gibbons, whose foraging skills were forged in grinding poverty, whose spirit was open to all, and who invented the genre that sustains me, literally and figuratively.

To these, and to pioneers of every kind, this book is dedicated.

CONTENTS

74   four: The Remarkable Talents of Common Flowers

ACKNOWLEDGMENTS

*S*o many people help get a book into print that thanking them all by name would require another book. That said, I would like especially to thank the following people, who have been instrumental in putting this manuscript in readers' hands:

My wife and family, for supporting my transition from productive member of society to writer, and whose frank criticism continues to be an asset to my career. I would especially like to thank my mother, who suffered the raised eyebrows of others when I forgot my lunch in Grade 6 and foraged one from schoolyard weeds.

Jim Schley, Hannah Silverstein, and the whole Chelsea Green staff, for their patience and can-do attitude.

Andrea Pedolsky of the Altair Literary Agency, without whose nose for the business this book might never have happened.

The DeJong family, for their support, encouragement, and foraging rights on their property.

And finally, my heartfelt gratitude to Sir John A. MacDonald, founder of Canada, my home and chosen land.

— Detail: The spoon test.

Wild edibles are "in." Magazine articles are exploring the subject from every angle, from edible garden blossoms to foraging for homebrewing and winemaking ingredients, while continuing education programs increasingly include courses on wild herbs and foods. The cause of this sudden resurgence is no secret: North Americans are seeking simpler, healthier lifestyles, and it's only natural (so to speak) that they turn to the most organic of foods, those that grow without any human intervention at all. A bigger mystery is why so few books address the concerns of the majority of wild food foragers. Though most of the interest is among suburbanites, most guidebooks emphasize rural settings for wild gathering activities. This book sets out to change that. A new kind of guide, one that emphasizes foraging in one's own neighborhood, *The Neighborhood Forager* bridges the gap between rural theory and suburban practice.

The conventional view of foraging, as gathering wild food and medicine is called, obscures the fact that suburban areas actually offer richer pickings than more natural environments. The botanical diversity of an established residential neighborhood, with its weeds, intentionally introduced exotics, and feral or persistent plants, outstrips that of the average forest or meadow. Greater variety means greater opportunity for foragers. Certainly, the suburban environment presents challenges either absent or markedly reduced in rural areas. Chemical contamination is more prevalent, and there are a lot more property lines to deal with. Room for error is scant when surgically removing a dandelion from someone else's lawn. But the territory is familiar, the variety superb, and the bounty just beyond the door.

By taking advantage of little-known or forgotten resources in yards, gardens, and vacant lots, suburban dwellers can enjoy healthy and intriguing new foods, experience environmental dynamics first-hand, and get to know a fascinating, mysterious neighborhood other residents never see.

Grab a pith helmet. The safari begins on the front step.

A Brief History of Foraging

Before the start of the Industrial Revolution in the late eighteenth century, the forager played a vital if precarious role in human society. Tribal cultures, be they North America's First Nations, the Celtic and Germanic tribes of Western Europe, or Australian Aboriginals, all had a place for this figure. Some tribal foragers, called shamans, medicine men, or medicine women, exercised a largely religious function. Others were scouts or victuallers. In all cases, their secretive, eccentric lifestyle and arcane knowledge aroused the fear of the different that has been the root of all injustice since the dawn of time. Worse yet (for the individual forager, at any rate) was the fact that foragers often acted as healers. Insofar as knowledge of beneficial herbs implies knowledge of poisonous ones, the forager was viewed as a loose cannon. Perhaps the patient died of natural causes, and perhaps the forager's "medicine" helped her along. And what about the fellow who suggested as much, then slipped and bashed his brains out a few days later? Coincidence, or something else? Such ambiguity meant that healer-foragers frequently didn't survive the misfortune of others.

As tribal systems fell before the nation-state, foraging underwent a transformation.

Relieved of religious functions by a professional priesthood, foragers were free to specialize in healing and provisioning. Tribal scouts resurfaced as shepherds, wardens, and hired hunters. But the jealousy of the new religious elite, added to the eternal fear of different or solitary people, conspired to push foraging underground. Court records dating into the eighteenth century reveal that only an audience with the devil himself was more damning testimony in a witchcraft trial than "The accused was gathering strange herbs." Foragers continued to play a pivotal role in medicine and victualling, but from even deeper in the shadows. To society's gatekeepers, they remained suspicious characters.

The coming of the steam engine spelled the end of foraging as a practical skill. As urban society supplanted rural as the cultural ideal, traditional activities were suddenly viewed as backward. Grubbing for roots and weeds in the dirty outdoors was decidedly uncool. From useful if potentially dangerous specialists, foragers were busted down to unlettered, feeble-minded hillbillies.

Foraging didn't die out completely, to be sure. Appalachian mountain peoples, Latin Americans, Scottish Highlanders, African tribespeople, First Nations peoples, and other cultures already so marginalized that they had little to lose, continued to view foraging as a valuable skill. Yet anthropological monographs published before the mid-twentieth century contain surprisingly little detail about the plants these peoples gathered, or what they did with them. In the academic view, such information was of little value.

So matters remained until the end of World War II. Fueled by affluence, cheap gas, and army surplus gear, postwar North Americans took to the outdoors with gusto. A

What's in a Name?

Everybody knows the story of Columbus: he sailed west, bumped into the Americas, and declared that he'd discovered a shortcut to India. Whatever else Columbus may have been, he was no geographer; even the remarkably non-Asian peoples he met didn't faze him. He confidently proclaimed them all "Indians." To make matters worse, each successive wave of newcomers repeated his nonsense. Now, five centuries later, these peoples are weary of the joke.

But to date, most of the proposed alternatives have been hardly better. "Native American" is wrong on all counts: anyone born here is "native" regardless of race, and "American" usually means "from the U.S.," which excludes Canadian and Latin American bands. "American Indian" and the utterly logic-free "Native Indian" don't solve anything. And what about the Inuit and Aleut, Arctic peoples entirely different from the "Indians?" What's worse, many of the band designations that Europeans pinned on people are disputed today.

In Canada, where indigenous cultures enjoy a high political profile, this is a vital issue. Canadians have tried "Native," on the theory that the capital N makes it a proper noun, and therefore "above logic." When that argument proved unconvincing, they turned to "aboriginal peoples." This passes the logic test, and is still widely used in Canada, but many people associated "aboriginal" with Australia. So Canadians forged on to what seems to me to be the ultimate solution: First Nations. This designation covers all the bases: distinct cultural and political entities who aren't from India; who were here before Old Worlders arrived; who don't necessarily have anything in common with each other; and who live all over North and South America, but not in Australia.

So, in this book I usually refer to the aboriginal peoples of the Americas as the First Nations.

whole industry rose around outdoor sports. With the boom in camping, hiking, and other pastimes came a demand for information on "survival foods." These were wild plants that, however unpleasant, a lost person might eat, to stave off starvation until help arrived. Into the vacuum stepped master forager Bradford Angier, who penned a dozen books on this and other "outdoor" subjects. To his credit, Angier did suggest that wild edibles might be enjoyed for their own sake—that starvation wasn't a prerequisite to appreciating them. Nevertheless,

Angier is considered a writer of the survival genre, perhaps to his chagrin.

In 1962, Euell Gibbons's *Stalking the Wild Asparagus* slipped onto the market. The book was not an immediate sensation, but outdoorspeople and Scout leaders purchased copies in sufficient numbers to keep it in print. In the decade that followed, North Americans began to question the conventional worldview pitting humanity against nature, and to formulate a new one based on the concept of harmony and sustainability. Called "back-to-nature," the new doctrine urged a distrust of manufactured goods and an acceptance of lifestyles in which earning and spending money were not the sole objectives. *Stalking the Wild Asparagus* dovetailed perfectly with this new ethos, catapulting Euell Gibbons to continental celebrity and bringing him financial security for the first time in his life.

For a moment it looked as if foraging might even become mainstream. Its ultimate failure to do so is reflected in jokes from the early 1970s: "Did you hear Euell Gibbons died?" "No, how?" "He choked on Astroturf!" Gibbons's quirky television commercials ("Ever eat a pine tree?") did little to improve his eccentric reputation. His "many parts are edible" follow-up remained a comic catch phrase for years. Yet Gibbons's central message, that wild foods are superior to those sold in stores, had clearly struck a chord. Today, the gourmet wild foods genre he invented boasts a whole shelfful of books, of which this is one.

Foraging Today

Outside the military, where survival foraging is an art and a science, modern foragers gather wild herbs not for subsistence, but for their gastronomic or medicinal value, and for the thrill of the hunt. When questioned, we may appeal to healthy living, holistic medicine, or self-sufficiency, but in the end, these are just pretexts. Foragers gather and prepare wild foods for the same reason well-heeled city dwellers try a different restaurant every Friday night. We like pleasant surprises, and the only way to get them is to try new things. The sole difference between foragers and restaurant-hoppers is the effect our respective hobbies have on our bank accounts.

The passion for the chase and satisfaction of reward are identical.

Not that this has done anything to alter foragers' eccentric image. Polite society still regards us as weird, as indeed it always has. Yet I've found foraging to be an excellent icebreaker, a way to meet people in the neighborhood. One autumn my wife and I gathered butternuts beside a paved, heavily travelled trail in a local park. In the hour we spent picking pointy nuts out of the grass, we had a dozen pleasant conversations with passersby. Each began with a friendly, "Whatcha pickin' up there?" and ended with a smile and a new acquaintance.

Then too, some suburban foragers integrate themselves into society along lines strikingly familiar to those of us who know our history. When I moved into a trailer park a few years ago, my wandering around, poking into obscure corners, and "gathering strange herbs" excited a certain amount of consternation. But the neighbors soon realized that I was harmless, and the landlord even told me he appreciated my activities, since I knew the park well, covered the territory often, and would surely spot suspicious goings-on in time to alert the police. His remark made me smile. I had assumed the ancient forager role of tribal scout.

Foragers have been considered odd for millions of years. Today is no different, and there's no reason to expect tomorrow will be, either. Rather than fight it, I've decided to love it. Such cultural continuity is rare indeed, and I'm proud to carry on the tradition. Besides, every neighborhood needs local color, something that reminds folks of humanity's fundamentally irrepressible nature.

In my neighborhood, I'm it.

What Is a Suburban Wild Edible?

Suburban foraging differs from traditional rural foraging in several respects. To begin with, the preindustrial societies that sustained the first foragers engaged mostly in team-oriented tasks that blended work with recreation. They made specialized labor and machinery available on a partly or wholly reciprocal basis, and profited from the lulls in daily and seasonal cycles. By contrast, suburbanites lead scheduled, cash-based lives. Their work patterns remain constant, month in, month out, regardless of weather or season. Industrial society distinguishes sharply between work and recreation, and access to equipment, supplies, and skills is strictly on a cash basis.

For these reasons, if it's going to work, suburban foraging has to be time- and cost-effective. Tasks calling for specialized skills or equipment must be reduced as far as possible. Most importantly, it has to be fun.

In response to these needs, this book emphasizes plants that:

·   have many uses, or answer a few universal needs;
·   require about the same processing skills as cultivated crops;
·   are largely available in urbanized areas;
·   are common across at least two-thirds of subarctic North America (with a few interesting exceptions thrown in).

In the same vein, this book does not include:

·   wild edibles that require leaching, multiple boilings, or other intensive preparation;
·   species easily confused with poisonous look-alikes, unless there is a simple and reliable identification gimmick;
·   mushrooms, because identifying mushroom species is an exact science and errors can be catastrophic.

Tools of the Trade

As a hobby, foraging requires refreshingly little in the way of financial investment. The fact is, a whole legion of foragers could be amply outfitted with the budget of just one average golfer. Most of our equipment can itself be foraged from recyclable items and materials, and keeping a sharp eye out at thrift stores and garage sales may fill remaining gaps for very little money. The following tools will enable you to handle most foraging challenges. (Digging implements are discussed in chapter 6.)

Berry hook. Like the hobby itself, the standard foraging accessory is as low-tech as it gets: it's a walking stick with a hook on the end. This tool extends the forager's reach into trees and across ditches, and pulls branches and vines into picking range. When foraging was a rural activity, a natural crook formed the hook. These days, most berry hooks are no more lyrical than a broomstick or length of bamboo with a large hook screwed to one end. The ensemble must be light enough to manipulate easily with one hand, yet sturdy enough not to break under stress. One of the best berry hooks I ever had was what remained of a hoe after the blade

Berry hook.

had broken off. The bent metal shaft formed a robust hook, capable of pulling down branches without breaking or bending. Though the hardwood handle was a bit heavy, the broken hoe answered the call.

Field scale. The berry hook can also be made into a serviceable field scale. Hang an ordinary white plastic shopping bag (the kind in which supermarkets bag groceries, with two loops for handles) on the hook and place an 8-ounce unopened food can in it. Hold your free hand out as if preparing to shake hands with someone and balance the handle across the base of your index finger. Mark the point where it balances "$1/2$ pound." Then replace the small can with a 15- or 16-ounce can,

Pruning shears.

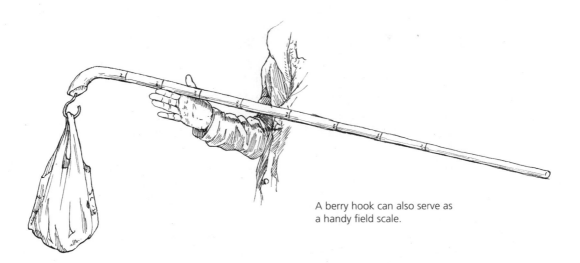

A berry hook can also serve as a handy field scale.

and balance the handle again. This time, label the balance point "1 pound." Return the small can to the bag with the large one, balance the handle again, and label the new balance point "1½ pounds." By continuing in this fashion, you can calibrate the berry hook to measure up to 3 pounds with sufficient precision to tell when enough berries for a pie have been picked. But if the weight of the berry hook changes, as when a green branch dries out or the bark peels away, all bets are off.

Plastic shopping bags. Available free from most supermarkets, these bags are an environmental disaster, blowing through the streets and green spaces of the entire world, choking wildlife and smothering plants. So it's just as well that we put them to good use. I stuff plastic shopping bags into the pockets of my coat, my bike's handlebar bag, the glove box, my backpack, my briefcase—in fact, anything that might come to hand when wild edibles turn up. Plastic shopping bags scrunch down to almost nothing, then unfurl like new when needed. They are also lightweight, and the plastic protects contents from drying out or wilting until I get it home. (Foragers must make sure that dirty or torn bags, having been reused until they can't be reused anymore, end up in a recycling bin or at least a garbage can, where they aren't free to tumble across the earth's surface, killing everything in sight.)

Pruning shears. For collecting berry clusters and small branches, my weapon of choice is a pair of pruning shears, the kind with curved blades that lock closed when not in use. Serviceable ones can be had for little money in hardware stores and garden centers. I slip them into my back pocket before going out on a foray, and they make short work of tasks such as grooming blackberry patches, nipping off sumac cones, or snipping the heads off marigolds. They also come in handy in processing.

A mortar and pestle is useful for grinding herbs and seeds. Consisting of a heavy marble cup, or mortar, with a matching marble cylinder called a pestle (some pestles are made of hardwood), this simple device has been grinding herbs for thousands of years. Many people are surprised to learn that mortars, while no longer common household tools, are available from many department stores and kitchen equipment stores. In the absence of a real mortar, a sturdy coffee mug and a length of broomstick or a wooden spoon handle may do the job. On the other extreme are home grain mills, available from rural hardware stores, homebrewing suppliers, and mail-order houses specializing in homesteading equipment. They vary widely in price and quality, but good ones cost a few hundred dollars new. Foragers who grind large quantities of seed may wish to invest in one.

Food mills, on the other hand, are a lot simpler and cheaper than the name suggests. The most basic one is a funnel-shaped colander in a wire stand. Soft fruits are piled inside and forced through the mesh with a round wooden pin. This creates a fine, seedless mash for jams, juices, and the like. Called a chinois (sheen-WA, French for "Chinese," though I don't know what the connection is), this tool was a common household utensil when most families made their own preserves. Today, chinois food mills are mostly found in antique shops and homesteading catalogues.

In the meantime, a minimally mechanical device called a hand food mill has taken its place. This looks like a large metal or plastic bowl with notched horizontal legs sticking out from the bottom like spokes and a crank fixed to a brace in the top. In place of the bowl's bottom is a cone-shaped screen. When the crank is turned, a metal plate rubs against this screen, forcing soft foods through. The notched legs fit over the rim of a pan or bowl to catch the seeded pulp and juice as it drips out. Hand food mills offer the advantage of interchangeable screens, allowing the operator to adjust the texture of the final product or exclude seeds of different sizes.

The most important feature of any hand food mill is sturdy construction. I purchased mine from a thrift store for three dollars. Though I was initially skeptical of this disco-era orange gizmo, the French-made device quickly won me over. Its heavy-gauge plastic has proven up to the task, earning it a garish place among our cast iron and enamelware.

Squares of muslin (the cotton cloth of which bed sheets are made) are another important tool. Generally about the size of a bandana handkerchief, such squares strain jelly and juice, wrap drying materials, and perform other tasks that call for light, strong, permeable fabric. Muslin squares are squeezed and wrung without mercy, so they wear out fast. I wash worn-out sheets and pillowcases and fold them away, ready to be recycled into replacement squares.

Lidded containers. Finally, foraging calls for a range of airtight storage containers. I like to keep as many promising bottles, tubs, and jugs on hand as possible. (My wife is less enthusiastic; in the course of our marriage, the Empty Vessel Treaty has been renegotiated many times.) The most useful containers are made of plastic or glass and have airtight caps or lids. (Many foraging-related liquids are salty, acidic, or alcoholic, so a nonreactive lid is a plus.) Clear plastic jars with plastic lids are ideal, as are the round plastic tubs that salsa and other deli foods come in. Corked wine bottles are perfect for wines, cordials, vinegars, oils, and tinctures. Green or amber ones are best, as they help shield their contents from the harmful effects of light. Plastic soda bottles and lidded buckets are also handy. But only food containers are eligible for consideration. Others may be contaminated with any number of spectacularly poisonous chemicals, even after repeated washing.

The Invisible Tools

Equally as important as the tools in the closet are those stored in the forager's skull. They're a little harder to acquire, since even wealthy foragers (assuming

Getting Those Stupid Labels Off

Plastic jars and bottles may be disastrous for the environment, but they are a boon to foragers. Lightweight, nonreactive, unbreakable, and usually airtight, plastic containers are perfect for storing dried herbs and other treasures. Reusing them reduces waste and environmental impact much more effectively than labor- and chemistry-intensive industrial recycling.

The only hitch is those stupid labels. Most glues don't stick to plastic, so the ones used to stick labels on it have to be practically bulletproof. Unlike glass containers, plastic ones can't be de-labelled by soaking in hot water. Scrubbing scratches up the plastic, and even then it only removes the paper. Tacky glue remains to stick to hands and attract dirt.

But removing labels from plastic containers is deceptively easy once you know how. For success every time, without scratched containers or residual glue, follow this simple procedure:

1. Apply a thick coat of cooking oil to the label in question.
2. Allow it to soak in, undisturbed, for 24 hours.
3. Try to peel the label off. If it comes readily, proceed to the next step. If it doesn't, repeat steps 1 and 2. (Many labels require two applications; some take several.)
4. After the label has been peeled off, some sticky, partly dissolved glue will remain. To remove it, coat the area with oil a final time and allow it to sit overnight.
5. Wipe off the oil and dissolved glue, then wash the container in hot, soapy water. No trace of label or glue will remain.

there are any) can't buy them. The good news is, they never break, they never get lost or stolen, and they're helpful for a range of life's challenges. Those who put in the effort to develop these skills soon wonder how they ever got along without them.

A Broad Palate

North Americans suffer from a notoriously narrow palate. Specifically, we like sweet or salty flavors. We tolerate tart foods if they are heavily sugared, but despise any hint of bitterness. Our draconian food preferences deny us delights that others relish. The joy of real Scottish marmalade, with bitter, sour, and sweet nuances that compete for the tongue's attention, is lost on North Americans. The substance sold as "marmalade" on this continent is just orange jelly, and cloyingly sweet at that. Olive oil, mustard, beer, cheese, chocolate, and lemonade have all suffered similar indignities here.

Broadening a narrow palate is really a question of values. Euell Gibbons noted the connection between palate and tolerance, and how rarely one finds narrowness of one and breadth of the other in the same individual. Of all perfunctory personality tests, I've found this one most reliable. Open, adventurous diners are seldom interested in enforcing conformity among their neighbors or closing their communities to those who are different. I've never met a bigoted forager.

The most effective way to broaden your palate is to make a simple resolution: "From now on, food will be given every opportunity to please me. Only after I've tried every possible angle will I write off any new food." This does not mean that every new food will please. Rather, it represents a commitment to try a new food until an acceptable way to enjoy it turns up. Many cherished dishes are an acquired taste.

Others simply require another approach. For example, I detest organ meat as a general rule. This might seem problematic for a person of Scottish origin, yet I love haggis, Scotland's national dish, which is made from several different sheep organs. Specialized preparation renders haggis not merely acceptable, but superb in my estimation. How much poorer I would be had I invoked my hatred of "innards" and struck it untried from my menu.

As new foods, wild edibles should be approached from several different perspectives. Those that taste unpleasant raw may be better cooked. Many are only palatable at a certain time of year, or differ widely with environmental variables. Those too strong to be eaten alone are often delicious in concert with other ingredients. And many are simply acquired tastes. Eaten sparingly but often, they can become valued foodstuffs. Try to take all of these points into consideration when a wild food first enters your diet.

Awareness

Most suburban residents live and work in temperature- and light-controlled environments. If they notice seasonal changes at all, it's from the viewpoint of the way they affect the daily commute to work. In winter, windshields must be scraped and snow chains mounted; summer is the time of hot, sticky car interiors and traffic jams.

By contrast, foragers notice every fluctuation in the earth's yearly journey around the sun. We use terms such as "very early spring" and "the last few days of summer." Since our hobby demands careful attention to the outdoors, suburban foragers are in daily contact with the natural world. We're not just along for the ride. We live on this planet.

One of foraging's most satisfying rewards is awareness of and connection to our surroundings. What others call a weed, the forager calls food. Human and animal activity have a direct impact on our lives. Squirrels compete for pine nuts, birds for rowan berries. The highway department wipes out a median stand of sumac, depriving us of an important resource. But the area comes up in evening primrose the following spring, offering new possibilities.

Keen observation and sensitivity to environmental change are important foraging tools. In exchange, foragers renew their maternal relationship with the planet. Even ruralites seldom live so close to nature today. Each time that construction, debrushing, or other ecologically unfriendly activity eliminates a foraging area from my neighborhood, I feel it acutely. Part of my heartache can be traced to the loss of wealth, to put it in economic terms, but most of it comes from the deep mother-child relationship the area inspired by feeding me. Aboriginal peoples have eloquently described the grief with which they witnessed the destruction of their surroundings. The invaders dismiss their objections as nostalgia, or a sentimental but unprofitable attachment to the area's former natural beauty. As a forager, I can affirm that the anguish goes much deeper than that.

Foragers observe details that are all but invisible to others. (Indeed, a whole tribe of suburban plants, the peripherals, specialize in not being seen.) In the process, foragers edge themselves back into the natural order. Foraging reestablishes the link between the earth and dinner, not as a philosophical abstract, but as immediate reality.

Trail Savvy

Just as a backwoodsman must be able to read the forest, so too must foragers cultivate an intimate knowledge of the suburban jungle. By interpreting the signs, suburban foragers estimate how much of what kind of edibles may be available in a given location.

Older neighborhoods boast higher biodiversity than younger ones, because successive generations of residents have introduced their favorite plants. They also tend to have larger yards and more public areas, both formal and informal. But perhaps the most striking feature of older neighborhoods is the number of fruit and nut trees they harbor. Today such species are seldom planted in new suburbs because they interfere with lawn care and automobiles, and the modern, upwardly mobile family isn't interested in their fruits. This doesn't mean that new neighborhoods have nothing to offer, however. Persistent shrubs and trees are common, and lots of weeds, of course. Newer neighborhoods are also more likely to have resources such as kousa dogwood and heirloom flowers, which have only become popular in the last few years.

To judge the age of a given block, it's handy to have a general knowledge of local architectural history and changing fashions in neighborhood layout. Large front porches, tree-lined streets arranged in a grid, and narrow alleys are hallmarks of older neighborhoods. Wide, serpentine streets ending in cul-de-sacs appeared in the 1960s, but those that lack sidewalks and curbs were probably built in the 1970s. Most large North American cities have produced at least one book, usually written by a local architect, on historical neighborhoods. A book on the nearest urban center will equip foragers to map neighborhood development according to house styles. The age and type of exotic (non-native) yard trees provide other clues, as do the dates embedded in sidewalks and the style of iron fittings such as fire hydrants and manhole covers.

Local History

The best way to gain knowledge of local native plants is to study local native cultures. Chances are, many of the foods they ate (and may still eat) are still around, and as tasty and nutritious as ever. First Nations lore is usually weak on introduced plants, but strong on indigenous ones that may not be covered in manuals of continental scope.

A bit of historical research may also reveal why previous generations introduced plants that have since become wild or feral. Though some exotics came to North America accidentally, most were intentionally planted to fill specific needs. Ironically, it's often harder to find such information about settler cultures than about the aboriginal cultures they displaced, but it is worth looking for. Probably the best-known and most widely available work on the subject is the Foxfire series, a multi-volume compendium on Appalachian culture written by high-school students in Georgia (see Further Reading).

The Botanical Bureaucracy

Botanical taxonomy—the classification of plants—is the key to positive identification and the confidence it fosters. Starting at the top, every organism on the planet can be sorted into a kingdom, phylum, class, order, family, genus, and species. The system is not immutable; even the kingdoms get reshuffled from time to time, while genera and species perpetually jockey for position. However, those

What's "Wild"?

Just as foraging differs in suburbia, so too does the definition of "wild" plants. Traditionally, wild plants are those not planted by humans. However, introduced plants that have escaped or outlasted cultivation have profoundly altered all North American environments, from the inner city to the deepest wilderness.

The greater part of intentionally introduced urban plants serve no material purpose; that is, they aren't used as food or to meet other constructive ends. Rather, most urban greenery is for decoration only. Many of these plants owe their presence in human-dominated environments to low maintenance and an ability to fade into the background. Insofar as they thrive independently of human intervention, they are "wild" in suburban terms. On the other hand, many species have ridden recent native plant gardening trends back into neighborhoods from which they had long vanished. Are such plants wild or domesticated? It's hard to say. What is certain is that ornamentals are not considered food in this place and time, and so are the province of foragers. By that definition, all of them are "wild."

organisms whose scientific names are in dispute can still be identified by their former or alternate names, and no two plants share the same one. The discipline of this system makes it a far safer guide for foragers than common names, which vary widely in different locales and periods.

Foragers are primarily concerned with the lowest two categories, genus and species. (Subspecies and variety names are usually insignificant for foraging.) Genus and species are italicized when both are cited. Genus may be abbreviated to its first letter after the first citation. When following a common name, genus and species citations are placed between parentheses. While genus names often appear by themselves, species names are never cited alone. Thus, the genus *Rubus* includes red raspberry (*Rubus idaeus*), thimbleberry (*R. parviflorus*), and blackcap (*R. leucodermis*).

Being able to identify different genera (the plural form of genus) is a most important skill, because species within a particular genus generally share culinary and medicinal characteristics. Generic relationships may also reveal surprising and useful details about certain plants, such as the close kinship of field mustard (*Brassica campestris*) with cabbage (*B. oleracea*). Members of a genus are not always interchangeable, however. Some taxonomists file poison ivy, poison oak, and poison sumac under the genus *Rhus*, alongside edible sumacs such as staghorn and squawbush. (Other botanists segregate the irritating species into a different genus, *Toxicodendron*.) The genus *Rumex*, on the other hand, claims both dock and sorrel—useful but remarkably different herbs. Such exceptions are rare, however. In most cases, different species belonging to the same genus have similar herbal properties.

Genus and species names are drawn from ancient common names, and, as such, they have meaning. While it can be illuminating to know what they mean, deciphering all of them requires a solid background in scientific etymology. Field guides may include translations of botanical names, but the following six turn up over and over and are worth knowing by heart:

- *edulis* (and forms thereof): edible.
- *esculentus* (and forms thereof): edible.
- *officinalis* (and forms thereof): for the laboratory. This title, which is something like a botanical knighthood, is conferred on about sixty plants judged most useful to herbal medicine. Species so honored are called "officinals."
- *oleraceus* (and forms thereof): garden vegetable. Most *oleraceus* species are still garden crops, but a few have struck out on their own in the wild.
- *sativus* (and forms thereof): domesticated. Some *sativus* species have since returned to weedhood, but the name remains between the parentheses to give new meaning to the term "inside joke."
- *vulgaris* (and forms thereof): common.

Due Caution

Nothing is as disheartening as those field guides that label practically every plant on the planet "poisonous." Certainly, if we are of a mind, we can prove that any plant is dangerous. Most edible plants cause allergic reactions in some individuals or have poisonous as well as edible parts. Some kill livestock that graze or overgraze on them. Yet if these considerations alone constitute proof of toxicity, almost no plant, wild or domestic, will make it to your table. Rhubarb, peaches, beans, tomatoes, and potatoes, to name just five, are virulently poisonous if the wrong part of the plant is eaten, or the right part is eaten the wrong way. In addition, all but potatoes have a high incidence of allergic reaction.

Certain pearls of folk wisdom regarding wild plant edibility are equally frustrating, and potentially much more dangerous. Perhaps the most prevalent of these myths is the infamous "bird principle." Anything that birds eat, so goes the saying, people can eat. What birds don't eat, people must earnestly avoid. This old canard came home to me rather dramatically one autumn day while I was collecting rowan berries. A man suddenly bolted out of a nearby apartment building, waving his arms and shouting, "Don't pick those! They're poisonous!" I assured him they were not, but he insisted. "Birds don't eat them! Stop picking those!" I was at a loss for words, since birds do in fact gorge themselves on rowan berries, but not until the nights dip toward freezing. I nervously continued nipping off clusters, and my would-be rescuer continued raving. Then a passerby joined in. "Look, the ground is covered with berries! The birds don't eat them! They'll kill you!" My bag full, I smiled apologetically and retreated. A few weeks later, neighborhood starlings stripped the tree bare.

So it is with great pleasure that I state here, for the record, that while animals eat or don't eat a given plant for any number of reasons, whether it's edible to humans is not one of their criteria. The most alarming aspect of the bird-based edibility test (aside from the fact that it may provoke onlookers

to go berserk) is that birds relish many foods that are poisonous to people. Bird-basers might decide to munch holly berries or the seeds of a leguminous tree, having observed birds doing likewise, and suffer serious consequences. Canny foragers do keep an eye on animals, because their behavior often signals seasonal changes. They are also our competitors. But however vocal starlings and jays may be in other contexts, they are silent on which plants we may safely eat.

Berry color schemes are another common fallacy. As a child, I learned that the mantra "white, no; red, maybe; blue, yes" would protect me from poisonous berries. Unfortunately, the first and last rules are demonstrably wrong. The only way to know if a given berry is edible is to identify it by botanical name and seek out reliable information about its edibility. There is no shortcut.

Commonsense Guidelines

When foraging, it is important to strike a healthy balance between raving hysteria and reckless abandon. Assiduously observed, the following rules replace both irrational caution and ill-informed folk dictums, and cut risk to manageable levels.

No plant is edible until it has been positively identified by its botanical name. This is the Prime Directive. Plants that "look just like edible plant X, except . . ." are not edible, nor are those identified by common name alone. Common names change from locality to locality, and the confusion can be lethal. For example, "thornapple" is a common name for both the genus *Crataegus*, which bears edible fruit, and the deadly poisonous genus *Datura*. Foragers must be certain of a plant's identity before they eat it.

- *The forager must know which parts of edible plants are edible, and under what conditions.* Until this information is known, no part of the plant is edible. Elder, for instance, bears tasty fruit, but its leaves and stems are virulently poisonous. What's more, red elderberries are edible cooked, but toxic when raw. Other wild (and domestic) edibles are similarly complex.

- *Any plant is poisonous to people who are allergic to it.* Those who are allergic to stone-bearing domestic fruits may be allergic to chokecherries as well. Allergies to beans and peanuts are common (and often violent), and clover, which is also a legume, may cause similar reactions in susceptible individuals. Some allergies can be fatal. Allergists can provide those who have known allergies with timely advice on which foods are suspect and how to test them. In any case, you must seek medical assistance immediately if you or others experience trouble breathing after eating a new food.

- *Successful foragers observe first-try protocol.* (The rest are dead.) When you have positively identified a new plant and its edible parts, taste just a little of it, prepared as required. Chew and swallow slowly, then wait at least two hours. If nausea, rash, sore throat, headache, or other reactions develop, more of the plant should only be eaten under an allergist's supervision. In most cases, you will experience no negative reactions. Next, eat about three times as much as before and wait again. If nothing happens, the food is probably safe.

  First-try protocol also affords an opportunity to limit damage from plants that are accidentally toxic, as when collected out of season or from a contaminated site. Further, any food can cause health problems if too much is eaten after a long abstinence, and as wild edibles are highly seasonal, they present the perfect opportunity to make this mistake. Regardless of past experiences, go easy on favorites when they reappear and work them gradually back into your diet. While allergic reactions are rare under such circumstances, nausea, diarrhea, and general misery often result from a sudden binge.

- *Most fruit pits enclose a poisonous seed.* Some, such as plum and cherry pits, are deadly. People can usually get away with swallowing a few, because the woody shell isolates the poisonous kernel from digestive acids. But should a hull be cracked for some reason, the swallower can find him or herself in real trouble. Children are particularly at risk. It's best to spit out all fruit pits, and teach children to do so as well.

- *Plants growing on roadsides and other high-traffic areas are best avoided.* In Euell Gibbons's day, this was Rule Number One because cars burned leaded gasoline. Horrifically poisonous lead compounds came streaming out of every exhaust pipe, and, being heavy, settled thickly on surrounding vegetation. Some plants, dandelions among them, fairly soak up lead, making them artificially toxic. Today leaded gasoline is all but extinct on this continent, and as a result, roadsides are less polluted. But plants growing along heavily travelled roads are still sprinkled with motor oil, gasoline, diesel fuel, other exhaust chemicals, and good old-fashioned grit. They aren't as poisonous as they were in 1962, but they aren't very appetizing, either.

Certain plants are toxic in large quantities. Even though they are perfectly all right in reasonable amounts, some plants can cause problems in people who gorge on them. Particularly noteworthy are acidic foods such as sumac, sorrel, strawberries, and tomatoes, and high-tannin ones such as acorns, rowan berries, and grapes. Although I have no allergies, I have experienced mild reactions from eating some of these foods to excess. Naturally, these foods also carry a high risk of bona fide allergic reaction, so foragers should rigorously observe first-try protocol before eating them or serving them to guests.

Eat wild foods only in season. Failure to observe this rule seldom has health consequences, though I once got sick on soup made from underripe knotweed shoots. However, while many foods are technically toxic when unripe or overripe, they usually taste unpleasant at this stage, so people rarely eat very much of them. But newcomers are likely to strike such foods off the list after the first try, denying themselves the pleasure of getting to know them in season. Wild plants are no different from domestic ones. Garden lettuce, radishes, and peas are unpalatable out of season, and so are wild lettuce, Japanese maple leaves, and dock. I wish I had a sack of young dandelion greens for every person who has told me that he or she tried dandelion leaves once, found them bitter, and never tried them again. Further investigation invariably reveals that the person ate the greens long after they could reasonably be expected to be palatable. Foragers must know what time of year a plant is edible, and eat it only then.

Using and Preserving the Harvest

Some recipes and preservation suggestions in this book call for skills that are becoming rare these days. The following paragraphs describe them in a general way, to give readers who may be unfamiliar with them an idea of what they entail. In addition, those who already have these skills may find a few hardearned pointers that will clear up the odd mysterious or persistent failure.

Canning

Canning many foods is a precise and expensive art, but suitable jars, canning lids, and a water bath canner are the only equipment required for the recipes found in this book. None requires the use of a pressure canner, and none is "processed," or boiled after the jar has been sealed. Therefore, any glass jar that will accept a canning lid can be used. Though the procedures are simple and straightforward, I strongly recommend additional reading beyond the basic instructions offered here. Many general-purpose cookbooks have sections on canning, and the Further Reading section lists some excellent sources of canning information and recipes.

When handling salty or corrosive food, including vinegar, pickles, wine, beer, and preserves, only implements made of impervious materials should be used. Such materials, called "nonreactive," include glass, crockery, wood, rubber, and plastic. Stainless steel is the only nonreactive metal used in kitchen implements. Aluminium, mild steel, copper, and cast iron are *not* nonreactive, and should not be used where nonreactive equipment is specified. Enamelware (iron or steel coated with a porcelain-like substance) in good condition is all right for cooking, but doesn't work for brining, fermenting, or other long-term projects. Hairline flaws in the coating, which is usually blue, black, or grey flecked with white, inevitably allow the metal below to contaminate such liquids.

Preserves are made by cooking fruit, pulp, or juice in sugar; these include jams, jellies, syrups, and sauces. This is canning at its easiest. Simply cook the recipe to a given point while sterilizing the jars and lids in boiling water. Then fill the jars with the mixture while both are still hot, screw the caps down tight, and leave the preserves to cool. When the slightly convex lid is sucked concave, usually with an audible pop, the process is complete.

Jams and jellies are jelled with pectin, a soluble fiber found naturally in many slightly underripe fruits, particularly apples. Refined pectin can also be bought in liquid or powdered form. Jam is made of fruit pulp and often contains seeds, though seedy fruits, or those with big seeds, are usually sieved or run through a food mill first. Jelly is made of juice strained through muslin. If appearance is unimportant, wringing the cooked and mashed pulp in the muslin after the juice has dripped through it produces a stronger-flavored final product. It can make the jelly hazy however. Insipid, overly sweet, or bitter fruits may make indifferent preserves by themselves, but complement other fruits nicely. In fact, pectin needs a certain amount of acid in order to thicken, so adding tart fruits or their juice may be necessary to get sweeter ones to jell. Some tart fruits, such as Oregon grapes, even supply their own pectin.

Getting jelly to jell is a bit of an art, even when all the necessary components are present. If jarred too soon, it doesn't jell. This is not an entire loss, as the result usually makes a nice sauce or syrup. When jarred too late, though, it becomes rubbery and doesn't spread easily. Such jelly may have to be dissolved in a little boiling water and jarred all over again.

Jelly makers have numerous tests for telling when a batch is ready to be jarred. The spoon test is the only one that works for me. In any case, experience is invaluable in jelly making, and any beginner's first few batches are likely to be an uneven success. My wife Nathalie is an accomplished jelly chef, and even she cans syrup a few times a year.

Here is Nathalie's approach to the black art of jelly making:

Before beginning, fill a glass with ice and stick a metal soup spoon in it. The ice will chill the spoon, which is important to get a valid spoon test.

Bring the syrup to a boil in a large pot filled no more than half full. Once it begins to bubble, watch it closely, as the syrup can boil over in seconds, resulting in an epic mess. You can stir the syrup to prevent a boil-over at this stage, but after it reaches an active boil, you must reduce the heat to the point where the syrup maintains the fastest possible boil without boiling over or stirring. Finding the exact burner setting requires trial and error, especially the first few times, but it gets easier with experience.

As the syrup cooks and thickens, the bubbles will grow bigger and glassier. When the light hissing sound becomes more of a smacking, the syrup is approaching the jelling point. You should start spoon tests every five minutes. As the tests indicate a progressive thickening, spoon test more often. (Storebought pectin usually sets much faster than natural pectin.)

Jelly recipes, including those in this

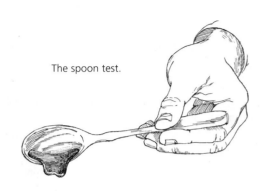

The spoon test.

book, usually describe this stage of the process by saying, "Cook until a spoon test indicates the jelly is ready to set," or words to that effect. In fact, the technique is touchier than those simple terms suggest. First, remove the spoon from the glass and with one quick motion, dip about half a spoonful of boiling syrup out of the pot. The syrup in the spoon must cool as much and as quickly as possible, so hold it over a plate and blow the syrup all over the bowl of the spoon. Watch for thick, viscous waves, indicating that the jelly is approaching the jelling point.

The next step is harder to describe than to do. Hold the spoon horizontally over the boiling syrup and roll it over quickly and completely using an overhand motion, turning the knuckles away from the body (the same motion used to throttle down a motorcycle, as opposed to rolling the knuckles toward the body, as if revving said vehicle).

It's the last few drops off the spoon that reveal the state of the syrup. They will drip like water at first, but as the syrup enters the jelling zone, these last drops will get progressively ropier until they leave strings of jelled syrup as they drop back into the pot. When the last drops fall two at a time, very slowly, with a sheet of thickened syrup between them, the jelly is ready to jar.

The drops will only reveal these stages if properly cooled first. To ensure this, store the testing spoon in the ice between tests, and blow the dipped syrup thoroughly cool before each trial.

With a little practice, this testing procedure will make jelly failures an infrequent occurrence.

Pickles are as far up the canning ladder as this book goes. In the broadest sense, "pickle" refers not only to whole fruits or vegetables preserved in vinegar, but also to chutney, relish, ketchup, and other vinegar-cured mixtures. Though some pickles are simply covered with vinegar and placed in the refrigerator, most are cooked and canned. Many, such as walnut pickles and butternut ketchup, require a brining period of several days, during which they are covered with salty water that must be periodically freshened.

Infusions

Infusions are a fun and easy way to use and preserve wild herbs. Essentially, an infusion is any liquid in which herbs have been soaked or simmered, causing the aromatic oils or other chemical constituents to dissolve in it. Vinegar, oil, and alcohol are all good mediums for herbal infusions. Water infusions, called teas or decoctions, don't keep well but are handy for making herbal medicines and beverages.

Herbal vinegars have recently become popular again after a century or more of absence. Sold at premium prices, herbed vinegars are nothing more than cider or wine vinegar in which one or more herbs have been infused. Usually a few stems of the plant are bottled with the finished product,

mostly for appearance. Garlic may also go into the bottle before corking to give the vinegar a savory, Mediterranean character. The process is so easy and cost-effective that foragers can put up a whole shelf-full of homemade herb vinegars, and they're great fun to experiment with in the kitchen.

Herbed vinegars can also be added to the bath and used as a hair rinse. Berry vinegars were used in times past to make cooling summer drinks. Diluted with iced water and sweetened to taste, they yield a tasty, refreshing cooler.

Herbal oils are infused like vinegar and serve similar purposes. Plant material should never be bottled in oil, however, since unlike vinegar and alcohol, oil is not a preservative and materials so infused may rot. Essential oils require a distillation process that is difficult to replicate at home. Further, like decoctions, essential oils are extremely potent and should never be ingested unless prescribed by a doctor.

Infused alcohol has both culinary and medicinal uses. Because alcohol evaporates readily, herbs can't be infused in it by simmering. Instead, stuff a wide-mouth jar full of the target herb, then fill it to the rim with wine, brandy, vodka, or rum. Seal the jar and store it in a cool, dark place for several months, after which the infusion can be strained and bottled.

Tinctures are strong alcoholic infusions intended for medicinal use. They are best made with high-test liquors such as authentic Russian vodka or Everclear. (Appalachian herbalists traditionally use "white lightning.")

Herbal teas can be enjoyed hot or cold, with honey, lemon, or other flavorings, depending on the type of herbs used and personal preference. Since dried plant matter releases only a modest amount of chemicals into the water, teas are generally a safe way to dabble in herbal self-treatment, but safety demands that foragers remain on their toes in this regard.

In the days when North Americans eschewed coffee, tea mixing was an important part of foraging in remote areas where imported black tea was expensive or hard to come by. Herbs of all kinds were gathered from every corner and dried for storage. They could then be mixed as needed to make a wide range of medicinal and beverage teas. Some foragers actually made a living selling their tea mixes. Today, tea mixing is a stimulating hobby, blending endless possibilities with negligible financial investment.

Decoctions are strong water infusions concentrated by simmering lots of herb in little water. Decoctions are both more effective and more dangerous as herbal medicine than simple infusions. They are usually used as topical medicinals and as cosmetic washes for skin and hair. In any case, decoctions should never be ingested except on the advice of a medical professional.

Wine

Perhaps the most appealing way to preserve and enjoy foraged herbs is in homemade wine. English farmers, possessors of arguably the most highly developed and least celebrated wine culture on earth, have teased exquisite wines from nearly every edible plant in Britain. Barberries, birch sap, cowslip, and clover are just a few of the foraged materials they have bent to their delightful purposes. Spruce, linden, and nettle are fermented into beer.

Freezing

Freezing is the quickest and easiest way to preserve many wild edibles. This usually involves no more than blanching (briefly boiling) the material in question, then sealing it in airtight plastic bags or containers and stacking them in the freezer. Fruit can simply be washed, drained, and frozen as is. Foragers fortunate enough to have a chest freezer can thus put up a year's supply with relatively little effort.

Drying

Drying fruits, vegetables, and herbs is the method of choice for foragers who don't have a large freezer. Even those who do fall back on this timeless method to preserve herbs that don't freeze well. The concept is simple. Since water is necessary for microbial growth, eliminating it prevents organic material from rotting. The challenge is to get the water out fast enough to prevent tissues from rotting during the drying process.

Paper bag drying is best for herbs that naturally lose water at an efficient rate. They can simply be placed loosely in a paper bag and stored in a warm, dry place for a week or so. Frequent fluffing accelerates the process and helps ensure that the material doesn't mat down and mold. The paper bag method is especially good for aromatic herbs that are sensitive to heat and light.

Rack drying is for thick or very moist materials. A drying rack can be as simple as a bed sheet spread over springy long grass or hung hammock-fashion between trees, or as sophisticated as a large frame with sliding racks lined with nylon window screen, permanently installed in the backyard. Slice very thin material destined for rack drying, and remove any peel. Protect food dried outside from insects by covering it with nylon screening or cheesecloth, and bring it in before damp night air slows down the drying process and invites rot. Direct sunlight destroys flavor and nutritional value, so in spite of the "natural" sound of sun-drying, place outdoor drying racks in shady areas. A simple and handy indoor technique is to sling a swath of cheesecloth or muslin from the beams or rafters. It's out of the way, and warm ceiling currents speed drying.

Line drying is best for whole plants. Hang the plants upside down from a clothesline until completely dry, then strip off the leaves or seeds and seal them in an airtight container. Line drying can be done outdoors or, if there is enough space, indoors. I used to string a winter's worth of mint down my trailer's narrow hallway. The cord was a hazard to navigation, especially in the middle of the night, but it got the job done.

Commercial electric food dryers vary widely in cost and design; the best have a variable temperature setting and a fan to circulate air through the racks. This remarkably shortens processing time, drying wet foods such as apples and Jerusalem artichokes in hours. As a kid, I dried apples on the forced-air furnace register beneath my bed. The method was highly effective, but as the register was only a foot long by four inches wide, production was limited. Since then I have been itching to design a multi-level food dryer that fits over such a furnace register. Unfortunately, I haven't yet had the correct balance of time and resources to do so. Perhaps a reader with greater ambition and manual skill will jump my claim.

Hot-car drying is the quickest and easiest method to dry currants and other berries. These fruits must be dipped in boiling water to crack their skins before rack drying or mashed and dried as fruit leather, but why bother when Henry Ford's self-propelled food dryer makes such short work of them? Just park a car in the sun, line a flat interior surface (a sedan's rear window deck is perfect) with newspapers, paper towels, or an old sheet, and spread the fresh, untreated berries on top. With windows rolled up and the doors shut, the berries turn to raisin-like morsels in little time. Whatever food value is lost to heat and sun is made up by the wonderful practicality of this method. As an added bonus, the car remains perfumed for days with the rich scent of fruit.

Though some sources suggest drying food in the oven, food dried this way may half-cook in the process, leading to disappointing results. However, the oven is handy for crisping already-dried herbs before pulverizing or stripping them from the stem. To do this, heat the oven to 150°F, then turn it off. Pop the dried herbs in for two or three minutes. (If the oven's lowest setting is higher than 150°F, allow some heat to escape before shutting the herbs inside.) It's important not to heat dried herbs too long, as this destroys vitamins and vaporizes the volatile oils that give them their flavor.

Plant material is more than 90 percent water, so it shrinks to a mere shadow of its fresh size and weight when dried. Foragers who haven't got much storage space greatly appreciate this fringe benefit. On the other hand, dried food must be sealed in an airtight container, as contact with the air leads to partial rehydration from water vapor, leading to decay. Plastic zipper bags are acceptable long-term storage containers if they are completely sealed and seldom disturbed. Moving them around a lot inevitably leads to pinholes, even when heavy freezer bags are used. Herbs that are to be used on and off over time should be sealed in a jar or other rigid container.

How to Use This Book

Each chapter is composed of entries dedicated to a distinct resource, arranged alphabetically by genus. The Special Notes that accompany these sections contain specific warnings and other interesting information.

The Dyers' Notes are a response to the recent swell of interest in natural dyeing. While the information presented here is too general to serve as a sole source, it will give readers a notion of the potential usefulness of common suburban wild dye-stuffs. Readers who wish to explore this engaging branch of foraging will find several excellent sources listed in Further Reading.

At the end of each chapter, readers will find a Foraging Advisory, listing hazards suburban foragers are likely to confront. However, there are literally thousands of potentially harmful plants in the world, only a fraction of which are listed in this book, so foragers must follow the common-sense guidelines outlined below and exercise good judgment at all times. *Common Poisonous Plants and Mushrooms of North America*, by Adam F. Szczawinski and Nancy J. Turner (see Further Reading) is a thorough source of detailed information on toxic plants.

Readers should use not one but several reliable field guides in conjunction with this book. For the suburban forager, these include field guides to wild plants and reference works on landscaping and garden plants. All should have comprehensive coverage of local plants, meticulous descriptions, and clear color photos or detailed line drawings. The most thorough guides are couched in dense botanical jargon, but even though they require regular flipping back to the glossary, it's time well invested. The forager who can affirm confidently that a collected plant has "ebracteate racemes, compressed, retuse silicles that are slightly stiptate, and a hirsute to stellate stem" is unlikely to ingest a toxic look-alike by accident. Learning the lingo also enhances the powers of observation. People who don't know what silicles are seldom notice them. (They are the skinny, pointy seedpods typical of mustard plants.)

Material on medicinal herbs found here is for information only. Barring allergy, foragers can get away with cautious use of the herbs for minor complaints, but medicinal herbs should only be used in consultation with a qualified professional if the herbs are taken in concentrated doses, if the condition is chronic, or if the patient is pregnant.

— Detail: Bigcone pine (*Pinus coulteri*).

The well-loved smell of a Christmas tree triggers a range of feelings but hunger is seldom one of them. In fact, the resinous tang of needle- and cone-bearing trees, called conifers, is all but absent from North American gastronomy. Nevertheless, in the words immortal of Euell Gibbons, many parts are edible.

Those not raised on resinous herbs may find they take some getting used to. First encounters are likely to elicit references to turpentine or Pine-Sol, yet the pungent, bitter-tart bite of needle-bearing trees is an integral part of many cuisines. For the average North American, resinous herbs are a true adventure, and familiarity with them marks an experienced gastronome. The fact is, nothing tastes even remotely like the evergreens, and once the taste is acquired, nothing else will do.

And there's more to resinous herbs than flavor alone. In the winter of 1536, natives living along the St. Lawrence River were amazed to find Jacques Cartier's party dying of scurvy in the middle of a conifer forest. The locals promptly boiled a few handfuls of needles in water and passed the tea to the strangers. Their quick thinking saved the Frenchmen not only their lives, but also an eternity of embarrassment. Scurvy is the common name for vitamin C deficiency, and the evergreens are chock-full of that vital nutrient.

Foragers can sort the resinous herbs into three categories. Pine nuts have the first to themselves, since they are a unique if somewhat rare wild edible with a flavor all their own. Next come young spruce, hemlock, and fir buds, which are interchangeable enough to be considered a single herb. Juniper brings up the rear.

Pine Nuts

Pine nuts, the only food from a resinous plant widely used in North America today, can be hard to come by in the backyard wilderness, since only a few pines (genus *Pinus*) produce them. Those that do include piñon or pinyon (*Pinus edulis*), a southwestern species and the only native pine cultivated for commercial nut production. Californian First Nations peoples gather the seeds of other species as well, including California's digger (*P. sabiniana*) and bigcone pine (*P. coulteri*). Italian stone pine (*P. pinea*), the primary Mediterranean source of pine nuts, occasionally turns up in sunbelt landscaping, while Swiss stone pine (*P. cembra*) and Swiss mountain pine (*P. mugo*) are the most frequently encountered nut-bearing pines in the North.

In the American Southwest, Mexico, and the Mediterranean, pine cones are gathered from eligible pines just before they open and then dried until they do.

Monkey Business

The monkey-puzzle tree (*Araucaria araucana*), a bizarre conifer that looks and sounds like something from Dr. Seuss, is an important source of food for indigenous peoples living in its native Chilean forests. They harvest the seeds from the monkey-puzzle's hedgehog-like cones and use them like pine nuts, with which monkey puzzle nuts are often compared.

Landscapers in the 1920s and 1930s adored this odd-looking immigrant, and its spiny, pipe-cleaner branches are still a fixture in older neighborhoods. The common name allegedly comes from monkeys' habit of scampering up the tree, only to find climbing back down difficult because the tree's spiny scales poke them when they try. Like juniper, only female monkey-puzzle trees produce cones, and even these "fire blanks" (the seed hulls are empty) unless a male tree is nearby. Thus, monkey-puzzle nuts are a rare find in suburbia.

The increasing appearance of young monkey-puzzles in new yards may herald a comeback for this distinctive exotic. Foragers lucky enough to have weird monkey-puzzle trees in the neighborhood may have a chance to try this unusual suburban wild edible.

Douglas fir (*Pseudotsuga menziesii*).

The seeds are then pried out, hulled, and dried, and sometimes roasted. The tear-shaped golden "nuts" (also called pignolias, pignons, or piñons) lend their rich, mellow savor to salads, sauces, and stuffings. They are also a principal component of pesto, a savory, all-purpose Italian seasoning. Believed to have evolved from a sea cook's gimmick for enlivening drab shipboard fare, pesto is essentially a paste of pine nuts, garlic, and basil. With such vitamin C–rich ingredients, it must have fended off scurvy as well.

Monkey-puzzle tree (*Araucaria araucana*), with cones.

Processing large quantities of pine nuts is a chore, but foragers who can collect enough nut-bearing cones may find it worth the effort. Prospects are especially good for Southwesterners who have access to a piñon. Pine nuts are generally used raw or lightly toasted. They should be stored in the freezer, since they are high in fat and quickly go rancid.

In addition to vitamin C, pine nuts supply a traditional treatment for bladder infections

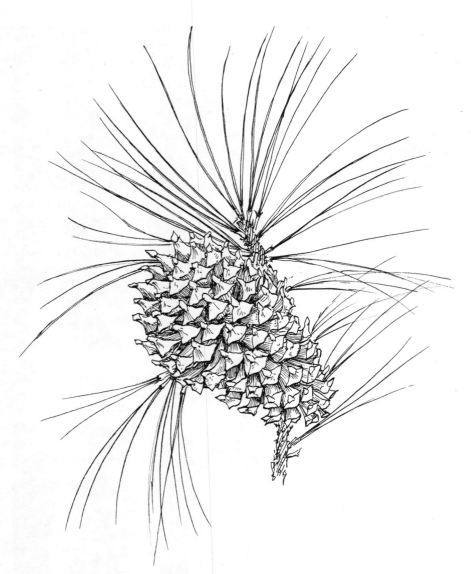

Bigcone pine (*Pinus coulteri*).

in southern Europe. (Folk healers also prescribe infusions of young pine needles, taken regularly over time, to dissolve bladder and kidney stones.) Pine nuts also have a reputation for stimulating the digestion when eaten sparingly, but if too many of these rich nuts are eaten in one sitting, they may cause heartburn.

Picea and Company

The soft, pale new needles of most evergreens are comparable in flavor and nutrition to pine nuts, and are much easier to find and use. Most species bear tasty buds, each with its own unique flavor and high vitamin C content. But for service above and beyond the call of duty, none surpasses spruce (genus *Picea*). Even the pitch of this tree is edible. The Cree chew spruce gum to combat sore throats and freshen breath, and for the inexplicable but universal human joy of pointless chewing. Before commercial chewing gum became widely available, farm children also chewed lumps of spruce pitch, which they picked from scars in the tree's trunk. Once they'd collected a respectable wad, they were set for the day.

As strange as this habit may seem, few of humanity's myriad "chaws" are as inoffensive and as good for the chewer as spruce gum. The turpentine flavor is overpowering at first, so experts spit several times while working up their plug. After a minute or so, the powdery pitch becomes elastic and settles down to a vaguely sweet, resinous taste. I like to flatten it against the roof of my mouth and lick the glassy, resinous surface, rather than chewing it per se.

With all this work some might wonder what the attraction is, but once the habit is cultivated, it's hard to pass up the clean bite of a good spruce plug. Black (*P. mariana*) and red spruce (*P. rubens*) are most often mentioned in connection with chewing. I've also had some success with Sitka spruce (*P. sitchensis*) pitch. Some spruces are sweeter than others, so if you find one species unpleasant, you may find that another suits your tastes. Naturally, anyone spotted putting this stuff in his or her mouth will get some strange looks. But as I pointed out in chapter 1, being considered a little unusual by one's neighbors is a time-honored mark of distinction among foragers.

Squirrels are famous for grabbing up pine nuts before anyone else has a chance at them, so human foragers have to look sharp if they want any. Cones are most promising while still on the tree and just about to open, but it is difficult to know exactly when to pick them. A particularly sly way around this problem is to keep the neighborhood squirrels under close surveillance. When they start into their annual pine-nut frenzy, during which they litter the ground with cone scales and spindles, foragers can rush out and snatch a few ripe cones before the professionals get them all.

To stir up trouble in a crowd of homebrewers, just ask, "Anybody ever tried spruce beer?" The room will immediately split down the middle, into those who swear spruce beer is on tap in every pub in Heaven, and those who clean paintbrushes with it. With apologies to the brush cleaners, I'm not on their side. Cultivating a taste for resinous beverages is admittedly a challenge, but having done so, I find I can't live without them.

Spruce and other conifers have been a favorite beverage flavoring for centuries. The Greeks produce their distinctive *retsina* by introducing a touch of Aleppine (*Pinus halepensis*) resin to the fermentation stages of a dry white wine. Well-chilled, piney retsina goes perfectly with spicy food and hot weather. Perhaps an intrepid home winemaker will parlay the sweet resin of a North American spruce, or California native sugar pine (*P. lambertiana*), into a New World retsina.

Spruce (*Picea* sp.)

Retsina notwithstanding, beer is the most common resinous beverage. British sailors brewed spruce beer as a scurvy-prevention measure, while a more refined version has been a winter tonic in Northern Europe since Viking times. The people of Québec still drink *bière d'épinette,* a pungent, carbonated soft drink available in supermarkets in that province.

Adventurous homebrewers sometimes try their hand at spruce beer or ale, substituting new conifer buds for a portion of the hops at various points in the brewing process, often in conjunction with ginger, orange peel, honey, or other flavorings. Traditional spruce beers are made from black spruce, but Sitka and red spruce produce good results, too. I suspect hemlock's (genus *Tsuga*) sweet young foliage would do equally well. (This conifer should not be confused with poison hemlock [*Conium maculatum;* see chapter 6], the parsley-like plant that killed Socrates.) The journals of Captain George Vancouver's 1792 voyage to the North Pacific mention a party sent ashore to brew beer from Puget Sound "spruces" that were almost certainly Douglas fir (*Pseudotsuga menziesii*). Shrubby, low-growing spruces have recently been developed by landscapers, and are particularly popular in northern suburbs. In my experience they are usually mild of flavor, and their young tips are well suited to this and other culinary uses. Even restrained use of Colorado blue spruce (*Picea pungens* 'Glauca') has proven successful, though as the botanical name suggests, this popular ornamental has a rather outgoing personality.

Most evergreens bud late in the spring. The buds swell larger and larger, chafing against their papery brown cover until at last they burst out. Flavor-wise, they reach the perfect balance between strength and mildness just before they blow.

Snap the soft tips off by hand or nip them from the tree with garden shears, and pull off the papery sheath, if present. The tips left behind remain palatable for weeks, though the older, darker, and glossier they get, the tougher and more phenolic they'll be in the kitchen. Because resinous herbs are so strongly flavored, there is little danger of overharvesting a mature tree. However, very young trees rely on new growth for survival, so foragers should be careful to take no more than a few tips from saplings.

Which species is best? The best way to find out is to chew a few needles. The flavor will be quite strong (imagine eating a fresh rosemary needle or a leaf of sage), but after tasting all available species the sweetest will be immediately apparent.

In terms of artificially applied poisons, conifer tips are a good news/bad news scenario. Unless the tree has been sprayed since the buds appeared, new growth will be toxin-free. On the other hand, if the new growth has been sprayed, it will be very recently and the toxins will be exceptionally potent. The best defence is to know for sure whether the tree has been sprayed. Where any doubt exists, tips should be fastidiously washed before use.

Conifers in the Kitchen

Young conifer tips' resiny-sweet tang invigorates many ordinary dishes. Newcomers to the resinous herbs should add just a few tips at first, adjusting the quantity as they become more familiar with them, as they can quickly overpower more subtle flavors. The following are good ways to get to know these unusual herbs:

· Minced new needles add zing to creamy garlic sauces.

· Whole buds integrate nicely with tomato soup, tomato-based sauces, and meat stews.

· Simmered in water over low heat, strained, and sweetened, young conifer tips make a tart, vitamin C–rich tea. Hemlock and spruce are my favorites. Douglas fir tea is tasty too, but consumption should be limited to one cup per day, as healthy drinkers may not appreciate the properties that make it an effective treatment for diarrhea.

· Lamb, rabbit, or turkey, braised in strong red wine with young conifer tips, garlic, and rosemary, have a lively Mediterranean zip.

· A cup of conifer tips pushed into a wine bottle with a sliced garlic clove, then covered with white, cider, or wine vinegar, creates a novel herbed vinegar for salads and cooking. The bottle should be filled to within two inches of its mouth, then corked securely and allowed to infuse upright in a cool, dark place for at least a month to develop its full flavor.

Spruce and other young conifer tips taste best when very fresh, but can be lightly blanched and frozen for later use. They can also be dried using a commercial food dryer, set on low if possible. Or, simply scatter new buds on a tray, cover loosely with muslin or newspaper to keep the dust off, and leave them in a dry place out of direct sunlight for a week or so. When the tips are completely dry, seal them in an airtight container and store in a cool, dark place.

Aside from supplying vitamin C, spruce acts as a diuretic and antiseptic, and oils infused with spruce needles can be used as a rub for arthritic or rheumatic joints. Conifer infusions have been used to treat diarrhea and dysentery (some species are more effective in this respect that others; see "Conifers in the Kitchen," page 29), cold symptoms, and as a gargle for sore throats. Antifungal conifer-bark infusions combat yeast infections, while infusions of spruce or hemlock needles are used as an antiseptic mouthwash and wash for wounds and burns. People of the First Nations in Canada rub the resin from young spruce tips into rashes and scrapes and squeeze it into wounds.

> **Spruce gum is highly adhesive.** People with braces or delicate dental work should avoid chewing it. Evergreen pitch of all types is famously hard to remove from hands and tools. While soap and water are powerless against it, charcoal lighter, paint thinner, or turpentine, followed by soap and water, are quite effective. Wearing gloves while gathering protects hands and fingers from staining in the first place.

Juniperus

For sheer numbers, no suburban evergreen eclipses juniper (genus *Juniperus*). Markedly different from its pine-shaped cousins, prickly juniper has been a landscaping standby for centuries. In the Middle Ages it was said that a witch could not cross a doorsill shaded by a juniper, though she might disarm this security system by correctly guessing the number of needles it had. This belief established juniper as a courtyard shrub, a tradition that European colonists later established in the New World. Today, juniper is one of the most common ornamentals in suburbia. I have even identified the sites of houses long since vanished by the junipers still guarding their foundations. Ubiquity alone makes this versatile herb worth knowing.

Suburban junipers are usually low, untidy-looking bushes, though some reach head height, and a few even attain tree size when conditions are favorable. Female junipers produce their pellet-like berries only in the presence of males, but junipers are so numerous that coed pairings are commonplace. People sometimes wonder why juniper is considered a conifer when it has no cones. A magnifying glass reveals the truth: Juniper's hard, blue to grey-green berries actually are tiny cones, whose scales are so tightly clenched that they appear round.

Juniper berries have been flavoring food for centuries. Their musky bitterness is the source of gin's characteristic bite. In fact, "gin" is a corruption of genièvre, the French word for juniper. Gin's ancestor, also called genièvre, was invented by French Flemings in the 1500s and is still a speciality in northwestern

France. When a noxious bathtub version became the crack cocaine of eighteenth-century London, patriotic "beer societies" promoted wholesome English lager as an antidote to the epidemic. But the reputed power of juniper berries to induce miscarriage ensured gin's continuing popularity in houses of ill repute, earning both liquor and herb an unsavory reputation neither has completely lived down.

Juniper (*Juniperus* sp.), with berries.

Nasty bit of luck for the honorable juniper, which people prize the world over as a medicinal herb. In Europe, the Middle East, and Asia, juniper infusions fight kidney and urinary tract difficulties. Europeans have also taken them for menstrual complaints and nausea, and, of course, English doctors once prescribed juniper berries as an abortifacient. Externally, juniper ointments and solutions treat joint and skin disorders in European and Middle Eastern folk healing.

Juniper berries have a distinct taste all their own. The strong, slightly "green" tang of whole, dried juniper berries lends a resinous touch to herbed vinegars. It also plays a role in the complex flavor of Italian pastrami and the Rhine country's succulent sauerkrauts. Ground roasted juniper berries have a rich, smoky savor that must be tasted to be believed. Stews, sausages, strong meats, mustards, and cheeses all benefit from a touch of this remarkable spice.

Winnow freshly picked juniper berries by floating them in a pan of water, then combing through them with your fingers. Needles and other detritus will stick to your hands and can be rinsed off under running water. When clean, allow the berries to drip dry in a sieve, then spread them in a single layer in a shallow pan.

Dyers' Notes

Juniper and hemlock are the only resinous herbs extensively used in dyeing, but what they lack in quantity, they make up in quality.

Strong juniper infusions impart a tenacious, earthy beige to wool mordanted in a solution of alum and cream of tartar. Juniper berries give the richest color, but bark and foliage can also be used. Some species give muted purple with alum alone.

Eastern hemlock (*Tsuga canadensis*) was an important dyestuff in colonial times. Hemlock bark gives alum-mordanted wool a ruddy hue, while a copperas mordant produces grey tones. Though this dye produces only feeble, temporary shades on cotton, tanners in Atlantic Canada and New England drew heavily on hemlock to cure and color leather.

Slow roasting in a 250°F oven turns them dark brown, almost black. (The sumptuous incense that fills the house is one of the best reasons to make this spice.) After they cool, grind finely with a mortar and pestle, coffee grinder, or grain mill and store the aromatic meal in an airtight container until use.

An intriguing coffee-like beverage can be drip-percolated from ground roasted juniper berries, though picking and preparing enough little berries for a whole potful is a saint's labor. Less patient foragers mix the dark juniper grind with real coffee. It also makes a hearty tea. (New juniper foliage can be infused as well, using the procedure outlined in "Conifers in the Kitchen," page 29.)

Most junipers set berries haphazardly and slowly. They ripen in two years, going from green to powdery blue or grey, and finally turning black and dropping from the branch. For culinary purposes, juniper berries can be used at any stage, particularly if roasted, but are best when blue or grey.

Foraging Advisory

While flavor and medicinal properties vary from species to species, few evergreens are toxic. However, there are two important exceptions:

Conifers that don't have true needles warrant suspicion. This includes cedar (genus *Thuja*, and others), cypress (genus *Cupressus*, and others), arborvitae (genus *Thujopsis*), and other species bearing lacy or scaly, bright green, non-scratchy fronds. By comparison, juniper has bottle-brush, grey-green to yellowish foliage that is scratchy against bare skin. Other edible evergreens have separate, non-segmented needles that can be plucked individually from the twigs, and which often prick the skin as well. Lacy-scaly trees and shrubs are extremely common in hedges and wind screens. Many contain high levels of thujone, which may be harmful if ingested. Their foliage can be safely steamed, though some have a fragrance reminiscent of white spruce. (See "Freshen Things Up a Bit," opposite.)

Never put any part of a yew tree (genus *Taxus*) in your mouth. This needle-bearing evergreen, prized by English longbowmen, samurai warriors, and First Nations peoples for bow wood, has flat, glossy, plastic-looking needles. Females bear eye-catching red berries. Most

---

The effect of juniper's scratchy needles on human skin is insidious. The scratching is hardly noticeable while you are picking berries, but a short time later, the tender skin on the underside of the forearms remembers every prick and scrape. This is because juniper needles, though small, are razor sharp. They make microscopic cuts in the epidermis, then deposit tiny grains of pitch or pollen under the skin, which irritate it later. I haven't heard of anyone suffering medical consequences from rubbing a juniper the wrong way, but in theory it could cause an allergic reaction in susceptible individuals. Foragers can easily avoid these problems by wearing a long-sleeved shirt or jacket during picking.

Though juniper berries contain oils that may be unhealthy in large quantities, the bitterness of most species rules out consuming enough to cause harm. However, the large blue berries of California juniper (*J. californica*) are sweeter than those of other junipers, and some people eat them out of hand. Foragers who encounter these berries, native to southeastern California, should limit their snacking to an infrequent handful.

Freshen Things Up A Bit

The antiseptic properties of conifers have been known for generations, as pine-scented commercial cleansers attest. First Nations cultures use the smoke from burning evergreen foliage ritually to purify people and places, while Europeans in times past disinfected disease-infested buildings with the steam from boiling conifer branches. In Europe and the Middle East, cold, bronchitis, and asthma patients, as well as those suffering chest pain and headaches, are traditionally advised to inhale the steam from boiling juniper or other conifer branches.

Stale household air can be freshened up by placing coarsely chopped evergreen twigs and needles in a wood stove humidifier or a pan of water and simmering them on the kitchen range. The water must be carefully monitored and topped up before it steams away. Otherwise the needles may scald and stink, or even start a fire.

Barring allergy, steamed conifer foliage vapors are harmless. However, Canadian backwoodsmen assiduously avoid white spruce (*Picea glauca*), known in rural Canada as "cat-pee" spruce, when cutting the family Christmas tree. Care to guess why?

common in residential areas are the Canadian yew (*T. canadensis*), a shrub often used in hedges, and shrubby nursery varieties of English yew (*T. baccata*). The berries and shiny foliage make yew a popular ornamental, but both are poisonous. (Actually, I understand the berry's flesh is edible, but the large pit is lethal. All things considered, I'd rather not test that hypothesis.)

An interesting footnote: Pacific yew (*T. brevifolia*) bark yields a chemical that combats breast cancer when scientifically refined and professionally administered. Like many poisonous plants, yew saves lives in measured, tightly controlled doses.

Recipes

Mediterranean Turkey with Conifer Tips

SERVES 6.

This hearty dish is a refreshing change from the ordinary, especially served with this Greek approach to mashed potatoes.

TURKEY AND SAUCE:

2 tablespoons olive oil • $^1/_4$ cup olives, sliced
6 turkey thighs, skinned and boned • $^1/_2$ cup new conifer tips
12 small boiling onions, peeled • 2 bay leaves
2 cloves garlic, crushed • 1 teaspoon cinnamon
Two 16-ounce cans tomato sauce, or 4 cups fresh • $^1/_4$ teaspoon ground allspice
1 cup hearty red wine, such as Burgundy • $^1/_4$ teaspoon red pepper flakes
2 medium carrots, sliced • $^1/_2$ cup mushrooms, sliced
Salt and pepper to taste

Heat the olive oil over medium-high heat in the bottom of a Dutch oven and briefly brown the turkey. Remove the turkey from the pan and it set aside.

Add the onions, and sauté until they turn translucent. Add the garlic, and sauté for a minute longer.

Pour in the tomato sauce and wine, and stir to mix. Add the rest of the ingredients and stir well. Return the turkey to the pan. Cover and bring briefly to a boil, then simmer over low heat until turkey is tender, about 2 hours.

MEDITERRANEAN MASHED POTATOES:

10 medium white potatoes, peeled and quartered
4 teaspoons olive oil • 4 large garlic cloves, peeled
Milk to moisten, about 1 cup • Parmesan cheese (optional)

Put the potatoes in a large saucepan and cover with water. Place the lid on the pot and bring it to a boil. Reduce the heat to medium and simmer until the potatoes are tender, about 20 minutes.

While the potatoes are cooking, place a small saucepan over medium heat and swirl in the olive oil. Drop in the garlic cloves and sauté them until soft.

When the potatoes are done, pour off the water. Place the uncovered pan on the hot burner and shake to dry the potatoes. Remove from heat, add sautéed garlic cloves and oil, and mash, adding milk as needed to produce a stiff purée.

Keep the mashed potatoes warm until serving.

Serve the turkey and sauce together in the same dish. Spoon the sauce over the mashed potatoes and sprinkle with Parmesan cheese, if desired.

Spruce Beer

MAKES TWENTY-FOUR 12-OUNCE BOTTLES.

This simple recipe is based on brews made by Québécois farmers centuries ago. Unlike modern, grain-based spruce beers, it requires little in the way of specialized ingredients or equipment. (Yeast, hops, and bottling paraphernalia can be purchased anywhere homebrewing supplies are sold.) Cleanliness is crucial, as is tightly capping the brew in old-fashioned returnable bottles (recognizable by their thick glass and scuffed exterior), or those sold expressly for home brewing. Flimsy modern disposables may explode and the ensuing mess must be cleaned to be appreciated. This black brew can be enjoyed in as little as a week, but mellows with age. Some connoisseurs recommend cellaring it up to a year before drinking.

> 2^1/2 gallons soft water (if local tap water leaves a white residue when it evaporates,
> use commercial bottled drinking water)
> ^{1}/3 cup fresh ginger root, thinly sliced
> 1 ounce dried hops (about 2 cups loosely-packed)
> 5 cups molasses
> 4 ounces hard peppermint candy, such as a broken-up candy cane (about ^{2}/3 cup)
> ^{1}/2 pound young spruce tips (about 4 cups)
> 1 packet brewer's yeast dissolved in ^{1}/4 cup warm water

Sterilize the fermentation vessel (a large, airtight, nonreactive container, such as a wine-making carboy or food-grade plastic pail with a hole cut in the lid for the airlock), cheese-cloth, airlock, and implements by washing them well and rinsing in a solution of 1 tablespoon bleach to 1 gallon of water. Drip dry in a sterilized rack. (Failure to sterilize everything that comes in contact with the beer may result in contamination, leading to an unpleasant final product.)

In a very large, nonreactive pot, bring the water to a boil and sustain it for 2 minutes. (The pot must be large enough to hold the whole recipe without boiling over.)

Bruise the ginger slices by pounding them with a knife handle or the butt of a cleaver. Add the ginger, hops, molasses, candy, and spruce tips to the water and boil them to-gether for 15 minutes, stirring occasionally.

Strain this liquid, called the "wort," through sterilized cheesecloth into the fermen-tation vessel. When the liquid has cooled to 70°F, add the yeast.

Seal the fermenter (if using a food-grade pail) and fix the airlock in place. Allow the wort to work at about 70°F until the airlock "burps" about once every 45 seconds.

Siphon the wort, which will be black and opaque, into sterilized bottles and seal with a bottle capper and metal caps. (Avoid bottling the last inch or so of wort, as this is mostly sediment.) Leave the bottles in a warm place (about 70°F) for one week. At this point it is ready to drink, but will benefit from further cellaring.

Cellar the beer upright in a cool, dark place. Chill and decant the beer carefully into a glass before drinking, to avoid stirring up the yellow sediment that accumulates on the bottom.

Christmas Tea

This dark, aromatic tea is especially well suited to the holiday season. For a single cup, place a tea strainer in a mug of boiling water and infuse:

2 teaspoons ground roasted juniper berries
One 1-inch piece of cinnamon stick, shredded
1 thin slice ginger root
2 whole cloves
1 teaspoon dried orange peel
Dash ground nutmeg
One 1-inch piece of peppermint candy cane

Or place the ingredients in the bottom of a teapot in the following quantities:

4 teaspoons ground roasted juniper berries
1 cinnamon stick, shredded
2 thin slices ginger root
5 whole cloves
2 teaspoons dried orange peel
1/2 teaspoon ground nutmeg
One 6-inch candy cane, broken up

Fill the pot with boiling water, steep for 5 to 10 minutes, and strain. Serve with milk or cream.

Juniper Marinade

Though best with dry or strongly flavored meats such as game, range-fed beef, or buffalo, this marinade can also be used on ordinary supermarket cuts.

1 bottle dry white wine
1 cup white wine vinegar
1/2 cup olive oil
1 large onion, chopped
2 large garlic cloves, crushed
1/4 cup fresh chickweed or parsley, chopped, or 2 tablespoons dried
1 tablespoon soy sauce
1/2 teaspoon thyme
6 crushed peppercorns
6 crushed juniper berries (may be roasted, dried, or fresh, according to taste)

Mix all the ingredients together and allow them to infuse, at least a couple of hours. Pierce the meat all over with a fork. Place it in a nonreactive dish or pan, cover it with marinade and marinate in the refrigerator 2 hours to overnight, depending on the strength, toughness, and thickness of the cuts. Turn frequently to marinate evenly. Marinated meat can be grilled, fried, or broiled. Leftover marinade can be used as a sauce base, or frozen and reused later.

Winter Air Freshener

This is a potpourri that freshens and humidifies dry and stagnant air during the heating season, and creates a warm and cozy atmosphere.

1 tablespoon whole cloves
2 bay leaves, or 1 tablespoon dried mint
2 cinnamon sticks, shredded
1 cup conifer twigs and needles, chopped (Christmas tree trimmings work nicely)
2 tablespoons dried orange peel
3 cups water

Bring all the ingredients briefly to a boil, turn the burner down to the lowest point, and simmer. Replenish the water as necessary. Store in the refrigerator between uses.

— Detail: chokecherry *(Prunus Virgiana)*.

Beyond the few that bear familiar fruits, trees are generally over-looked as a food source. While many people are taken aback at the thought of eating tree leaves, blossoms, or bark, they're missing out. Many are fun and delicious edibles, and some are effective medicines.

As perennials, trees demand special respect. The fact that they produce year in, year out, with little or no maintenance is a definite plus, but the resource must be properly maintained. Nuts and fruits often set high off the ground, and I have seen people break branches in order to get them. This is extremely harmful to the tree, as the wound bleeds sap and offers an entry point to fungi and predatory insects. What's more, simple self-interest would seem to argue against the branch-breaking approach, since the following year's crop will be set even higher on the tree.

Picking from high branches is best accomplished with an "apple picker," which is a small wire basket mounted under a hook at the end of a long handle. If available resources don't justify making or buying this tool, a berry hook wielded with intelligence and sensitivity can accomplish much. Take care not to break the branches or score the bark while pulling the harvest within reach, especially if the hook is made of metal. Take leaves and flowers only from well-established trees, since saplings need all the help they can get. Branches taken for bark should be those that have been or were going to be pruned anyway. Further, all parts of a tree are subject to spraying. New leaves and flowers are particularly susceptible since they come on in early spring, about the same time the spraying starts. Foragers should collect from unsprayed trees only, and always wash the harvest thoroughly.

An especially nice thing about trees is that their long branches frequently extend well beyond property lines. Although I understand that tree owners have legal grounds for preventing passersby from taking even the fruit that falls beyond their property, I've never known such a niggardly landowner. (I have, however, seen more than one feud erupt between the owners of such trees and neighbors who regard fallen fruits, nuts, or leaves as a nuisance.) While it is not a good idea to pick anything from a privately owned tree, whether or not the branch overhangs a public area, blow-downs are usually free for the taking, provided they are not on private property.

In these days when suburban trees are more often regarded as a liability than an asset, those of us who know better must actively cherish them. Insurance agents compel homeowners to cut them down to avoid property damage from roots and falling branches, while automobile owners fell them to protect paint jobs from falling sap, fruit, and the effluent of perching birds. But beautiful, bountiful trees add immeasurably more to a neighborhood's true worth than they subtract from its monetary value. Whether or not their merit can be calculated in dollars, foragers must do their part to preserve them.

Arbutus (see chapter 5)

Acer

Japanese maple's (*Acer palmatum*) just-opened leaves are one of suburbia's most surprising wild edibles. These delicate spring greens (if translucent red leaves can truly be called greens) bring stained-glass color and tangy, sorrel-like zip to salads and sandwiches. Floating on a bowl of miso or other clear soup, they become a sort of edible haiku, as much art as entrée.

An apple picker makes harvesting from high branches easier.

Japanese maple
(*Acer palmatum*).

These delightful salad greens are only briefly available during the early spring leafing-out. Used soon after picking, they are tender and tart, but not sour; if refrigerated for more than a few hours, though, they lose their tenderness and tang and begin to taste like, well, leaves. Nor is there any satisfactory way to preserve Japanese maple leaves for use out of season. Such rarity serves to make this sublime herb that much more exquisite.

Japanese maple is a common centerpiece in formal landscaping, seldom if ever occurring feral. Cultivars abound, some waist-high bushes with very lacy leaves, others tree-sized with more conservative foliage. The new leaves of most are pink to maroon, though some turn green with age. Only young Japanese maple leaves are tangy and tender. No other maple in my acquaintance bears palatable new leaves. But because they are grown for their beauty, Japanese maples are often dowsed in toxins, particularly at leafing-out time, when the luscious young leaves are susceptible to predatory insects. Foragers should be certain that new Japanese maple leaves have not been sprayed, and wash them carefully before use.

Zen Buddhist monks labored for centuries to produce Japanese maple, whose foliage suggests cascading water, a common metaphor in their religion. The leaves' lacy "fingers" resemble an individual spray of water or, as the species name suggests, a palm tree. In formal Japanese gardens, Japanese maples symbolize the serenity inspired by the sound of falling water, and are often planted within earshot of a waterfall.

Betula

The twigs and bark of yellow birch (*Betula alleghaniensis*) and sweet birch (*B. lenta*), also called black or cherry birch, smell of wintergreen when crushed or broken. The volatile oil responsible is almost indistinguishable from the oil of true wintergreen (*Gaultheria procumbens*), even to chemists. In fact, most commercial "wintergreen" oil is actually distilled from sweet birch sap.

Both sweet and yellow birch have dark, broken bark, in sharp contrast to the shiny white or metallic bark of most birches. Sweet birch contains more volatile oil than yellow birch and is therefore more valuable as a flavoring, but yellow birch has a much greater geographical range.

Sweet and yellow birch were once in great demand as beverage ingredients. Birch beer, with a flavor something like modern root beer, is an old-time favorite in the Northeast. Some specialty brewers still market non-alcoholic birch beer. Northeastern backwoodsmen also tap birches for their sap, which is boiled down to make syrup, just like sugar maple. There's even a company in Scotland that produces a choice wine from European white birch (*B. pendula*) sap.

European white birch (*Betula pendula*) showing catkins.

Salicylates present in Betula species bear a close resemblance to aspirin. Children, pregnant women, and people who are allergic to aspirin should avoid birch products.

To make a refreshing, wintergreen-flavored tea, break sweet or yellow birch twigs or bark into small pieces and cover with boiling water. Steep ten minutes and sweeten with maple syrup for an authentic Big North Woods treat.

Birch twigs and bark also spice up ordinary black tea and add an aromatic kick to herbal tea mixes. They may be gathered year-round, but are most potent in the budding season. I find the wintergreen zing an especially good accompaniment for tea made from young conifer tips, which become available at the same time. Twigs and bark should be salvaged from pruned branches to spare trauma to the tree. Both may be dried for later use. The volatile oils readily evaporate when exposed to direct sunlight or heat, so birch bark is best dried using the paper bag approach (see page 20), then sealed in an airtight container and stored in a cool, dark place.

First Nations and Southern mountain cultures take sweet birch tea against cold and fever symptoms, upset stomach, internal parasites, and dysentery. Strong infusions and decoctions of sweet or yellow birch bark are used as a wash for scrapes, sores, and rashes. In ointments and soaks, birch extracts treat joint and muscle pain. European white birch enjoys respect as a medicinal throughout its home continent. (The weeping birches trendy in northern landscaping are European white birch cultivars.) Tea made from the leaves or bark of this ubiquitous ornamental is said to have much the same effect as willow tea. Some people gargle with it for sore throats and ulcers in the mouth.

Carya

People who really know their nuts consider hickory (genus *Carya*) the finest of all. It is certainly the toughest. *Carya* closely resembles its near relative *Juglans*, but sets fewer, less uniform leaves per shoot. Green hickory nuts are rounder and smaller than green walnuts, with a thick, seamed husk that looks sewn together. In the autumn this husk curls open, dropping its payload on the ground below. Hickories are virtually absent from the western half of the continent, but fairly well represented in the East.

Shagbark hicory
(*Carya ovata*).

Of several hickory species, only the nuts of the two "barks"—shagbark (*C. ovata*) and shellbark (*C. laciniosa*)—are good foraging prospects. The others are either wholly inedible or require acorn-style processing (see Foraging Advisory, page 66).

Like other nuts, hickory nuts are very high in fat and should be used in moderation, especially by those who are watching their weight.

Hickory nuts are best gathered as soon as they drop, to minimize insect damage. Ripened in the shell like walnuts, the kernels' green edge mellows to a sweet, buttery flavor. After a month or so of drying using the paper bag treatment (see page 20), take out a few and crack with hammer, vice, or channel-lock pliers to test the meats for ripeness.

Devotees prefer properly aged hickory nuts to any other in baking, salads, sauces, stuffings, and rice dishes. Even pecans (*C. illinoinensis*), technically hickory nuts themselves, take a backseat to shellbark and shagbark in rural areas of the American South. There, roasted and salted hickory nuts are considered the best snack nut there is.

A Death in the Family

American chestnut (*Castanea dentata*), whose delicious nuts are memorialized in Christmas songs and stories, was once the most widespread nut tree in North America. Also a source of valuable timber, native chestnuts flourished over most of the East when Europeans arrived. Their subsequent westward expansion carried American chestnuts all the way to the Pacific and all points between. Past generations cherished chestnut as a shade tree, and the streets of the first suburbs were lined with it. Tragically, chestnut blight (*Endothia parasitica*) has pushed this beautiful, economically valuable tree to the edge of extinction. Scientists have struggled unsuccessfully to produce a blight-resistant variety. To date, each new cultivar has survived only a year or so before contracting the blight and dying. Though a few trees in the Pacific Northwest have managed to escape the epidemic, the prognosis is grim.

The loss of American chestnut is a disaster for everyone, foragers foremost. But foresters still haven't given up. They continue to blend together genetic material from disease-resistant individuals, and some are confident they will yet produce a blight-proof cultivar. Foragers can help in the struggle by reporting any healthy adult American chestnuts to the nearest agricultural college, county extension agent, or provincial Department of Agriculture.

Perhaps our children will live to see this beautiful, useful tree reclaim its place on the continent. In the meantime, it is with a heavy heart that I exclude American chestnut from further consideration in this chapter.

Hickory nuts play an important role in Eastern Woodlands cultures, being very high in protein, as are all nuts and seeds. They are also a good source of iron, phosphorus, and magnesium, and have less sodium than most other nuts.

Cornus (see chapter 5)

Crataegus

North America boasts more than a hundred native hawthorn (genus *Crataegus*) species. Throw in half a dozen introduced varieties and a strong tendency to cross-pollinate, and telling one *Crataegus* species from another becomes a thorny prospect (in a manner of speaking). Fortunately, none are toxic and all are useful resources to some degree. A bit of experimenting quickly determines which local hawthorns bear the most palatable fruit. After that, it's just a matter of harvesting the plentiful "haws" from the chosen tree.

> **Hawthorn has been known to** amplify, sometimes dangerously, the effects of prescription heart medications. Heart patients should take hawthorn only under the supervision of a cardiologist.

Hawthorn is closely related to apple, and is often called thornapple. In the South it is also called mayhaw. Most species grow to tree height, with spines that vary in length and sharpness. The leaves are small and dense, coarsely-veined, serrated, and usually lobed. Hawthorn fruits, called haws, are pea- to marble-sized and red, orange, blue, or black. They set in small clusters, a happy coincidence since harvesting such small berries from the thorny branches would otherwise be a chore. Haws ripen in early autumn, at which time they are at their best, but often persist well into winter.

Hawthorn has much in common with rowan (genus *Sorbus;* see below), whose range it shares, and for practical purposes the two can be considered sibling resources. Both play an important role in Northern European folklore. Both are ritually associated with death: one probably Druid-inspired tradition has it that Christ's crown of thorns was made of hawthorn branches. Beauty and vigor have made both rowan and hawthorn fixtures in suburban landscaping. Like rowan berries, haws vary widely from place to place and tree to tree, but are almost always uninteresting when eaten raw.

The little bunches of haws can be cleanly snapped from the tree with a quick jerk, eliminating the need for tools. If leather gloves are worn, several pounds of clustered haws can easily be bagged in less than an hour. Without the gloves, hawthorn's stout, sharp spines turn haw-picking into the sort of heroic trial that Greek mythology made famous.

Once gathered, the haws may be dried for use in tea by hanging the bunches in a dry place. Collected haw clusters usually retain a spine at their base, and I have dried them by sticking this "tack" into a bulletin board or sheet of cardboard. For use in cooking, fresh haws can be snipped from their stems with scissors. It's all right if some stem remains, since the haws will be pulped or juiced before use. A good wash, and they're ready for action. Haw juice or pulp can be used alone or in concert with sweeter fruits in preserves, pies, and beverages.

Hawthorn (*Crataegus* sp.).

Haw jelly is excellent, although it usually requires the additional tartness of sumac or lemon juice. Mixed half-and-half with rowan berries, haws yield a jelly that is almost impossible to distinguish from cranberry sauce. European farmers also press them with apples when making cider, or mash them with sweeter fruits to impart a more complex color and flavor to wines. Dried haws are a popular tea-mixing ingredient, owing to both the visual appeal they lend to jarred mixes and the fruity, astringent flavor they contribute to the beverage itself.

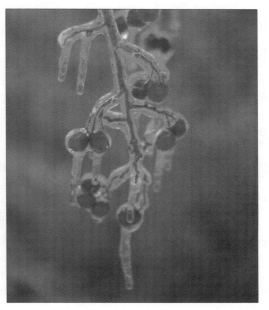

Hawthorn berries in winter.

Hawthorn has exciting potential as herbal medicine. Its leaves, flowers, and berries are a clinically proven tonic for the heart and circulatory system. Hawthorn appears mainly to suppress extreme changes in heart rate, whether up or down, making it particularly useful in cases of congestive heart failure, angina, mild arrhythmia, and hypertension. In addition, haws fight arthritis, periodontal disease, and insomnia. European tradition values hawthorn berries as a diuretic and treatment for disturbances of the urinary tract, such as kidney and bladder stones. Scientific studies have confirmed all these applications. Hawthorn

Hawthorn (*Crataegus* sp.) in flower.

flowering tops intended for medicinal infusions are collected in late spring and early summer, and dried for later use.

Fagus

Beech's (genus *Fagus*) shiny toothed leaves and prickly, chestnut-like seed clusters are a common sight along many residential streets. The small, wedge-shaped seeds, called beechnuts, were once marketed commercially in North America. Pressed in quantity, they still render a rare oil that sells for usurious prices in Europe.

Pairs of beechnuts set in bristly husks, which turn gold and begin to open in autumn. Gather the husk-bearing nuts in a paper sack and shake vigorously to free most of the triangular kernels, which collect at the bottom. Roast these in a 250°F oven until dark and crisp. When cool, remove the hull and outer skin by rubbing between the fingers or hands or chafing (not grinding) with a mortar and pestle.

Roasted beechnuts can be munched like popcorn, but they are small and preparation is tedious. Most foragers grind them to make a coffee-like beverage, using a coffee grinder or mortar and pestle. Infused and drunk as is (the grounds need not be strained out), ground roasted beechnuts are said to be one of the best natural coffee substitutes. They may also be mixed with real coffee or cocoa.

Though beechnuts contain saponins that can cause gastric disturbances in high concentrations, a person is unlikely to consume enough of them under normal conditions to cause harm. Roasting reduces the risk even further. If ingesting beechnuts or beechnut products leads to an upset stomach, stop ingesting them.

Feral Fruits (and Wild Cousins)

The gnarled, broken, lichen-covered fruit trees that persist in many neighborhoods bear witness to the fact that much of suburbia was once farmland. Intentionally planted, yet neglected now, such trees are best described as feral. Their misshapen, blemished fruits often taste better than store-bought produce,

Beech (*Fagus* sp.).

for two reasons. Feral trees must adapt to pests and local soil and climate conditions, which brings out different flavors in their fruits just as it does in their wild cousins. Then too, postwar consumer culture has prompted the development of picture-perfect fruits that ship and store well. These engineered crops imitate wax fruit, right down to the taste. By contrast, many feral trees date back to a time when the market was less obsessed with appearance and more interested in flavor. Today, such fruit literally cannot be bought for any price.

Genuinely wild species also persist in some neighborhoods. Typically smaller than their domesticated cousins, wild fruits have larger seeds and are sour or bitter enough to discourage casual browsing. Nevertheless, a modicum of processing renders many of them delicious.

Feral apples (genus *Malus;* still listed as *Pyrus* in some sources) abound throughout southern Canada and the United States. Their small, worm-eaten, unevenly shaped or colored fruits almost always taste better than the prom queens found in the produce section at the local supermarket. Many are baking or cider varieties now rare or completely unavailable. While some are less than inspiring as fresh fruit, feral apples are great fun to experiment with in the kitchen.

Wild apples, called crabapples, are the ancestor of the domesticated varieties and belong to the same genus. Crabapples come in all colors, shapes, and flavors. Pacific or Oregon crabapples (*Malus fusca*) are oblong, yellow-orange,

Chokecherry (*Prunus virginiana*), flowers and fruit.

and berry-sized. Eastern crabapples (*M. coronaria*), which look like green golf balls, may remain on the tree well into winter. These trees, whose branches bear long, rather dull thorns, are native to the East and Midwest, but have been introduced all over the continent. Exotics such as Siberian crabapple (*M. baccata*) are widely planted for their beautiful spring blossoms. Oddly, the copious, neon pink fruit that follows is usually left to rot. While crabapples are astringent and unpalatable raw, they make a delicately flavored jelly counted among the finest. Crabapples' very sourness dissuades worms from molesting them, hence they are usually perfectly shaped and uncompromised.

Both feral apples and crabapples make excellent preserves and pies. Their fresh, tart bite complements other fruits, and they are a major source of pectin for jellies and jams (see "Using Apples in Jams and Jellies," page 49). Fresh, unbruised apples keep for several months when stored in a cool, dark place. Dried, they keep even longer. To prepare apples for drying, peel, core, and slice them thin, then dip the slices in an acidic solution such as orange juice or water mixed with a tablespoon of sumac or lemon juice. This prevents the slices from oxidizing, which robs them of vitamins and turns them brown. They can then be

Using Apples in Jams and Jellies

Each summer my wife and I put up several dozen jars of preserves. One year she used store-bought pectin, while I jelled mine exclusively with pectin from underripe foraged apples. Our techniques were otherwise identical, and we used the same equipment, yet nearly all of her batches failed on the first try, while mine produced not a single runny jar.

Not only does apple pectin jell readily, it adds depth of flavor to the finished product. Crabapples contain the most pectin and add snappy tartness, but any kind of apple will jell, provided it is slightly underripe. (Completely ripe and very green apples contain less pectin, and therefore they yield disappointing results.) Because there is no need to peel or core, pectin duty is perfectly suited to wild or feral apples, which are typically small or misshapen.

To make jelly with apple pectin, wash the apples, cut out bruises or worm damage, and chop. Add one pound of chopped apples to two or three pounds of other fruit. Simmer, mash, and allow to drip as usual. Add sugar as specified in the recipe and proceed accordingly. Apple pectin can also be concentrated in liquid form for later use (see Homemade Apple Pectin in the Recipes section, page 73).

Note: When making jelly, ignore time-based instructions such as "boil 10 minutes, then jar." Always get a positive spoon test before jarring, as described in Chapter 1, whether using foraged or commercial pectin.

dried on a rack or in a commercial food dryer. (Fresh slices can also be frozen without pretreating.) Dried apples are an excellent snack food that is also handy in baking.

The relationship between apples and general health is legendary. In addition to their impressive vitamin C content, fresh apples' crunchy flesh provides fiber for the digestive tract and a cleansing workout for the teeth. Apple pectin unblocks obstructed bowels in small amounts, tightens up loose bowels in large amounts, and contributes nonfattening bulk to weight-loss diets. Pectin is also believed to play a role in lowering cholesterol levels.

When I was teaching, I frequently suffered excess acid brought on by stress and an empty stomach. Several store-bought remedies met with imperfect success. Eventually I discovered that dried apple slices absorbed and neutralized the acid in real time, curbed the hunger, and left a pleasant taste in my mouth. After that, I kept dried apple slices in my desk at all times, and suffered no more.

Wild or feral cherries and plums (genus *Prunus*), like apples, are often more appealing than their modern descendants. Cherries in particular were once widely used in cooking and preserves. The tart, firm fruits of many vacant-lot trees are still better for these purposes than commercial varieties, almost all of which are too sweet and too juicy to be of much use in baking.

Feral cherries occur anywhere farms once existed. Most are red, but pink, purple, blue, and black varieties turn up as well. One pie cherry commonly found growing feral is a striking yellow.

Wild species such as pin cherry (*P. pensylvanica*), bitter cherry (*P. emarginata*), and black cherry (*P. serotina*) may or may not bear usable fruit, depending on personal preference and local growing conditions. However, with the addition of sugar or sweeter fruits, most become valuable edibles.

Though chokecherry (*P. virginiana*) owes its name to the astringent nature of its unripe fruit, ripe chokecherries are among the most sought-after cooking cherries. First Nations peoples dried them in quantity for the winter, and early European settlers held chokecherry pie and jelly in high esteem. Appalachian hill cultures still make wine and syrup from them. Bright red chokecherries set in heavy, almost grapelike bunches, an efficient configuration for picking.

Wild cherry species are found throughout most of North America. Some, such as chokecherries, have been so widely introduced beyond their native range that they are practically universal. Wild cherries are rarely larger than a marble and usually black or red. Large stones in all wild and some feral cherries make them a pain to pit. Instead, they should be cooked, mashed, and sieved or strained. The pulp and juice can then be used in syrup, jelly, beverages, and pies.

High in iron, cherries nourish the liver and circulatory system. They also stimulate digestion, flush the intestines, and combat urinary disorders. Their laxative effect made them the, er, butt of many jokes when I was a kid. Cherries are also recommended for joint disorders such as arthritis or gout. Cherry syrup was once so popular as a sore throat treatment that cherry remains the dominant cough syrup flavor to this day.

Wild and feral plums are less widespread, but foragers may encounter them all the same. Canada (*P. nigra*) and American plum (*P. americana*) are native to the eastern half of the continent, and have been widely introduced elsewhere. The smooth, translucent skin of both recalls a nectarine in color and texture. American plums are a uniform red and somewhat powdery. Canada plums tend to blush red over a yellow foundation, and have no powdery yeast bloom. Their juicy yellow flesh tastes sour, particularly around the large, flat pit. Blue garden plum (*P. domestica*), or prune, is the most common feral plum. Its distinctive, powdery blue half-moons are easily spotted in late summer and early fall. Juicy and tart, with amber flesh, they are tasty fresh or dried and integrate nicely into recipes.

Plums are highly flavored, if somewhat messy, table fruit. Though rarely used in savory dishes here, plums garnish roasted meats in the Near East, and dried prunes are a traditional ingredient of cockaleekie, Scotland's robust chicken soup. (But I leave them out, because poaching prunes in chicken broth multiplies their laxative effect exponentially.) Wrapped in fried bacon and pinned with a toothpick, dried plums are a simple and novel Norman hors d'œuvre. Prunes also traditionally fill French *clafouti*, a chewy pastry. *Pruneau*, a high-test French liquor, is distilled from plums.

Leonard Louis Levinson's *Complete*

Book of Pickles and Relishes (see Further Reading) contains an intriguing recipe for ersatz olives that calls for unripe plums. I haven't had an opportunity to try this, but it looks a great deal easier than the elaborate brining procedure that real olives require.

Ginkgo

At 200 million years of age, the ginkgo (*Ginkgo biloba*), or maidenhair tree, is the world's oldest living tree species. Though ginkgo forests blanketed the planet in primordial times, today no naturally seeded stands remain. In fact, the sole surviving species would have followed the rest of the Ginkgoaceae family into the fossil record, had Buddhists not adopted it as a religious symbol. Lovingly attended by Asian monks over the past two thousand years, ginkgo beat the odds. Today it is even reclaiming some of its lost territory, albeit sporadically, as an ornamental rather than a forest tree.

> **Cherry and plum stones contain** toxic cyanogenic glycocides. Cherry stones are particularly hazardous, as they are more likely to be swallowed. The stone's impervious wooden shell usually protects the swallower from harm, but poisonings have occurred, especially in children. The best defense is to spit out all fruit pits and teach children to do likewise.

As a living time capsule, ginkgo is a fascinating evolutionary case history. Although it bears a superficial resemblance to broadleaf trees, most tree identification guides list it with the conifers. Nature had yet to finalize these categories when the first ginkgo spread its branches to the sun, and as a result it has components of both. (As a prototype, ginkgo also has experimental features nature has since abandoned, such as its unique reproductive structures.) Considering that the first platypus frolicked in ginkgo forests already millions of years old, ginkgo's ambiguous design is perhaps not so odd as it appears.

Ginkgo is a good-news bad-news scenario for foragers. Few foods have stood the test of time like ginkgo nuts; humans have horded them since we were tree shrews. Called *eunheng* in Korea and *baiguo* in China, ginkgo nuts are prized in Far East cuisines to this day.

On the other hand, to get at these sought-after seeds, marauding hominids must overcome ginkgo's otherworldly prehistoric defenses. To put it bluntly, ripe ginkgo fruit smells remarkably like vomit. And the nuts are inside the fruit. One autumn I watched passersby in Portland, Oregon, gag in disgust as elderly Vietnamese women filled shopping bags with mushy fruits from a downtown sidewalk. To longtime Portlanders, the "stinko" was nothing more than an annual nuisance. The immigrants knew better.

The fact is, once the smelly yellow pulp is cleaned away, ginkgo nuts are completely inoffensive. Leave them to dry for a week or so, then gently crack and peel their shells off. Scald the kernels briefly in boiling water to loosen their brown

Ginko (*Ginko biloba*).

outer skin, which is also peeled off. The yellowish result, which must be cooked before eating, is the honored "nut."

> **High in starch, ginkgo nuts** quickly go bad at room temperature. Refrigeration extends shelf life to a week or so, freezing to several months.

Emerald green when cooked, ginkgo nuts are the "eight jewels" in classic Chinese dishes of the same name. Ginkgo nuts' creamy texture and rich flavor are equally welcome in appetizers, main dishes, and desserts. Threaded on long pine needles, they are barbecued over hibachis in Japan. But many Asians insist the simplest approach is best: Just fry newly shelled nuts in vegetable oil, rub them on paper towels to remove the brown skin, salt lightly, and munch with sake or cold beer.

Chinese doctors prescribe ginkgo for a litany of disorders, including indigestion, respiratory difficulties, hypertension, and hangovers. Gingko is also reputed to cleanse and stimulate the circulatory system. Recent studies suggest ginkgo leaf extract may prevent or even reverse memory loss, apparently because it promotes circulation to pertinent parts of the brain.

Though ginkgo forests once spanned the North American West, it has been extinct on this continent for millions of years. Today, ginkgo's superb resistance to air pollution has spurred a comeback in urban areas. Landscapers tend to snub female ginkgoes because they bear the strong-smelling fruits, but the odd female inevitably slips through. Older neighborhoods are especially good prospects for sidewalk spoils. (No pun intended.)

Gleditsia

Finding the sweet pods of honey locust (*Gleditsia triacanthos*) can be a challenge in residential areas. Though a popular landscape tree in hot, dry regions, most nursery-produced cultivars are both thornless and fruitless. But wild honey locusts persist in some yards and parks, as well as on undeveloped land. Further, birds and squirrels greatly appreciate honey locust's long, corkscrew-shaped seedpods, and their attentions account for many random occurrences in and around suburban neighborhoods.

A member of the Fabaceae family, honey locust bears thin, yellow-green seedpods that recall those of fellow legumes such as beans and peas. Honey locust's twisted, leathery pods are significantly larger though, attaining fifteen inches in length. Up to fifteen pairs of two-inch

I have never seen or heard a warning about honey locust pulp, though some sources question the practice of brewing coffee from the ground roasted seeds. There are also accounts of people becoming sick after eating pulp from other leguminous trees such as mescal bean (*Sophora secundiflora*) and black locust (*Robinia pseudoacacia*). Some toxic look-a-likes are even called "honey locust" locally. Accept no substitutes; consult a reliable field guide before collecting, and be sure that only genuine *Gleditsia triacanthos* pod pulp makes it to the table.

Honey locust (*Gleditsia triacanthos*).

oval leaves adorn the shoots, which vaguely resemble domestic pea plants. The branches of natural varieties are armed with two- to three-inch, make-my-day thorns. Curved like sabers, with smaller spines jutting from their bases, they are enough to give the most intrepid forager pause.

In exchange for braving these defenses, the collector gets a quantity of sweet, spongy pod pulp. After splitting open the pods and removing the toxic seeds, scoop this pulp out of the shell and use it as a flavoring and sweetener for other foods. It can also be made into jam. Some Southern African tribes take advantage of honey locust pulp's high sugar content to ferment a beer-like drink.

Soviet doctors investigating honey locust pulp as a potential chemotherapy resource discovered that an extract of the distilled pulp was effective against cancerous tumors. Unfortunately, it was too harmful to healthy tissues to warrant widespread use. The pulp is also taken for respiratory complaints in Africa, while Eastern Woodland cultures use it in cold medications and as a stomachic.

Juglans

Nuts were an important source of protein and fat otherwise wanting in winter diets in the days before refrigeration. Today's suburbanites resent nut trees for interfering with lawn care equipment, littering driveways, and pelting cars. Still, many soldier on, particularly in older "porch swing and back alley" neighborhoods. And it's no accident that the most common suburban nut trees are also the most useful. Surviving against the odds, their once-prized crop rotting in storm drains and leaf piles, they wait patiently for people to return to their senses.

While living in an old residential section of Chilliwack, British Columbia, I was pleasantly astonished to find that nearly every block had at least one walnut or butternut tree (genus *Juglans*). Squirrel-related occurrences notwithstanding, the sheer number of these trees so far from their natural range was astounding. Early Chilliwack residents clearly had more than shade in mind when they planted these handsome trees.

Black walnut (*Juglans nigra*) and butternut (*J. cinerea*) are both native to eastern North America, where they are a common forest tree. As my Chilliwack experience suggests, both have been widely planted in yards and parks across the continent. A third species, English walnut (*J. regia*), which bears the familiar commercial walnut, is also common in residential areas, particularly on former farmland. The nuts of all are edible both green and ripe, and yield a light, delicately flavored oil for which gourmets pay exorbitant prices. Throw in valuable timber and one of the most effective natural dyes (see Dyers' Notes), and you have a veritable retirement plan with leaves.

Young saplings of this genus are sometimes mistaken for sumac, whose foliage resembles their own. *Juglans'* narrow, pointed leaves grow in pairs on opposite sides of the branch tips, ending in a single terminal leaf. Both foliage and fruit give the tree a tropical air. Clustered, unripe walnuts resemble large unripe plums, while green butternuts, drooping in long, double strings, look like limes. *Juglans* fruits are easily sliced or pierced when they first appear. By midsummer a woody shell begins to form inside, and by autumn the nut is fully developed inside a leathery green husk as thick as an orange peel, but much tougher.

Ripe nuts are traditionally picked before they fall, then the tough husk is removed, a procedure that can leave unprotected hands stained for weeks. Left undisturbed, many trees carry their fruit until the husk opens, dumping the nuts on the ground. This relieves foragers of tedious husking, but they must compete with squirrels, crows, and insects for the harvest. Once on the ground, nuts also mildew quickly. Butternuts and some walnuts drop their fruit, husks and all, and the nuts lie about in the decaying pulp, looking like rotting apples or plums. Unhusking these varieties is a royal mess, but may be worth the trouble. Once the husk is removed, the nuts assume recognizable form.

English walnuts are the easiest *Juglans* nuts to shell. The shells of some varieties are easily opened with the fingers alone. Commercial varieties have to withstand shipping conditions, so their shells are heavier and harder to crack, but none are as tough to open as black walnuts and butternuts.

Naturally, black walnuts and butternuts are preferred by connoisseurs, but their rock-hard shells are difficult to crack. (Butternuts' nefarious "beak" is an added challenge. The first attempt to slide a hand into a pocketful of foraged butternuts is invariably the last.) A hammer or rock is effective but clumsy. In an interesting case of role reversal, one West Virginia forager even scatters black walnuts on his driveway and drives over them. A less radical strategy is to squeeze each nut in a carpenter's vice until the shell pops, then pry out the meats. This allows nutmeats to be extracted in relatively large pieces.

Juglans nuts must be dried before the meats are extracted. Place the unopened nuts in a pillowcase, old pair of pantyhose, or paper bag, then hang them in a dry place until the nutmeats are firm and crisp and have the characteristic mellow walnut flavor. This generally takes about a month. They can then be shelled for use in snacking or baking. Undried nutmeats are edible but have a harsh edge and rubbery texture. Eating too many of them may cause gastric disturbances. They may be cooked, however, and are particularly well suited to stir-frying.

Juglans nuts will keep up to a year in their shells, but once shelled they quickly go rancid owing to their high oil content. Nutmeats that are to be kept more than a few weeks should be frozen in an airtight container.

Most people assume *Juglans'* usefulness ends there, but in truth we've barely started. Long before the nuts ripen, before the shells even begin to develop, they are a delicacy appreciated in Europe since pre-Roman times. Though these green nuts cannot be eaten fresh, or even cooked, they make sublime pickles and condiments. England's traditional jet-black walnut ketchup predates the tomato kind, while green walnut pickles crossed the Atlantic with the first settlers and entered the cuisines of New England and the Upper South. Chutneys and relishes are also made from these unusual fruits. Strain leftover brine through wet muslin, bring it to a boil, bottle, and allow it to cure for a week or so before using like soy sauce. The Italians even make an elegant liqueur called *nocino* from green walnuts.

Black walnut
(*Juglans nigra*).

Gather green *Juglans* nuts no later than the end of June, when the nutshell begins to coalesce. If a long, ungalvanized nail or darning needle passes all the way through without meeting resistance, the nut is good for pickling. Pickling stock should also be fresh and unblemished. Recent blowdowns are suitable if undamaged, but avoid those that have lain about in the sun for several days.

The sticky, velvety substance that covers green butternuts quickly coats pickers' fingers with duct-tape-strength adhesive. A plastic sack pulled over the hand averts a gummy mess. Also, unripe butternuts and walnuts ooze an indelible yellow-brown dye when pierced or cut. Foragers who prefer the original color of counter tops, kitchen implements, clothing, and skin should use an apron, rubber gloves, plastic sheeting, and an expendable cutting board while working with them.

Juglans nuts set liberally on lower branches, so bucketfuls can usually be gathered in minutes with no more equipment than a berry hook. Strings of butternuts can be nipped off with a long-handled tree pruner. I find butternuts better suited to ketchup than pickles, if only because their felty covering feels a bit odd on the tongue. I have tried dipping them in boiling water and scrubbing, as some sources advise, without success. Butternuts also tend to be smaller than walnuts, and need be brined only three-quarters as long in pickle and ketchup recipes.

Recent studies suggest polyunsaturated and monounsaturated fats in ripe walnuts may lower the risk of heart disease. Whether these health benefits balance their high calorie count is a matter for debate.

Butternut Alert

A microscopic fungus with the jaw-breaking name of *Sirococcus clavigignenti-juglandacearum* is wiping out butternut trees across North America. Sores full of black muck appear on infected individuals, giving rise to the fungus' common name, butternut canker. Scientists have had some success developing canker-resistant strains, but the battle is far from over. Foragers should report any healthy butternuts growing near diseased trees to the nearest agricultural college, provincial Department of Agriculture, or county Extension agent. Genetic material from such trees might save the species from the sad fate of the American chestnut.

Magnolia

When I was a graduate student in Angers, France, the local botanical garden was my favorite place to study. One sunny afternoon I found it impossible to focus on my books. Eventually I became aware of a rich perfume that was swirling around me, dissolving my concentration. Searching for its source, I spied a huge white blossom on a branch overhanging my bench. Twisting to see the plaque at the base of the tree, I read, "*Magnolia grandiflora. Sud des États Unis.*" For the first time I understood the Southern obsession with this elegant, aristocratic tree.

Saucer magnolia (*Magnolia soulangiana*).

Magnolia is a common yard and street tree throughout North America. Some are evergreens; others leaf out after the spring bloom and drop their leaves in autumn. Blossoms may be small and bright, like star magnolia (*Magnolia stellata*), tulip-shaped like saucer magnolia (*M. soulangiana*), or huge and voluptuous like the glorious Southern magnolia (*M. grandiflora*). Many bloom twice, once in early spring, when deciduous magnolias are all flower and no foliage, and again in late summer. Symbol of America's subtropical South, magnolias actually occur throughout the continent, though cool northern nights rarely draw out the fulsome scent of southern magnolias. Leathery, oblong magnolia leaves decompose slowly, and unless the groundskeeper is particularly attentive, both ever-

> **Redbud (genus *Cercis*) blossoms** can be used like magnolia in salads and rice dishes. Redbud is common in eastern North America and California.

green and deciduous species can be identified by the accumulation of cardboard-crisp dead leaves at the base of the tree.

Magnolia is most useful to suburban foragers as an intriguing culinary herb. The flower buds, picked just after they break free from their downy, oval husk but before they open, lend a faint horseradish tingle to soups, salads, and sandwiches. The husks and any green parts, which may be bitter, should be discarded before use. Saucer magnolia buds are my favorite, though others can be used as well. In Asia, pickled yulan magnolia (*M. denudata*) buds are stirred into steamed rice.

Magnolia is also a healing resource in traditional medicine. Chinese magnolia (*M. officinalis*) is used to treat anorexia, malaria, alcoholism, sexual dysfunction, and several dozen other complaints in Asian folk medicine, while in the American South, sweet bay magnolia (*M. virginiana*) fights fever, dysentery, and rheumatism. Mexican herbalists treat scorpion stings with a local magnolia and Japan's Ainu make cold remedies from another.

Morus

In spite of their sweetness and abundance, surprisingly few mulberries (genus *Morus*) make it to the table. Instead, heavily fruiting mulberry trees are excoriated for fouling vehicles and sidewalks. It's time this attitude was overhauled.

Black mulberry (*Morus nigra*).

North American suburbs harbor three Morus species. In order of fruit quality, they are black (*M. nigra*), red (*M. rubra*), and white mulberry (*M. alba*). All are more typical of eastern than western neighborhoods, evidently because eastern neighborhoods are often older. Mulberry leaves vary in shape—sometimes heart-shaped, sometimes lobed, even on the same branch—and the twigs bleed milky sap when cut. Mulberries are aggregate fruits, and black and red ones look remarkably like domestic blackberries. Unlike most tree fruits, mulberries generally ripen randomly over several weeks. This relieves foragers of the gathering and preserving frenzy all-at-once fruits provoke and allows time to perfect recipes. Since fresh mulberries also spoil quickly, this is an important advantage. An efficient collecting technique is to cover the ground beneath a tree with a sheet or tarp and shake the branches. Ripe mulberries fall readily into the net, leaving unripe ones on the tree to be harvested later.

Unripe mulberries, raw mulberry foliage, and mulberry sap are all potentially toxic. They may cause contact dermatitis, and should not be eaten.

White mulberry is native to Asia. Introduced to North America in a nineteenth-century bid to challenge China's silk monopoly, its leaves are practically the only thing silkworms will eat. When the North American silk industry failed, it left white mulberries to threaten native woodlands with their aggressive growth. Historically cultivated for their foliage, many white mulberry cultivars don't even bear fruit. (Even this is not a total loss; Euell Gibbons found new spring mulberry tips a delicious potherb.) Those that do fruit bear pale, edible berries that many foragers find too insipid to be worth the trouble. Others, while acknowledging that white mulberries are too sweet to anchor a recipe, use them to thicken and sweeten pies and puddings of other fruits.

By contrast, red and black mulberries have a pleasant, dry, slightly chewy sweetness. They can be eaten raw, either straight from the tree or with sugar and milk, and are delicious in pies, jams, jellies, and juices. If allowance is made for their sweeter, drier nature, mulberries can be substituted for blackberries in most recipes. Summer pudding, a British dessert well suited to the season for which it is named, is a particularly good way to enjoy mulberries (see Recipes, page 71). Near Eastern cultures sun-dry mulberries and use them year-round like raisins or prunes.

In Europe, mulberry root bark infusions have a long history as a vermifuge. The same concoctions are used as a laxative. Mulberries themselves are high in vitamin C, minerals, and plant proteins, and mulberry syrup is a traditional digestive aid, used to soothe ulcers.

Rhamnus

During the Great Depression, cascara buckthorn (*Rhamnus purshiana*) vanished around Pacific Northwest towns as cash-strapped inhabitants plundered medicinal bark from whole trees and sold it to pharmaceutical companies. The irony of restoring regularity to an obstructed economy by means of this powerful laxative was not lost on backwoods humorists. Even today in some remote logging towns, the mere mention of cascara touches off a torrent of ancient puns.

Small understory trees, buckthorns occur naturally on deforested land and in clearings. Though seldom planted intentionally, they are frequently introduced to residential areas by birds, who relish their glossy black berries.

All of the buckthorns are famous for their leaves, which persist long after other deciduous trees have dropped theirs. Cascara, common to the central and north Pacific coast, has large oval leaves seamed with coarse veins. The leaves of Carolina buckthorn (*R. caroliniana*), native to the Southeast, are narrower and more pointed, with fewer veins, while birchleaf buckthorn (*R. betulaefolia*), a Southwestern species, bears leaves that are narrower still. Introduced European buckthorn (*R. cathartica*) has oval, pointed leaves with a few coarse veins. Its thorny branches gave the genus its common name. Fellow immigrant glossy buckthorn (*R. frangula*) has shiny, many-veined leaves and hairy rather than thorny twigs. Taken together, the species of this expansive genus cover most of temperate North America.

Backyard herbalists can take advantage of buckthorn bark's famous properties by pouring a cup of boiling water over dried, shredded bark, and steeping about an hour over very low heat. (Some sources recommend aging collected bark for at least a year, citing potentially

Cascara buckthorn
(*Rhamnus purshiana*).

violent reactions. I've found the effect varies widely. The bark of some buckthorns is quite weak, even when fresh.) Though the berries of most buckthorns are not considered a valuable medicinal, and some are even reported to be toxic, syrup made from European buckthorn berries has been a remedy for constipation since at least the Middle Ages.

Salix

Rhamnus bark and berries have been known to cause gastric upset and spasms. Users should start with half a teaspoon of shredded bark per cup of water, gradually increasing strength in treatments spaced two hours apart until they reach the desired effect. Fresh bark and unripe berries are considered toxic and should not be infused or ingested.

Vigorous growth under virtually any circumstances has earned the willow (genus *Salix*) an enduring place in parks and yards. By happy coincidence, willow bark is also the oldest and most respected painkiller in history.

Willow has been honored by healers nearly everywhere in the world. No less a luminary than Hippocrates, father of Western medicine, advised his patients to drink willow bark tea and call him in the morning. Nineteenth-century practitioners of the new science of chemistry managed to isolate willow's active ingredient. They dubbed it salicylic acid, after genus *Salix*. A synthetic version, acetyl salicylic acid (ASA), hit drugstore shelves under the brand name "Aspirin." Thousands of years after its discovery, willow bark remains "the pain reliever most often prescribed by doctors," albeit in altered form. Few other drugs can boast such thorough time trials.

Weeping willow (*Salix babylonica*).

There are literally hundreds of willow species. Most have soft, narrow leaves without prominent teeth or lobes. Most are little more than shrubs, though some, such as weeping willow (*Salix babylonica*), attain great height and spread. White willow (*S. alba*) is the traditional favorite of European healers, and the species from which salicylic acid was first isolated, though I have also had good results with several other species. Flavor varies between species, mainly between bad and worse.

The constant pruning required to control these trees means that bark is seldom hard to come by. Bark gathered while the tree is in bud is said to be most potent, though bark collected at other times is effective, too. For best results, strip bark from freshly cut branches. If the branches are large enough to have rough, rigid bark like that found on the trunk, the moist, sweet-smelling white cambium should be stripped out and dried for use in tea, and the tough, thick outer bark discarded. The smooth, leathery, easily-peeled bark of smaller branches can be shredded whole and infused with the darker part intact.

Like the over-the-counter medication it inspired, willow bark tea soothes minor discomfort of all sorts, helps cool fevers, and is a mild sedative. Modern herbalists also treat the symptoms of menopause with it. Astringent willow bark decoctions are used topically to combat acne.

Willow tea's acrid, aspirin flavor is quite frankly revolting. Other herbs, such as sumac and mint, plus a dollop of honey, greatly improve the taste and medicinal value of willow infusions (see Flu Lawyer in Recipes, p.72).

Sorbus

A rowan (genus *Sorbus*) in fruit may be as red as it is green. In fact, the word rowan comes from the Germanic root word for red. Pre-Christian Europeans held this striking tree, with its fiery red or orange berries, in high esteem. According to Scottish folklore, malevolent spirits finding a house protected by a rowan will elect to harass the neighbors instead. Similarly, a barnyard or pasture rowan acts as a sort of spiritual flea collar, deflecting misfortune away from the stock. But rowan's power also commands respect. Traditionally, its shadow poisons those who linger in it.

Called mountain-ash or dogberry in the New World, rowan is a popular ornamental. With five to seven pairs of narrow, serrated leaves per shoot and a final leaf growing straight out of the tip, rowan trees resemble small-leaved sumacs. Their flashy fruits, called sorbs, hang in dense clusters and are so vibrant they look as if they're made of plastic or porcelain. Rowan fruit varies greatly in color and flavor from species to species and tree to tree. Where many rowans are available, a berry should be tasted from each to determine which bears the best before picking a large supply.

Rowans typically blaze with orange, red, or (rarely) yellow sorbs from midsummer through late autumn, and are an important source of food for wildlife. I once watched a cacophonous flock of migrating birds strip a large, heavily laden rowan of every last berry in a single hour. Such incidents explain why one-rowan neighborhoods are rare.

Quantities of rowan fruit can be gathered in little time by nipping off the clusters with pruning shears. The sorbs can be separated from the twigs later, or dried by hanging the clusters in a warm, dry place until the berries shrivel and become rubbery.

Sorbs are edible straight from the tree, but most have a disagreeable raw-cranberry taste. When cooked they take on a bittersweet quality that is easy to appreciate. Jewel-like red-orange rowan jelly (see Recipes, page 72), with the lively bite of British marmalade, is one of my all-time favorites. Those who find it too extroverted for toast or scones will appreciate rowan jelly as a glaze or condiment for meats, in which role it is a worthy substitute for cranberry sauce. Sorbs also add character to jams and jellies of sweeter fruit.

A good frost sweetens rowan berries considerably, and recipes made with these "shocked" sorbs have little of the sophistication (i.e., bitterness) of those made with pre-frost fruits. Some find this an advantage. Personally, I prefer the complex bouquet of unshocked rowan berries.

Sorb wine, brandy, and liqueur are much sought after in Northern European countries. Rowan berries are also pressed and the juice fermented into a tangy, reddish, cider-like beverage, or fermented with apple cider to add tannin and color. Rowan berries' color, tannin, and flavor also make them a useful additive to fruit and flower wines.

Rowan fruit is high in vitamin C. With its pectin and tannin, sorb jelly is a pleasant-tasting response to diarrhea. Folk

> **Salicylic acid levels in willow** bark infusions are fairly low, so healthy adults can enjoy multiple cups, gently boosting the cumulative effect with each. Nevertheless, willow bark tea is essentially an aspirin-delivery system. Children, pregnant women, and those allergic to aspirin should steer well clear of it.

Rowan, or mountain-ash (*Sorbus* sp.).

> Since sorbs are seldom consumed in quantity, their high tannin content is rarely hazardous. Still, discretion is the better part of valor where rowan is concerned. Rowan seeds contain amygdalin, a toxin present in the pits of many tree fruits. For this reason I prefer to make jelly or seedless jam, and I limit my intake of fresh sorbs to pre-picking tastes. My wife, who is allergic to most tree fruits, has a mild reaction to rowan berries.

healers recommend applying astringent rowan berry infusions topically to shrink hemorrhoids. Gargled, the same infusions are said to be an effective treatment for a sore throat.

Tilia

During my time as a student in Angers I lived with a local couple, both of whom were products of large Angevin peasant families. Each Sunday the entire clan came together on someone's farm. The men immediately repaired to the barn, where the host passed out jelly glasses full of outstanding homemade wine, tapped directly from his huge, ancient wooden cask. Then we leaned on the tractor, sipped wine from bottomless glasses, and engaged in the international farmer pastime of grousing about the government. French farmers know what living is all about.

After an hour or so we rejoined the women in the house for a pot of fragrant, yellow-green *tilleul*. The sweet, lemony fragrance of this soothing herbal tea always takes me back to those lazy Sunday afternoons.

Tilleul is the French word for linden (genus *Tilia*), also called basswood or lime (no relation to the citrus fruit of the same name). American linden (*T. americana*), native to the eastern half of North America, and European linden (*T. cordata*) are common yard trees throughout the continent. More exotic lindens also crop up in landscaping from time to time.

Linden bears heart-shaped leaves with serrated edges, hand-sized on the North American species, smaller on the European. The branches often droop in a semi-weeping fashion. Small, yellowish green, highly perfumed blossoms hang in sprays among the leaves in early summer. These flowers, which produce a delicate, much-sought-after honey, are the reason beekeepers frequently plant linden near their hives.

Tea drinkers pull down the flower clusters and dry them for year-round use. This necessarily involves tearing off part of the tree, so foragers should be careful only to take the flower sprays and leave the foliage. Traditionally, fresh linden flowers are spread on a sheet in the sun until dry and papery, then sealed in airtight jars. They may also be placed in a paper bag and left on a warm dry shelf for a week or so, then stored in jars or resealable plastic bags.

Linden tea has widely recognized medicinal properties. French country folk rely on it to calm nerves and induce drowsiness. *Tilia* infusions also treat weak heart, high blood pressure, and the moodiness occasioned by pregnancy. As stress

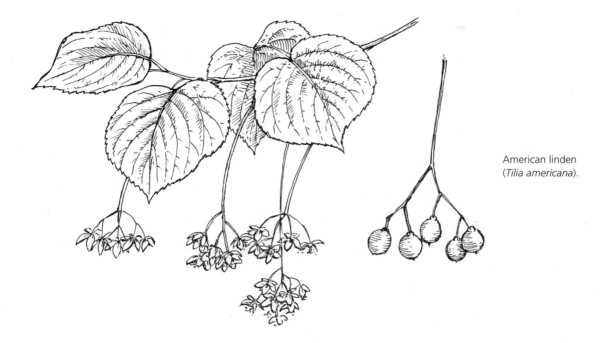

American linden
(*Tilia americana*).

aggravates all of these afflictions, linden's true effect is probably related to its well-known sedative properties. Yet linden tea is also unusually benign. It remains one of the few medications obstetricians allow pregnant patients to take. (Nevertheless, pregnant women should consult their own doctor before drinking it.) Linden tea is also a common beverage in Europe, taken day after day without adverse consequences.

To make linden tea, cover the dried flowers with boiling water and infuse for five minutes or so. I use about a tablespoon of crushed dried flowers for a mugful. The result is sweet enough to drink without honey. Linden blends well with other flavors such as mint, and is a favorite tea-mixing ingredient. In addition to tea and cosmetic infusions, dried linden flowers are added to beer in the fermenting stages to give it a sweet mellowness.

> **A very strong linden infusion,** made by soaking a pint of flowers in a quart or so of boiling water, is said to keep Eastern European country girls' skin clear and glowing when used as a facial rinse. In Western Europe, the same concoction is a rinse for blond hair.

A Pleasant-Smelling Plague

In the early part of the twentieth century, California speculators planted eucalyptus (genus *Eucalyptus*) trees by the thousands. At up to 15 feet of growth per year, promoters said the Australian native would make fortunes overnight. And it might have, if California-grown eucalyptus had any timber value. In the end, the only enduring result of the eucalyptus rush was the entry of an aggressive intruder into native Californian habitats, one whose camphorous leaves feed only koalas and forest fires. The former are rare, the latter all too common in California.

Nevertheless, foragers can wring some benefits from this admittedly beautiful, pleasant-smelling tree. A gunny sack or pillow case stuffed with long, aromatic dried eucalyptus leaves makes nontoxic, anti-flea bedding for pets. Eucalyptus leaves can also be layered into folded blankets and clothing to repel moths and keep linens smelling fresh, or added to potpourri and humidifying air fresheners.

During a visit to Oakland, California, I pocketed several showerhead-shaped eucalyptus seed cases. They were promptly forgotten, and passed into the wash with the pants I had been wearing. On emptying the dryer, I found that warm, heady camphor vapors had freshened the whole load. Eucalyptus nuts don't have the heavy, overpowering perfume of commercial dryer sheets, and the price is right. Now I pester friends visiting the Bay Area to bring me back a sackful of them.

Foraging Advisory

For reasons of practicality, I have not discussed using acorns (nuts of the oak, genus *Quercus*) as food in this chapter. While acorns are a staple of hunter-gatherer societies, their high tannin content renders the unprocessed kernels of many unpalatable, even toxic. Such acorns require labor-intensive leaching, drying, and roasting before they can be eaten. This is particularly true of red oak acorns. While the sweeter acorns of some white and chestnut oaks are sometimes eaten without leaching, I find their bitter-bland flavor doesn't justify the effort. Readers interested in acorn cuisine will find detailed information on the subject in *Edible Wild Fruits and Nuts of Canada*, by Adam F. Szczawinski and Nancy J. Turner, and *Stalking the Wild Asparagus*, by Euell Gibbons (see Further Reading).

Leguminous trees, those that bear pea- or bean-like seed cases, are very often toxic. These trees usually have thorny branches and bear lovely chains of white or yellow blossoms in spring. With the exception of honey locust, they should be avoided. This includes Kentucky coffeetree (*Gymnocladus dioicus*).

Although settlers apparently made coffee from its roasted seeds, most authorities agree this practice is dangerous. Given that many safer wild coffee substitutes are available, foragers should sidestep this one.

Black cherry (*Prunus serotina*) bark has a long history of medical service, but like all Prunus bark it contains cyanide and should not be used by amateurs.

Horse chestnut (*Aesculus hippocastanum*) may be the best-represented ornamental tree in suburbia. Fragrant blossom chains appear in mid-spring to blanket the ground with unseasonal snow in early summer. In autumn, its beautiful, piano-finished nuts break free of their thick, bristly husks to litter streets and driveways. Horse chestnuts closely resemble edible chestnuts, but are rounder and toxic to horse and human alike.

The most effective way to collect bark for dyeing is to take advantage of windfalls and prunings. Stripping bark from standing trees opens them up to all manner of pests and disease, and is not good foraging form.

Dyers' Notes

Juglans bark, husks, and green nuts are the big dyeing news in broadleaf trees. All species tint just about anything a colorfast olive, grey, or brown. Legend has it that the thirteenth-century Scottish patriot Sir William Wallace dyed himself with walnuts, then took up a harp and spied on the English royal family for weeks posing as a sun-bronzed minstrel. Chopped green nuts, husks, or bark, boiled in water, produce a dye that is even more permanent on fabric than it is on skin. Butternut dye was so widely used on Confederate uniforms in the American Civil War that "butternut" became the name of the color itself.

I dye new, freshly laundered white cotton tee-shirts in brine left over from pickling *Juglans* nuts. I first strain the brine through wet muslin to remove impurities, then bring it to a boil, remove the pot from the heat, and poke a shirt into it with a wooden spoon. When cool enough to handle, I transfer shirt and brine to a large lidded plastic container to steep for several days, during which time I stir it often to distribute the dye evenly. I then remove the shirt and allow it to drip-dry on a clothesline. A cold-water machine washing and it comes out an earthy, vaguely military grey-brown. Further treatments deepen or refresh the hue.

Juglans dyes require no mordant, though adding different substances brings out alternate shades. For example, *Juglans* dyestuffs boiled in an iron kettle or with iron filings yield black dye.

Rowan berries are a traditional source of tannin for mordanting.

Dyers use birch and apple leaves and bark to produce a variety of earth tones in conjunction with alum.

Beech bark produces soft grey with an iron mordant.

Mature Japanese maple leaves yield plum purple with an iron mordant.

Cherry bark yields salmon pink, willow bark a lighter pink, on alum-mordanted wool.

Buckthorn bark and berries are said to produce a light brown on alum-mordanted wool, and a slightly lighter, colorfast brown on cotton mordanted with alum and tannin.

Oak (genus *Quercus*) bark yields dark brown or black, and requires no mordant. Acorns are a source of tannin. Oak galls, nut-like growths caused by parasitic wasps, were prized by preindustrial weavers as a source of particularly excellent tannins.

The Amish make Easter egg dyes by infusing oak, maple, and apple bark, crabapple leaves, blossoms, and bark, and walnut hulls with water, vinegar, and alum.

Recipes

Walnut Pickles

YIELDS ONE PINT.

These pickles are traditionally served with roast beef or other strong meat, to cleanse the palate so diners can continue to appreciate the meat's full flavor. Walnut pickles are a surprising treat, and make a colorful garnish for cold plates.

10–12 green walnuts
3 cups pickling salt
1 gallon water

Pierce each nut all the way through three or four times with a darning needle or ungalvanized nail. (Galvanized nails may provoke a toxic reaction with the nuts' natural juices.)

Dissolve the salt in the water. Place the nuts in a lidded, nonreactive container and cover with one-third of the brine. Let them stand in a cool place for 3 days, stirring at least once a day. Change the brine and repeat, then change the brine and repeat again.

At the end of the third brining, drain the nuts. Dry them for 3 days, ideally in direct sunlight. (If drying outside, bring them in at night to prevent them from absorbing moisture from the night air.) When completely dry, the nuts will be jet black, pulpy, and wrinkled, and weigh practically nothing.

To make the pickling liquid, place the following ingredients in a large, nonreactive saucepan:

2 cups cider or wine vinegar
1/8 cup sugar
4 whole cloves
2 whole peppercorns
1/4 teaspoon ground allspice

R
E
C
I
P
E
S

Bring all ingredients to a boil, cover, and simmer over low heat for 30 minutes.

Place the dried nuts in a hot, sterilized pint jar. They will fall far short of filling it at this stage. Fill the jar to the rim with hot liquid and wait 5 minutes, while the remaining liquid simmers in its covered pan.

When the nuts have absorbed about a quarter of the liquid and have swollen considerably, refill the jar to the rim with hot liquid and seal.

Allow the pickles to cure 1 month before eating. They will keep at least a year in the brine, but should be refrigerated after opening.

Butternut Ketchup

An aromatic, jet-black condiment especially good with broiled or grilled meats, this traditional English recipe is a real conversation-starter at barbecues. Green walnuts can substitute for the butternuts.

25 green butternuts
2 tablespoons pickling salt, divided
1 large clove garlic
1/2 cup chopped onion
Cider or wine vinegar

Pierce each nut all the way through three or four times with a darning needle or ungalvanized nail. (Galvanized nails may provoke a toxic reaction with the nuts' natural juices.) Place them in a large, nonreactive container with a watertight lid.

Add 1 tablespoon of pickling salt and cover the nuts with water.

Cover and turn the container gently end-over-end to dissolve the salt. Place in a cool place and turn it daily the same way for 7 days. (If the butternuts are smaller than average, brine them for only 5 days.)

At the end of the brining period, drain the nuts, cover them with fresh water and add the second tablespoon of pickling salt. Brine nuts for another 7 days, as above.

At end of the second brining period, drain the nuts and place them in a large, nonreactive saucepan with the garlic and onion. Cover with vinegar and bring to a boil. Lower the heat to medium-low and stew the nuts until they are completely soft, about half an hour. Remove the pan from heat and allow the nuts to cool to handling temperature.

Mash the nuts in the vinegar with a potato masher, then grind them fine in a blender or food processor. Finally, pass the mash through the finest screen on a hand food mill, or force it through a sieve. (The whole process can be accomplished in a food mill by passing the mash through each screen from coarsest to finest, but this is time-consuming.)

At this point, the mixture will be a uniform black sludge. Return this to the saucepan with the following:

1 tablespoon brown sugar	1 teaspoon ground cloves
1 teaspoon pickling salt	1/4 plus 1/8 teaspoon cayenne
1 tablespoon black pepper	1 teaspoon celery seeds, tied in a bag
2 teaspoons ground ginger	1 cup water
2 teaspoons ground allspice	1/2 cup dry white wine

Cover loosely and simmer for 45 minutes to 1 hour at medium-low heat. Bottle or jar the mixture when it reaches the consistency of tomato ketchup. If it thickens too quickly, thin it with a little brine.

Allow butternut ketchup to age at least a week in the refrigerator before using to allow seasonings to infuse and to mellow the green edge. (Butternut ketchup reaches optimum flavor in about 2 months.)

Mulberry Summer Pudding

SERVES 6.

This traditional British recipe requires only cursory cooking and is served chilled, two features that make it ideal for the dog days of summer. Other soft fruits, such as black-berries or pitted cherries, can be mixed with the mulberries.

6 cups ripe red or black mulberries
$1/2$ teaspoon ground cloves
$1/2$ teaspoon ground cinnamon
$1/2$ teaspoon ground nutmeg
1 cup sugar
About 8 slices of bread (homemade bread works best)

In a large, nonreactive saucepan, gently stir together the fruit, spices, and sugar. Heat the mixture very lightly, about 5 minutes, to dissolve the sugar and bring the juice out of the berries. The mulberries should be only slightly mashed in the process, turning the whole into a syrupy, cohesive mass. Remove from the heat and set aside to cool.

Trim the crust from the bread slices. Wet a 1-quart pudding basin or mixing bowl and line it with plastic wrap. Cut the bread slices so as to line the edges of the bowl. (The slices should overlap on one side, domino-style.) When they are in place, cut a slice to fit snugly in the bottom.

Gently spoon the berry mixture into the bread-lined basin, being careful not to displace the bread. Cut a few more slices of bread to cover the fruit.

Place a plate face up on top of the final bread layer. Put enough weight on the plate to compress the pudding over several hours (four 16-ounce cans typically do the job) and place the whole thing in the refrigerator. Chill overnight.

To serve, remove the weight, hold another plate face-down against the bowl, and flip them over together. Jiggle the pudding gently out of the bowl and remove the plastic wrap. Cut thick slices of pudding and top them with whipped cream, or serve with cheese or ice cream on the side.

Flu Lawyer

MAKES ONE MUG.

A steamy, aromatic tea that combines willow bark's famous pain-relieving properties with better-tasting medicinals and a generous dollop of honey. Just what the doctor ordered for cold and flu symptoms.

2 teaspoons dried willow bark, crumbled · Two thin slices fresh ginger root
1¹/₂ cups water · ¹/₄ cup sumac juice (see p. 113) or lemon juice
¹/₂ teaspoon dried mint leaves, crumbled · 1 tablespoon honey

Simmer the bark, water, mint, and ginger over low heat for 10 to 15 minutes. (Do not boil.) Strain the infusion into a mug, add sumac juice and honey, and stir. If the willow flavor is too strong, add more honey.

Warning: willow bark contains salicylic acid (aspirin). Pregnant women, small children, and those allergic to aspirin should avoid willow bark infusions.

Rowan Jelly

YIELDS 2 PINTS.

Crystalline, resembling cranberry sauce in flavor, rowan jelly is especially good with turkey and game. I like it on toast or scones, where its marmalade qualities come to the fore.

6 cups rowan berries, washed
¹/₂ pound underripe cooking apples, chopped. (About 4 medium-sized pie apples,
or 12 crabapples)
1 teaspoon sumac juice (see p. 113) or lemon juice
1 cup sugar per cup of juice (ordinarily about 4 cups)

Dice the apples and place them with the berries in a nonreactive saucepan. Add the lemon or sumac juice and cover with water. Cover the pan and simmer until the fruit is completely soft, 30 to 45 minutes.

Remove the pan from the heat. When the fruit has cooled enough to handle, mash it to a fine pulp. Return it to the heat and simmer 5 minutes more.

Tie up the mash in a square of wet muslin and allow the juice to drip into a bowl for several hours or overnight.

Gently wring the remaining juice through the muslin and discard the pulp. Measure the juice back into the pan, add sugar in the proper proportion, and stir until it dissolves. Boil the syrup until it yields a successful spoon test (see p. 17–18).

Pour or ladle the syrup into hot, sterilized jars and seal.

Homemade Apple Pectin

It takes a lot more apples than store-bought pectin to make a batch of jam or jelly (4 pints of homemade apple pectin equal 6 ounces of commercial liquid pectin), but the results are worth it. The foraged product easily outperforms commercial liquid pectin at the cash register, too.

Slice slightly green apples or crabapples and place them in a nonreactive pot. (No need to peel or core, but long-stemmed crabapples should be stemmed.) Add 2 cups of water per pound of apples and boil for 15 minutes, or until the apples are soft.

Mash the apples with a potato masher. Strain the liquid through a square of wet muslin. Allow the juice to drip out naturally, without squeezing, pressing, or wringing.

When the dripping slows to a drop per minute, return the apple mash to the pot and add the same amount of fresh water as the first time. Bring it briefly to a boil, then simmer over medium heat for another 15 minutes. Turn off heat and let the mash steep for another 15 minutes.

Repeat the straining process, adding the juice to that already collected. When mash has cooled enough to handle, gather it up in the cloth and thoroughly wring out the remaining juice. The pectin can then be used or frozen for later.

Japanese Maple Leaf Gelatin Mold

SERVES 6.

Equal parts sculpture and salad, this dish never fails to enchant. Be sure to use only very young, very fresh Japanese maple leaves.

2 packages strawberry-flavored gelatin powder
About 12 just-opened Japanese maple leaves
One 8-ounce can grapes, drained
One 8-ounce can pears, drained and sliced

Mix the gelatin according to the directions on the package for molding. Chill 1 hour.

Wet the Japanese maple leaves and spread them individually on the bottom and sides of a 2-quart mixing bowl, so that they are not touching. (The moisture will hold them in place.)

Stir the fruit into the gelatin and spoon the mixture carefully into the lined bowl, so as not to displace the leaves.

Refrigerate 2 hours, or until the gelatin has set.

Before serving, gently loosen the edge of the gelatin with a knife or spatula. Dip the bowl very briefly to the rim in warm water. Holding the bowl at a slight angle, rotate it slowly to loosen the contents. Invert a chilled plate on top and hold it against the bowl while flipping both over. The salad should slide onto the plate intact.

four | # THE REMARKABLE TALENTS
OF COMMON FLOWERS

— Detail: Evening primrose *(Oenothera* sp.*)*.

Throughout most of history, human life has been, in the words of Thomas Hobbes, "solitary, poor, nasty, brutish, and short." Common people struggled daily for the means to survive, and any time or energy left over went to building reserves against even harder times. Indeed, many people in the world still live this way.

Into such a world the first garden flowers were born. Gardeners are often surprised to learn that their favorite blossoms were once hard-working crops, cultivated not for their beauty but for material gain. Their contributions to our ancestors' well-being earned them their current comfortable retirement in the suburbs. Yet, subsequent genetic manipulation permitting, these herbs are as useful as ever. Suburban foragers can count on the quantity and quality of these old friends.

Garden flowers may not be "wild" in the literal sense, since they are often carefully tended, but they are wild edibles in the suburban sense. They are not considered food crops, and often go feral, or establish perennial or self-renewing stands in neglected corners. Conversely, a few wildflowers are establishing themselves in cultivated gardens at the behest of gardeners involved in the native gardening movement and those sowing meadow seed mixes. California poppy and evening primrose, to name two, frequently turn up in yards, parks, and highway medians, thanks to these seed mixes.

Though several books have appeared on the subject of cooking with flowers, some of them exhaustive (see Further Reading), this chapter focuses on the most common, the most easily processed, and the most flavorful edible garden flowers.

Flower Lore

Original uses aside, a century or more of playing dumb-but-pretty has left its mark on many garden flowers. So many colors, shapes, and (coincidentally) flavors have been drawn from single gene pools that a substantial amount of trial and error is necessary to identify the best-tasting varieties. Blossoms are especially variable, because the pigments that create different shades also taste different. Foragers should try several of them before forming an opinion on an entire species.

It will come as no surprise that ancestral forms, the ones gardeners call "heirlooms," are the most valuable to foragers. Fortunately, heirloom gardening has become widely popular in recent years. Archaic varieties are riding this movement back into neighborhoods all over the continent, and since most are hearty, tenacious plants, they will probably be around for a long time to come.

One advantage of foraging flowers is that blossoms are rarely poisonous. (But see the Foraging Advisory, page 94, for exceptions.) Gardeners, on the other hand, pose a definite threat to foragers. Because they cultivate their flowers for appearance, they often drench plants with toxins to ensure perfection. Systemic pesticides are the worst. These are mixed into the soil and taken up by the roots to become part of the flower itself, in effect converting a harmless plant into a poisonous one. Fortunately, most common systemics have a fairly short cycle, or active period. Once the host plant cycles the foreign substance out of its system, flowers and foliage revert to their natural, benign state.

For safety, foragers must know what chemicals flowers have been treated with and when. This information should come from the gardener. We must also be familiar with common pesticides and their properties. This information comes from either the product's label or local dealers. In any case, in spite of the "dirty" reputation of truly wild plants, closely tended ones such as garden flowers demand scrupulous cleaning. While harmless dust or insects sully the average weed, immaculate garden flowers are often thickly coated with invisible poisons. For this reason, foragers need to take special care when collecting and processing them.

Calendula

A humble border flower today, calendula (*Calendula officinalis*) casts a long shadow in herbal traditions from India to Northern Europe. The name comes from the same root word as "calendar," a reference to the Roman myth that calendula blooms on the first day (the "kalends") of every month. Accorded spiritual

Calendula, or pot-marigold
(*Calendula officinalis*).

properties since pagan times, in the Christian era calendula became associated with the Virgin Mary. Its vibrant orange or yellow, daisylike blossoms suggest coins, giving rise to the common name "Mary's gold," or marigold, an alternate common name. (See "Know Your Marigolds" for a full description.) Believed to repel evil, calendula is traditionally planted around houses, hospitals, churches, and other sites susceptible to diabolic infiltration.

Calendula was once common in European kitchen gardens. This is partly because it protects other crops from predatory insects and fungi, and partly because calendula itself is an invaluable culinary herb. Slavic cuisines still make use of calendula petals to impart an appetizing gold color and subtle bitterness, sparing cooks the ridiculous expense and potential toxicity of saffron. Calendula petals traditionally season and color cheese, butter, soups, sauces, dips, egg dishes, wine, baked goods, and cereals such as rice and bulgur wheat. The young leaves, which are tart and vaguely gritty, integrate nicely with salads or cooked greens.

Calendula's reputation as a talisman against evil may be rooted in its outstanding healing properties. Calendula infusions, powdered petals, or a simple poultice of fresh petals, are all effective against rashes, acne, abscesses, urticaria, burns, fungal infections, and other skin disorders. These topical applications are the reason calendula is still a popular ingredient in herbal soaps. Calendula's astringent effect on blood vessels makes it handy for scrapes, cuts, and varicose veins. Taken internally, calendula itself, or infusions thereof, soothes gastric disturbances including ulcers and dry hives.

Chrysanthemum

Oxeye daisy, also called marguerite, is a familiar blossom with the melodious, contradictory botanical name of *Chrysanthemum leucanthemum* ("gold flower, white flower"). A favorite in European gardens, oxeye daisy arrived here early in the colonial period. *The History and Folklore of North American Wildflowers*

Know Your Marigolds

Plants belonging to the genera *Calendula* and *Tagetes* are both popularly called "marigolds," though in fact they have little in common. This is one instance where identification by botanical name is crucial to avoid making mistakes.

Tagetes species are wiry little plants with ruffled yellow or orange blossoms that suggest cabbages and have a strongly musty odor. Their foliage is stiff and usually feathery, sometimes reddish or purplish in color. An important medicinal and agricultural herb in Central and South America, *Tagetes* was unknown in Europe until the sixteenth century. Although some species are called "African" or "French" marigold, all are native to the Americas.

Calendula is a lithe flower with large, somewhat sticky leaves that are tonguelike in appearance, and open, orange or yellow blossoms that look like daisies with a double row of petals around the edges. Calendula has been a prominent culinary and medicinal herb in the Old World since ancient times. Europeans call it "pot marigold" because cooks in times past threw it in the pot.

Even the experts sometimes confuse these flowers. One gardening guide illustrates its description of *Calendula* with a drawing of *Tagetes*. Mistaking one for the other is rarely dangerous since both are edible, but recipes and other projects risk unforeseen and probably undesirable results if the wrong one is used. For clarity, I adhere to the increasingly common practice of calling *Tagetes* "marigold" and the Old World genus "calendula."

As if matters weren't complicated enough, two other common genera, *Dimorphotheca* and *Osteospermum,* go by the name of "Cape marigold." Both are inedible, and should not be used in cooking or herbal preparations.

(see Further Reading) notes that none other than John Winthrop, Jr., who would become governor of Connecticut Colony, purchased oxeye seed immediately prior to his 1631 voyage to Massachusetts Bay Colony. History does not record whether his were the first oxeyes in North America, nor indeed if he ever planted the seed, but oxeye daisy did appear in New England about that time. The species immediately set off on its own, and now occurs most frequently in the wild. In fact, oxeye is now considered a wildflower, even a weed. Ironically, the wildflower-gardening movement has brought oxeye daisy back into yards. Once established, this deceptively delicate-looking flower quickly becomes a permanent fixture.

Oxeye daisy is one of the most widely recognized flowers in Western culture, popping up from mid to late spring in moist fields, roadsides, and beds sown with wildflower mix. The bright, simple flowers suggest the sun, with a row of clean white petals surrounding a bright yellow disc. Balanced high on thin, sparsely

Oxeye daisy
(*Chrysanthemum leucanthemum*).

foliated stems, the blossoms nod at the slightest breeze. On the ground below, a hummock of somewhat shiny, toothed, spoon-shaped leaves, whose shape recalls the "spork" of fast-food restaurant fame, anchors the plant.

These leaves were much appreciated in preindustrial times as a spring green. The tender, sweetish foliage, whose flavor some compare to anise, makes a novel garnish or addition to salads and sandwiches.

Oxeye daisy is also a traditional diuretic and treatment for blood in the stools and urine, as its astringent properties are believed to stanch blood flow in ulcers and internal lacerations. European folk healers prescribe oxeye blossom infusions against illnesses involving discharges, such as bronchitis, colds, and vaginal infections. Powdered flowers are said to drive pests from plants and pets that are dusted with them.

Taxonomists have shaken up genus *Chrysanthemum* in recent years. Some related genera have been eliminated and their species added to *Chrysanthemum,* while new genera have been created from species that were carved out of *Chrysanthemum.* Older guidebooks may identify oxeye daisy by its former botanical name, *Leucanthemum vulgare,* but list potentially toxic tansy (*Tanacetum vulgare;* see Foraging Advisory, chapter 6) as a *Chrysanthemum* species. Most garden chrysanthemums are useful as herbs in some capacity. One, called edible chrysanthemum (*C. coronarium*) is an ordinary vegetable in Asia. As ever, foragers must be certain they know which species they're dealing with and which parts, if any, are edible, before eating untried chrysanthemums.

Dianthus

The ubiquitous florists' carnation (*Dianthus caryophyllus*) of bouquet and boutonnière fame is actually descended from one of the world's most respected herbs. Dianthus flowers are or were an important culinary and medicinal resource across Europe and through the Middle East to India, China, and Japan. Syrups made from these flowers were commonplace in kitchens and apothecary shops right up until the mid-nineteenth century, and the petals themselves were used to flavor baked goods, teas, and sauces. Popular along sunny margins of suburban lawns, large quantities of these blossoms can often be gathered in little time, a task rendered especially pleasant by their strong, sweet scent.

Clove pink (also *D. caryophyllus*), ancestor of the florist carnation, has the vibrantly colored blossoms and grassy, sea-green foliage of its glamorous descendant, but not the leggy, vase-friendly stems or the demanding maintenance schedule. Under the common name "border carnation," clove pink continues to fill its traditional role in landscaping. Its petals, which smell and taste like their spicy namesake, were used as such in the days when cloves were literally worth their weight in gold. Gillyflower, another common name for this plant, shares ancestry with *girofle,* the French word for clove. Clove pink's flavor isn't as strong as genuine cloves, but it is pleasant and sweet and well worth the effort to pick and process.

Historians infer that cottage pink (*D. plumarius*), once a seaside wildflower, was the first *Dianthus* species to come under cultivation. Cottage pink's greyish, somewhat matted foliage, densely covered with single or double blossoms from summer into early fall, is still a favorite in walkway and wallside beds. The fringed flowers are strongly fragrant and can be used like clove pinks. Cheddar pink (variously listed as *D. gratianopolitanus* or *D. caesius*) and maiden pink (*D. deltoides*) are similarly useful in herbal applications. Pink is the most common blossom color in all these species, naturally, though some "pinks" are actually white or candy-striped.

No one walks past a sunny strip of pinks unaware, since the heavy, spicy-sweet perfume seems to suffuse the very air around them. This fragrance translates into flavorful sauces, vinegars, wines, and liqueurs. Pink syrup (see Recipes, page 98), which resembles grenadine, was a common household product in the days before the Industrial Revolution. A healthy swirl of pink syrup turns a vanilla milk shake into something special. Dianthus petals can also be kneaded into scones, pastries, and sweet breads, stirred into pie fillings, and sprinkled over salads and cream desserts. Pinks are also cooked into jamlike preserves.

Dianthus was formerly much used as a nerve tonic or sedative, particularly when infused in wine or brandy. Alternatively, the petals themselves were fermented in floral wine. Such "physiks" were frequently prescribed to heart patients in the Middle Ages. Dianthus was also believed to improve energy levels in patients exhibiting the symptoms of what we now call depression, and a spoonful of pink syrup was the first line of defense against colds, flu, and basic misery.

Eschscholzia

Most garden flowers arrived in North America as seeds carefully packed among immigrants' belongings. Intentionally planted, lovingly attended, some of these flowers have since struck out on their own and become "weeds." But California poppy (genus *Eschscholzia*) has done exactly the opposite. The first non-aboriginal settlers in the West found it already thriving there. Later immigrants built cities and residential areas, where California poppy often pops up on unattended land. Recently this charming little flower has begun to insinuate itself into commercial seed packets, making it one of the few North American natives to make the transition from weed to ornamental, and one of the few Western natives to colonize the East.

California poppy is the official flower

California poppy
(*Eschscholzia* sp.).

Eschscholzia **is chemically distinct** from other poppies, including opium poppy. Unlike its infamous cousin, California poppy is neither narcotic nor addictive. Poppies of many genera are popular garden flowers, but, except for *Eschscholzia,* they have dangerous side effects and should not be used for self-treatment.

of the American state of the same name, which is also its region of origin. It frequently turns up in wildflower seed mixes, and has now been introduced to suburbs across the continent. Once established, this tenacious annual reseeds year after year without further intervention, provided conditions are suitable.

California poppy raises its brash little orange flag over well-drained fields, gravelly waste areas, and sunny roadsides from late spring to late summer. Heralding as it does the end of the school year, California poppy was my favorite flower when I was a child. Sadly, my attempts to assemble a bouquet produced vase after vase of wispy foliage; the petals drop minutes after picking.

California poppies have classic poppy morphology, with feathery, dusty grey-green foliage, weak, stringy stems, and floppy orange petals about an inch across. They typically occur in sparse patches or widely strewn over vacant land.

Chopped together and infused, *Eschscholzia's* aerial parts make a gentle but effective sedative. They may also be dried for later use. Tea made from the petals alone is highly perfumed, but care must be taken to leave plenty of blossoms behind to reseed the patch.

Unlike other poppies, California poppy is mild enough for children to use. European doctors prescribe it for hyperactivity and bedwetting. *Eschscholzia's* sedative effect is also useful for insomnia, while antispasmodic properties of *Eschscholzia* syrup quiets coughs. (See Pink Syrup in Recipes, page 98.) First Nations peoples masticated the roots to dull toothaches.

Hemerocallis

A handful of plants seem to have it all. Beautiful, hardy, and prolific, they are also nutritious, medicinal, and delicious. Most parts are edible. They are the plants foragers love best. Daylily (genus *Hemerocallis*) is one such plant.

Daylilies abound in suburbia, partly because they are pretty and partly because they propagate ferociously. Often they become truly wild, spreading unasked along roadsides and fences. Botanists now estimate that there are more daylilies in North America, only a century or so after their arrival, than in their native Asia.

Daylily (*Hemerocallis* spp. and hybrids).

A common crop in the Orient, daylily tubers, young shoots, leaves, flower buds, flowers, and seedpods have all been staple foods since prehistoric times. Dried daylily buds, sold as "golden needles" or "gum jum" in Asian groceries, are an essential ingredient of many Asian soups.

Daylilies owe their name to their large, brightly colored blossoms that burst open all of a sudden, only to shrivel up and die within twenty-four hours. The heirloom variety is the pale orange tawny daylily (*Hemerocallis fulva*), but daylily breeders have since produced a full range of hues, from vibrant yellows to deep reds, as well as white. The flowers set at the ends of wiry, branching stalks, two to three feet tall, that rise from the center of a long, grasslike "fan" of leaves. A plant in full production bears embryonic buds, ripe buds ready to blow, a blossom or two, shrivelled blossoms, and seedpods, all at the same time.

The daylily harvest begins in early spring when the shoots appear. These can be cut at ground level while no more than four inches high. Peel away the coarse outer leaves, leaving the tender inner shoot, which may be lightly steamed and served as a vegetable with butter or wine vinegar. Some foragers like to cut off the sprout crowns, the white part that grows just above the soil, to be chopped and tossed in salads.

Getting the Most from Unfamiliar Ingredients

Practically every kitchen has a shelf of "one-hit wonders," where exotic flavorings purchased to season a single recipe molder in dusty neglect. Eventually they are thrown away, making that first and only tablespoon an extremely expensive investment.

Any food that lands outside its home territory risks the same fate. A French friend still has the jar of peanut butter I gave her over a decade ago. It just never comes to mind when she's hungry. Unlike North Americans, she has no peanut butter sense. By the same token, an Italian cook would have emptied my five-year-old bottle of balsamic vinegar a long time ago.

Wild edibles suffer the same problem. Hardest hit are those that bear little resemblance to "normal" food, such as flowers. With their strange flavors and textures, they risk falling by the wayside. A few hints will help integrate wild foods into the daily routine:

·   International cookbooks and Internet newsgroups are fun and practical sources of information on new or unfamiliar foods. For instance, Russians have seasoned dishes with calendula petals for centuries, while the average Chinese housewife has a stack of daylily recipes. Enjoying many wild edibles is as simple as finding out where they are considered "normal" and borrowing a few techniques.

·   Similarly, new foods integrate most comfortably with ingredients from their native cuisines. For example, as a Latin American herb, marigold goes well with corn, white or sweet potatoes, chili, and beans.

·   Strong or oddly flavored ingredients that are unappealing alone may complement other foods perfectly. If oxeye daisy leaves are too sweet, one or two torn into bits may be just the thing for a vinegary salad.

·   Ideas generate themselves while a new flavor is on the tongue. When tasting new foods, I keep a pad handy to jot down my impressions. The notes I take while enjoying that first dish help me improve that recipe and develop new ones.

Sprouts left to attain full height eventually produce flower buds. These buds are a staple in China, where they are cultivated on an agricultural scale. Harvest daylily buds just before they blow, when they swell and lighten noticeably in color. They impart taste and texture to soups, stews, and stir-fries, and may be steamed as a tender, subtly flavored vegetable. Very ripe buds may burst open when heated, but if this is undesirable, harvesting them a few days before optimum ripeness will solve the problem. Ripe daylily buds can be dried on racks or in a commercial food dryer for use throughout the year.

As to what daylily buds taste like, well, they taste good. More than that I decline to say. The fact is, daylilies impress every tongue a little differently. One fan claims they taste "exactly like scrambled eggs." Others snort. The buds taste nothing like eggs, they say. Rather, daylily buds taste like beef soup. "Beef soup?" others laugh. "Sweet corn!" Varying in taste widely from plant to plant and person to person is a favorite daylily prank (see Special Note, page 84). Apparently the plants are highly sensitive to local conditions. The buds may also react differently to individual body chemistries, causing disagreement among connoisseurs.

Unpicked daylily buds become blossoms, which are also tasty edibles. Since they wither within hours, daylilies must be picked immediately. But the plants replenish their blossoms daily, so a bed of them can be picked bare without causing undue stress to the community, so long as it isn't repeatedly plundered in this fashion. Failing this, a few petals can be stripped from each blossom, leaving the rest to complete the job of reproduction.

Daylily petals go anywhere lettuce goes, and are suitable for salads and sandwiches. The entire blossom is delicious stuffed and fried. First, pull out the reproductive structures (the center "bristles"), then stuff the flowers with cheese, cooked rice, couscous, or fresh, seasoned bread crumbs. Push the petals into the middle or twist them to seal the stuffing inside, then dip the blossoms in batter and fry them. An alternative is to dip them in beaten egg, roll in fresh bread crumbs, and sauté quickly in butter or olive oil. Lightly crisp, fried daylilies are a first-rate hors d'œuvre.

Like the rest of the plant, daylily blossoms vary in flavor, so it's a good idea to taste a petal before gathering a lot of them. The pigments that create different shades also taste different. Red ones especially are liable to be bitter.

Daylily seedpods, consisting of three fused chambers, follow the blossoms. They too are edible when green and tender. Daylily seedpods can be steamed as a vegetable or sliced on the diagonal for stir-frying. They also pinch-hit in daylily bud recipes when the latter are unavailable. Some foragers pickle daylily seedpods using fresh-pack cucumber pickling recipes.

When the plant's aerial parts have given their all, it's tuber time. The dozen or so tubers a daylily produces are about the size of a peanut in the shell. They differ chemically from the stringy root, which is toxic, so only the swollen, yellowish tubers should be eaten.

Harvesting techniques differ according to the growth habits of the patch. If plants are crowded together, it's probably best for the colony to dig a few out completely. This gives remaining plants a chance to prosper. My favorite tool for this work is a potato fork. Grasp uprooted plants by the leaves and shake to remove most of the dirt. Later, immerse the root mass in a bucket of clean water and shake vigorously to remove more dirt. Then cut the tubers from the plant with a pair of garden shears and remove the remaining rootlets. In sparse patches, you can pry up a few tubers without disturbing the rest of the plant by probing in the ground with a digging stick (see chapter 6). Snip the tubers off the roots and tuck the roots back into the soil. Sensitively managed, a single patch will furnish tubers year after year.

Clean gathered tubers by tossing them in a metal sieve under running water, then roll and rub them between your fingers under the same stream.

Raw daylily tubers are sweet and crisp, reminiscent of water chestnuts or Jerusalem artichokes. Some people crunch them as is, but others find they have a disagreeable

Daylilies vary from location to location and, apparently, from diner to diner. Of potential importance are the various physiological reactions daylilies may provoke, which range from none (most common) to mild gastric upset, nausea, sore throat, or diarrhea. Peter Gail's *The Delightfully Delicious Daylily* (see Further Reading) contains a thorough discussion of this issue, as well as describing medicinal uses. Scrupulous first try protocol minimizes or eliminates most side effects. Daylilies should be eaten cooked and in moderation until allergies are ruled out. Foragers who intend to eat lots of them should start small at the beginning and increase consumption gradually to avoid shocking their bodies with unfamiliar chemicals.

aftertaste. Steaming or boiling for twenty minutes eliminates the aftertaste, though many aficionados insist their daylily tubers be served a specific way, such as in chili or mashed and fried as hush puppies (see Recipes, page 96).

Though daylily root is considered toxic, the Chinese regard it as a powerful medicinal, useful against complaints of the urinary tract, blood, and breasts. Nevertheless, Chinese studies indicate that daylily root toxins accumulate in the body, leading to vision problems and even blindness. Other studies suggest the roots contain carcinogens. In any case, daylily is not a suitable herb for home treatment. The Chinese also regard young daylily shoots as a sedative. Though I haven't found any documented cases of daylily shoot poisoning, some authorities report that they are mildly toxic in large quantities.

Oenothera

Evening primrose (genus *Oenothera*) is another wildflower riding the native gardening movement into flower beds. And well it deserves to. An evening primrose in bloom is a moving sight, its large, vibrant yellow flowers (pink or white in some species) bursting open atop a high, heavy stalk like fireworks trailing smoke. As the common name suggests, these blossoms remain open after dark, making evening primrose a favorite in moon gardens. (These specialty gardens, popular in the Renaissance, are meant to be enjoyed beneath the full moon. Recent interest in theme gardening has made them popular again among a tiny but dedicated minority of gardeners.) A deep taproot anchors the stalk, and from its crown a rosette of long, narrow, pointed leaves arcs over the ground. The blossoms cede their place to one- to two-inch seedpods, composed of four chambers and vaguely conical, with the larger end attached to the stalk.

Evening primrose is an important herb to First Nations people. Its resilient beauty and food value prompted European colonists to invite evening primrose into their gardens. By the eighteenth century it was under commercial cultivation as a vegetable root crop. But as rail and steam ushered in the era of mass marketing, evening primrose lost ground to more widely recognized Old World crops. Evidently, the customer isn't always right: I doubt many people today would choose a parsnip over the radishy goodness of an evening primrose taproot. Yet parsnips are sold in supermarkets, while evening primroses are often torn out of the ground and pitched on the compost heap.

Evening primrose is a biennial. Leaves, shoots, and roots destined for the pot must be collected early in the first year, but eligible plants can be located by scouting the dry flower stalks of deceased plants. Evening primrose prefers full sun and gravelly, well-drained soil, which often translates into relatively easy digging. Poisonous look-alikes, some of them deadly, share their habitat (see Foraging Advisory), so collectors must make positive identification before putting spade to soil.

Evening primrose
(*Oenothera* sp.).

Since zesty flavors are rare in northern plants, long, carrot-shaped evening primrose taproots were probably valued by indigenous peoples and European settlers for their peppery bite. Some people today find them too strong, and recommend boiling the peeled, sliced roots in several changes of water. However, the intensity of flavor varies considerably with age, season, species, and locality. Many are palatable in a single water, or sliced and fried after boiling. Alternatively, the roots can be pickled, or candied by simmering in syrup for thirty minutes. They are also sliced and scattered around a roast, minced like fresh ginger root and used to flavor other dishes, or added to stews.

Young evening primrose shoots and leaves

Evening primrose is at the center of the bitter debate over gamma-linolenic acid (GLA). Oil pressed from evening primrose seeds is high in this substance, which some claim is a miracle treatment for premenstrual syndrome, alcoholism, obesity, and AIDS, among other maladies. Clinical trials to date have proven inconclusive; the U.S. Food and Drug Administration has yet to endorse medical use of evening primrose oil.

are considered a spring tonic, and can be used in salads or cooked as a vegetable. The flowering tops are simmered in syrup or honey to make a cough suppressant, while the strongly flavored root is said to stimulate digestion and combat depression.

Primula

Literally synonymous with spring, genus *Primula* takes its name from a diminutive form of the Latin word for "first," referring to its position in the botanical year. "Primrose" is essentially the same name, a corruption of *prima rosa,* or "first rose." The Spanish come straight to the point; they simply call it *primavera,* which is the Spanish word for spring.

North America counts about a dozen of its own primulas, few of them common in residential areas. European primroses, on the other hand, are positively omnipresent. As gardening season opens, a full spectrum of primroses in Easter pastels blossoms in racks above nursery and hardware store parking lots like vertical meadows. Spring-starved northerners cart them off by the dozen, to heel the little flowers in along sidewalks and fence lines. For a few weeks, every street in town is Primrose Lane.

Any plant so long and so widely cultivated is certain to have a long history of folk uses, and true to form, primrose is one of the most important plants in European herbalism. Given the universal admiration this plant enjoyed right up until the twentieth century, it is amazing how quickly it was forgotten. Among flowers, only dandelion has fallen lower from a greater height in as little time.

For foraging purposes, primulas can be divided into two categories. Cowslip (*P.*

veris) has the first to itself. English-style gardens occasionally shelter this archetypical English meadow flower, but it is not as widely cultivated in Europe or North America as garden primroses, which form the second category. The most common varieties are forms of *P. vulgaris*. Both this species and its sister, *P. x polyantha,* are often called English primrose in gardening guides. However, though all primulas are fertile medicinal and culinary resources, they are not altogether interchangeable.

Cowslip has *Primula's* characteristic crown of tender, crepe like leaves laying close to the ground, but they are typically darker than those of garden primroses. Its long, narrow blossoms, trumpet-shaped and bright yellow, are about an inch long and clustered at the top of an otherwise naked stalk, where they suggest stadium floodlights clustered high atop a pole. Though cowslip is less common in gardens than its domesticated siblings, it crops up from time to time, especially in wildflower theme beds. In moist and mild climates reminiscent of its native land, cowslip may escape and establish itself as a truly wild flower.

English farmers have made cowslip blossom wine since Saxon times, as well as a pulpy jam for scones. The flowers were also crystallized (for instructions see Crystallized Violets in the Recipes section, page 96), used fresh in salads, and ground into a moist meal to be mixed with honey for a dessert filling. Unopened cowslip buds can be pickled, and the leaves are used fresh as salad greens.

Herbalists consider cowslip more potherb than medicinal plant, although it does have healing properties. Dried cowslip blossoms are infused for a calming tea taken against headaches and insomnia, and as a skin revitalizer. Cowslip root tea is an effective expectorant, indicated for particularly persistent coughs.

Garden primroses are far more common than cowslip in residential areas. *P. vulgaris,* the ancestral primrose, bears single blossoms in many soft colors, while *P. polyantha,* whose species name translates as "many flowers," bears smaller blossoms in showy clusters. Though the garden primulas were originally developed as medicinals, their flowers can be used in cooking like cowslip blossoms. Garden primrose foliage is tougher and stronger-flavored than cowslip leaves, and therefore not as interesting as a salad green. However, it makes a good cooked green, either alone or in concert with others. As such, primrose leaves are traditionally harvested in England as part of the Eatin' o' the Greens (see chapter 6), a role that they still fill admirably.

A staple of English folk medicine, primrose flowers, leaves, and roots are each prescribed for separate conditions, though they are sometimes taken together for cumulative effect. Primrose root infusions are a traditional sedative, taken for stress-related disorders such as insomnia and tension headaches. The blossoms are believed to provide a milder version of the same medicine. English farmers boost the sedative effect of primrose blossoms by fermenting them into wine, thus adding the depressant effect of alcohol. Primrose wine is a famous prescription for winter's cabin fever in the English countryside. Garden primrose leaves are a general tonic and blood purifier, as their reputation as spring greens suggests. Folk healers sometimes pull, wash, and chop the entire plant, then infuse it to relieve colds and flu.

Rosa (See chapter 5)

Tagetes

Little *Tagetes* marigolds are one of suburbia's hardest-working flowers. The tough ornamentals line sidewalks, driveways, and high-traffic flower beds from spring to late fall, shrugging off abuse and serving as bodyguards to more flamboyant blossoms. When autumn shrivels their fragile charges, marigolds march on alone, surviving to Hallowe'en and beyond before succumbing to the cold.

Marigold's low, dense growth contributes to its popularity as a border plant. (See "Know Your Marigolds," page 77, for a full description.) So many anonymous little blossoms adorn each plant that they form a single band in peripheral vision, rather than distracting the viewer's eye from the celebrity plants in the middle of the bed. Pests dislike marigold's aromatic foliage, so the wiry little plants are often dug in alongside vulnerable flowers and even vegetables to protect them from depredation.

Marigolds are called *cempazuchitl* or *zenspasuchitl* in Mexico. A fixture of Día de los Meurtos celebrations, they have been a symbol of death since Aztec times. Trails of marigold petals are said to help the dead find their way.

Occurring naturally from the American Southwest to Cape Horn, marigold has been cultivated for thousands of years in Latin America for its aromatic and repellent qualities and as a dyestuff (see Dyers' Notes). In addition to the protective properties of the foliage, *Tagetes* roots release chemicals into the soil that specifically inhibit those insects

French marigold
(*Tagetes patula*).

and diseases that prey on potatoes. Other chemicals prevent certain aggressive weeds from flourishing, thereby establishing a "red zone" around marigolds and the plants they protect. Guarding potato fields, a life-or-death responsibility in much of South America, has earned marigold the respect of peoples who depend on potatoes for survival.

Potato-field marigolds were engineered to endure Andean extremes without complaint, and rugged independence is still a hallmark of their descendants. North American suburbs may be a fraction less hostile than the Bolivian altiplano, but they present other challenges that pre-Columbian marigolds could never have imagined. In their ability to withstand

Gathering and Using Flower Petals

Processing flower petals for use in cooking and medicinal preparations isn't hard, but a few precautions will help ensure success.

· Blossoms are best gathered on a warm, dry day before they have been watered, as moisture collects in the calyx and promotes mildew or rot. Mid-morning is the best time to gather, since the plant is best able to recover at that point in the day.

· The white "heel" or base of most petals is bitter and unpleasant, and can spoil the taste of otherwise flavorful flowers. These heels are easily snipped or torn off before the petals are used.

· Remove seeds and heels from flowers that have a cup-shaped calyx, such as marigolds and pinks, by pinching the calyx with one hand and bending the petal mass back and forth with the other, as if breaking wire. The colored portions will tear free, leaving heels and seeds in the calyx.

· When used as a seasoning, petals should be crushed or chopped. Some, such as calendula or marigold, can be dried and powdered.

· Gathered flowers should be used or processed immediately, as the volatile oils that give them their unique scent and flavor quickly evaporate.

abuse, neglect, and climatic extremes, modern marigolds evoke *Tagetes'* long tradition of stoic service to humanity.

Marigolds are among the easiest blossoms to process. Simply nip off the flower heads behind the heavy green calyx and remove the petals. (See "Gathering and Using Flower Petals.") The petals are best used fresh, but they also can be spread on a tray in a dry place, air-dried, then stored in an airtight container for later use.

As a culinary herb, marigold petals are more or less interchangeable with tarragon, though their flavor varies. Signet or dwarf marigold (variously listed as either *T. tenuifolia* or *T. signata*) and sweet marigold (*T. lucida*), also called Texas tarragon or Mexican mint marigold, are considered the best types for use in cooking, though even the workaday French marigold (*T. patula*) complements egg and fish dishes when used with restraint. Tuna, egg, and potato salad all benefit from marigold's color and flavor.

Marigold petals also make an unusual herbed vinegar (see Recipes) for salads or fish and chips. Marigold butter is as easy to make as kneading petals into softened butter, then pressing it into a loaf or mold and refrigerating. Left two weeks to cure, this butter complements seafood and baked potatoes. Cream cheese, yogurt, and sauces all welcome marigold's golden touch, and the petals make an interesting tea.

Latin American peoples take *Tagetes* infusions internally as a vermifuge, and apply them externally as a fungicide, an insect repellent, an antiseptic wash for sores, carbuncles, and boils, and to fight lice infestation. Modern herbalists anoint fungus-infected toenails with the essential oil of *Tagetes* marigolds.

> **Like many herbs, marigold can be toxic in large quantities. To be on the safe side, foragers should ingest the strongly flavored petals in moderation.**

Tropaeolum

In my book (and, come to think of it, this *is* my book), garden nasturtium (*Tropaeolum majus*) is the best thing to happen to summer since blackberries. Easy to grow in most climates and soil conditions, with lush, ground-covering foliage, this delightful annual is one of suburbia's most popular garden flowers. It produces copious quantities of seed, and, where winter permits, self-seeds with gusto. As a result, nasturtium pops up uninvited, year after year, yet somehow dodges that hated epithet, "weed." Apparently, nasturtium is so beautiful that even order-loving gardeners can't despise it.

Better yet, nasturtium is delicious. Its crisp horseradishy zing contrasts sharply with other salad greens. Even the seeds are edible—excellent in fact. The vivid red, yellow, or orange flowers add honey-sweetness to nasturtium's characteristic bite. Whenever I see one, I am torn between its beauty and lyrical charm, and the urge to eat it.

Nasturtium
(*Tropaeolum majus*).

Sixteenth-century Spanish *conquistadores* encountered nasturtiums in Peru, where the Inca farmed them intensively for their beauty, perfume, and food value. The invaders appreciated them as well, and shipped sacks of seed home. Soon nasturtiums were trailing romantically down Spanish garden walls. From there, nasturtium departed for points north and south, to France, Italy, England, and Germany. An especially warm welcome waited in North Africa, where today nasturtiums are cultivated as an agricultural crop much as they are in native Peruvian cultures. Fresh nasturtium leaves and blossoms are sold in Moroccan markets, and they embellish courtyards and terraces across the Maghreb.

Latin America boasts almost a hundred *Tropaeolum* species, of which several are cultivated on a large scale. The potato-like tubers of *T. tuberosum* are a staple of Central and South American cuisine. But few *Tropaeolum* plants have crossed the Rio Grande, and the familiar garden nasturtium is by far the most common. Sun-warmed banks of blossoming nasturtiums release a sweet, fruity perfume discernible many feet away. The leaf stems attach in the center of the hexagonal, white- or yellow-veined leaves, giving them the appearance of little umbrellas. In the flowers, large, soft, deeply-colored petals join into a graceful horn-of-plenty balanced on a central stem, also attached midway. When the petals drop, they leave behind a fused pod of two or three wrinkled, immature seeds.

Nasturtium's peppery bite recalls the taste of the mustard family, hence the British common name, "Indian cress." Its leaves and stems are crisp and fiery, excellent in tossed salads and sandwiches. Chopped nasturtium leaves can be mixed into potato salad, while whole ones can line bowls of this or other cold dishes. Finely chopped nasturtium leaves and flowers may also be kneaded into butter or stirred into sour cream, yogurt, or cream cheese for use on baked potatoes or in dips.

Whole nasturtium blossoms add color and fragrance to cold Middle Eastern dishes such as tabbouleh and hummus. Mild salsas gain fire and flavor from a handful of blossoms, though strong spices quickly overpower them. Stuffed with a lump of cream cheese, feta, or cold meat, nasturtium flowers are an elegant, easily prepared hors d'œuvre.

Immature nasturtium seed clusters are an herb in their own right, contributing crunch and zip to steamed rice and vegetables. (They should never be cooked, however, as this robs them of texture and flavor; rather, they should be added after the dish is cooked.) Chopped, they do the same for egg salad, dips, and other buffet fare. Some people use nasturtium flower buds the same way, but I prefer to let the plant flower and then pick the seedpods, which are crunchier, when the blossoms have passed. (However, if flowers are the target harvest, they should be pinched regularly. This discourages seed production and optimizes blossom production.)

Nasturtiums produce pods erratically, generally at a rate of about a tablespoon per plant per month in peak season. This makes it hard to gather any quantity in a single pass, but they are easily dried for long-term storage. Drop them into a net bag and hang them in a warm, dry place until the pods are shrivelled, yellowish, and hard. I find that if I keep adding pods through the summer, they dry famously without further attention. Once thoroughly dry, store nasturtium seed clusters in an airtight container and reconstitute in soups and tomato sauces as demand arises.

> In spite of their confusing names, garden nasturtium (*Tropaeolum majus*) is unrelated to watercress (*Nasturtium officinale*; see chapter 6). The word *nasturtium* ("nose twister") refers to the spicy vapors that enter the nasal passages when either plant is chewed, causing the chewer to wrinkle his or her nose. Though both nasturtium and watercress contain mustard oil and taste remarkably alike, they belong to entirely different families. Some taxonomists resolve the confusion by disbanding genus *Nasturtium* altogether and reassigning watercress to genus *Rorippa*.

An even tastier solution is to pickle the harvest. Pickled nasturtium seeds are often compared to capers, though they aren't entirely the same. As with other wild edibles, pickled nasturtium pods are best taken on their own merits. Some cooks keep a brine pot in the refrigerator and pitch in the pods as they ripen (see Recipes, page 95). By autumn, they have a respectable crockful of hot little pickles. Because they pickle so readily, nasturtium pods are also good candidates for relish, or to lend character and visual appeal to pickles of other vegetables.

Nasturtium flowers' beautiful color, fragrance, and sweet-hot flavor ought to make an exquisite, savory jam to serve with cold meats if enough blossoms can be gathered to fill a few jars. Unfortunately I haven't had access to that many simultaneously blooming nasturtiums, but whole banks of these delightful flowers cascade into some gardens. I encourage foragers who have access to enough stock to try nasturtium flower jam.

Like most spicy foods, nasturtium is a reputed digestive aid and tonic. Recent studies indicate it may have antibiotic and antiseptic properties, vindicating Incan doctors who used it both internally and externally to combat infection. Both the leaves and flowers are high in vitamin C, confirming nasturtium's historical use as an antiscorbutic.

Viola

As a rule of thumb, the more folk names a plant has, the greater its historical value as an herb. By this measure, genus *Viola* is a force to be reckoned with. Violet and pansy are only the most prosaic of its common names. Among others are fighting-cock, kiss-me-behind-the-garden-gate, jump-up-and-kiss-me, heartsease, and heal-all. Native to most of the world, *Violas* grow wild in parks and other green areas and are an enduring garden favorite.

The literally hundreds of *Viola* species are perennials, though they behave as self-seeding annuals where winters are harsh. Their bright green, heart-shaped leaves and cheery flowers form a quiltlike ground cover in meadows, forest clearings, and shady suburban beds. Blossoms are blue, white, and yellow, usually with a dark, contrasting center. Larger species, called pansies or violas, can reach twelve inches, but most violets top out at about six inches.

Common suburban species include:

· Sweet violet (*V. odorata*), famous in song and legend. As both the common and botanical names suggest, sweet violets are exceedingly fragrant. Their blossoms were one of the first employed in perfumery. They also make flavorful syrups, infusions, and candied blossoms.

· Blue violet (*V. sororia*) is a garden variety that has gone free-agent in many areas. A symbol of the Confederate States of America, it is still called Confederate violet in some parts of the United States. Blue violet's petals are actually white, but heavy purple veins give the petals a bluish cast. The blossoms end in a stiff,

> **Pansy is a corruption of the** French *pensée,* or thought. In old Europe, pansy infusions or decoctions were widely used as love potions, believed to fill the object's head with thoughts of the first person sighted. Shakespeare twice mentions pansy's persuasive powers, an indication of how common the knowledge of them was in his day. Johnny-jump-up (*V. tricolor*) resembles a small pansy, to which it is closely related. The common name, an abbreviation of "Johnny-jump-up-and-kiss-me," is another reference to love potions. Interestingly, Johnny-jump-up was believed to cure as well as cause heartaches, evidently following the same principle by which digitalis (see Foraging Advisory) can strengthen an ailing heart or stop it altogether. This power gives rise to another common name, heartsease.

Violet (*Viola* sp.).

curved claw. Farm children noted the resemblance of this appendage to a fighting-cock's spur, and little boys have gloried in bloody "chicken fights" ever since. Combatants pluck violet blossoms and hook the spurs together. A miniature tug-of-war ensues, resulting in the beheading of the weaker violet. A knot of children can decimate a violet patch in short order this way. On a more practical note, blue violet blossoms are commonly used to make syrups, and their tender, mildly flavored leaves are perfect for salad or sandwich duty.

· Pansy (*V.* x *wittrockiana*) sports big, violetlike flowers and light green, scalloped, spoon-shaped leaves. Flats of them appear in supermarkets and garden centers in early spring and autumn. Where winters are mild, pansies may bloom through December, ushering out the old growing season just as Primula ushers in the new. The enigmatic wintergreen tingle of their leaves and flowers is especially welcome in tea and salads.

· Heal-all (*V. rotundifolia*) is a North America native that persists in and around residential areas of the Northeast. Also called round-leaved or early yellow violet, this modest little forest-dweller is an anodyne among Pennsylvania's "plain folk" and Eastern Woodlands tribes.

All Violas are tasty, healthy edibles. The foliage of most is best eaten raw, though it may be lightly steamed. The whole plant is rich in vitamin C; the leaves pack an additional shot of vitamin A. Violet leaves, whose fresh, subtle flavor recalls spring itself, are a traditional spring tonic in Appalachia. They can also be infused for a refreshing tea. I find tea made from dried leaves somewhat harsh in

Dyers' Notes

Marigold (genus *Tagetes*) blossoms are a traditional source of yellow-gold dye in Latin American cultures. Alum mordants give weaker shades; chrome, livelier ones; iron, darker ones.

Calendula infusions yield a pale yellow dye.

Oxeye daisy blossoms yield shades of yellow with an alum mordant.

The Amish make Easter egg dyes by infusing violets and pansies with water, vinegar, and alum.

flavor, and prefer to make violet leaf tea in season from fresh ones.

The flowers can also be added to salads or infused in tea. Violet jam or jelly is a special treat, though recipes call for large quantities of the little blossoms. *Viola* blossom wine, a sought-after delicacy among the elite in the Middle Ages, suffers the same limitation. Foragers who don't have access to a quart or more of flowers can, however, infuse lesser amounts in vinegar, vodka, or brandy. Queen Victoria reportedly insisted that her staff keep violet syrup (see Pink Syrup in the Recipes, page 98) on hand at all times, for both health reasons and culinary enjoyment.

In addition to flavoring desserts and drinks, violet syrup is a mild expectorant, indicated for coughs and bronchial difficulties in European folk medicine, as well as a gentle laxative. Pansy blossom infusions are applied externally to skin disorders such as eczema, itching, and rashes. Taken internally, pansy tea is a diuretic.

🌼 Foraging Advisory

Daffodil, iris, crocus, and narcissus are toxic and should be avoided. Special care must be taken when gathering daylilies, which superficially resemble these plants in the shoot stage.

Older guidebooks may place tansy and feverfew in genus *Chrysanthemum*, but botanists have created a separate genus for them, called *Tanacetum*. Unlike most chrysanthemums, tansy and feverfew can be toxic and should not be ingested. (See Foraging Advisory, chapter 6.)

Foxglove (genus *Digitalis*) is a garden flower in the eastern part of the continent, and a weed in the West. The blossoms resemble oven mitts a fox might wear, if so inclined, and come in several vibrant, eye-catching colors. Though *Digitalis* yields the powerful heart medication of the same name, it is deadly poison unless scientifically refined and administered. No part of this plant is useful to foragers. Those handling it should wash their hands to avoid accidentally ingesting the juice. *Digitalis* leaves resemble those of evening primrose (genus *Oenothera*) and burdock (genus *Arctium;* see chapter 6), and the plant often occurs in the same habitat. Foragers must be able to identify all three by foliage alone, and take care not to mix foxglove leaves or roots inadvertently with evening primrose or burdock when collecting.

Flowers from a florist are uniformly inedible, regardless of species. In fact, any cut or potted plant sold commercially is off-limits to foragers, since they are inevitably soaked in toxins to ensure visual perfection. But there's little reason to eat them in the first place. Not only are overcultivated florists' flowers very expensive, they taste like the manufactured products they are.

Recipes

Nasturtium Seed "Caper" Crock

MAKES UP TO 2 PINTS.

The downfall of most nasturtium-pod pickling recipes is that they call for a pint or more of fresh seedpods upfront. I have had little success convincing nasturtiums to fruit accordingly. Instead, they insist on setting a pod here and a pod there over several weeks. This recipe, on the other hand, is well suited to nasturtium's characteristically uneven pod production. The pickled pods resemble and can be used like capers, though they have their own unique flavor.

1 pint marigold- or tarragon-flavored vinegar (see p. 97)
1/4 cup sugar
1 teaspoon pickling salt
1 small red onion, chopped fine
1 clove garlic, thinly sliced
3 whole peppercorns
Fresh nasturtium seedpods

Place all ingredients except the nasturtium seedpods in a nonreactive saucepan. Bring to a boil, cover, and simmer over lowest heat for 30 minutes.

When cool, pour the liquid into a lidded jar, crock, or plastic tub and place it in the refrigerator.

Wash and drop nasturtium seedpods into the crock as they become available. (Pods develop at the base of the blossom after the petals wither.)

Allow the pods to cure for a month after the last one has been added before using.

Pickled nasturtium pods will keep through the winter if refrigerated.

Daylily Tuber Hushpuppies

MAKES ABOUT 12.

An update on the classic Southern recipe, crisp on the outside, tender on the inside. Daylily tuber hushpuppies are a good side dish for deep-fried fish.

Oil for deep frying
1 cup daylily tubers, scrubbed
1 egg, slightly beaten
1/2 teaspoon baking soda
1/2 teaspoon black pepper
1 tablespoon dried parsley or chickweed, or 2 tablespoons fresh, chopped
Approximately 1/4 cup flour

Heat the oil to 375°F in a deep fryer.

Boil the tubers in water for 15 to 20 minutes, or until tender. Drain, then mash. Allow to cool for 10 minutes.

Stir in the egg, baking soda, and seasonings. Sprinkle in the flour a bit at a time, until the mixture is about as stiff as mashed potatoes.

Drop heaping tablespoonfuls of the tuber mixture into the hot fat and fry until the lumps are crisp and golden outside. Daylily hushpuppies generally turn themselves as they fry. If they don't, flip them with a slotted spoon.

To make pan-fried hushpuppies, add just enough flour to the mashed tuber mixture to make a thick batter. Spread a quarter cup of batter in a hot, greased frying pan or griddle and toast until lightly browned. Flip the patty and repeat on the other side.

Serve hot.

Crystallized Violets

In times past, cakes were decorated with real violets, crystallized to preserve their delicate color and flavor. Crystallized violets are still an elegant garnish for desserts. However, the delicate blossoms begin to wilt the instant they are picked, so they must be crystallized as quickly as possible. Most effective is to move the crystallizing materials to the violet patch and candy each flower as it is picked. Other flowers and petals can also be candied using this method.

1 egg white, beaten foamy but not stiff
1 cup granulated sugar (superfine works best)
Waxed paper
A small artist's paintbrush
Viola blossoms

Spread a thin layer of sugar on a plate.

Pick sound blossoms, leaving the stems intact. Rinse gently and pat them completely dry between paper towels.

Take a violet by the stem and use the artist's paintbrush to moisten the entire blossom, front and back, with egg white.

Hold the moistened blossom against the layer of sugar and use a teaspoon to sprinkle sugar over it, turning it until evenly coated. Be certain all recesses, such as the flower's center, are coated as well. Wait about 10 seconds, then gently shake off excess sugar.

Pinch the blossom off the stem over a sheet of waxed paper. When the batch is finished, place it in a dry, mildly warm place (too hot and the flowers will wilt before the coating sets) until completely dried.

Crystallized flowers must be kept in an airtight container to prevent them from absorbing moisture from the air and spoiling. They will keep a week or so under refrigeration, up to a year if frozen.

Marigold Vinegar

MAKES ABOUT 3 CUPS.

A pretty, honey-colored vinegar for salads and cooking, marigold vinegar is also a good clarifying rinse for the hair. (**Note:** the same procedure can be used to make vinegars from any edible flower.)

> 4 cups cider vinegar
> 1 teaspoon dried orange peel, or 1½ teaspoons fresh
> 1 teaspoon dried lemon peel, or 1½ teaspoons fresh
> 1 cup *Tagetes* marigold petals, packed (about 2 cups whole blossoms).

Pour the vinegar into a nonreactive pan and bring briefly to a boil.

Reduce heat to its lowest point. Add the orange and lemon peel and marigold petals.

Warm the mixture over low heat for 1 hour. (Do not boil.)

Strain the infusion through wet muslin, then pour it into a sterilized wine bottle. (To sterilize, place 2 teaspoons of bleach in the bottom, half-fill the bottle with water, shake well, and rinse thoroughly before filling.) Cork securely.

Store this and other flavored vinegars in a cool, dark place.

Pink Syrup

MAKES ABOUT ONE PINT.

A culinary and medicinal standard in Europe until the nineteenth century, pink syrup is delicious on desserts and in mixed drinks. A pleasant and effective sedative can be made by substituting California poppy blossoms and foliage for the *Dianthus* petals in this recipe.

1 cup *Dianthus* petals, white parts removed
1 cup sugar
2 tablespoons sumac or lemon juice (see page 113)

Immerse a pint jar in a large pot of water, place it over high heat, and chop the flower petals while the pot comes to a boil.

When the pot reaches the boiling point, remove the jar and place the chopped petals inside it, then pour 1 cup of boiling water over them. Cover loosely and infuse the petals overnight at room temperature.

The next day, strain the infusion through wet muslin and discard the chopped petals.

Mix the infused liquid, sugar, and sumac or lemon juice in a nonreactive pan and bring to a boil. Reduce heat until the syrup maintains a vigorous boil without boiling over. Cook until it thickens. (The bubbles will become glassy and the smacking sounds will get louder.) Remove the syrup from the heat and allow it to cool to handling temperature.

Pour the syrup into a sterilized bottle or jar (for the sterilizing procedure see Marigold Vinegar, above) and cap. This syrup will keep for 3 months in the refrigerator. It can also be frozen.

— Detail: American highbush cranberry *(Viburnum trilobum)*.

Suburbanites generally divide plants into two categories. There are those we plant on purpose, such as garden flowers and ornamentals, and those that appear uninvited. Weeds and persistent shrubs and trees are representative of the second category. Yet the bulk of suburban flora falls into a twilight zone between the two categories. These are the "peripherals," plants that define limits and fill space. Peripherals live by their willingness to grow under unpromising conditions and by an uncanny ability to deflect attention away from themselves. Some form hedges, living fences that restrict traffic between human territories. Others stem erosion or plug visual voids with anonymous greenery.

Some peripherals are planted on purpose; others are naturally occurring plants that survive either because they accidentally meet with human approval, or because they are remarkably invisible to the casual eye. People pass day after day without really noticing these shrubs and ground covers, whose foliage softens the otherwise harsh lines of human-dominated landscapes. But to those who know their value, peripheral herbs stand out as beautiful, generous plants that are much more than a convenient screen or backdrop.

Arbutus

I once lived in the sparsely populated, semiarid countryside surrounding the southern French city of Marseille, an area inhabitants call *le terroir*. My part-time job afforded me little money, but plenty of time to tramp this fascinating Provençal wilderness.

Strawberry tree
(*Arbutus unedo*).

Noting both my financial status and my love of the back-country, a friend suggested I keep any eye peeled for a local shrub called *arbousier* (*Arbutus unedo*). Armed with her description, I located one on my next hike. Its branches sagged with soft, sunset-red *arbouses* about the size and shape of a ping-pong ball. I bit into one. The translucent yellow flesh was like seedy tapioca, with a faint aftertaste of spoiled orange juice. But I was in no position to turn down free food. I pulled out a plastic shopping bag and started picking.

Was I glad I did. As my advisor promised, the arbouses underwent a miraculous change in cooking. First I simmered them in just enough water to steam them soft. Afterward I forced them through a sieve to remove the seeds. The resulting pulp, simmered with sugar and lemonade mix (I had no lemon juice), produced a smooth, rosy orange spread. Slathered on a slice of France's renowned bread, with a cup of *tilleul* (see chapter 3) on the side, it made an appetizing, sustaining snack.

Arbousier is native to dry, mild Mediterranean climes, so I was shocked and delighted many years later to spot several of them, thriving and heavily in fruit, in the city center of Olympia, Washington. Municipal groundskeepers there have presumably taken a liking to the shrub. And why not? Defying Olympia's dour, overcast skies and drizzly weather, every arbousier in town boasted full, glossy foliage and orange-red fruits as firm and healthy as any I've seen in Provence.

I've since learned that this large, bushy shrub, called strawberry tree in North America, serves as an ornamental most anywhere below-freezing temperatures are rare. Further, this tree is first cousin to the West Coast's ubiquitous arbutus (*A. menziesii*), also known as madroña or madrone, as well as Texas (*A. xalapensis* or *texana*) and Arizona madroña (*A. arizonica*). Like its New World relatives, strawberry tree has leathery, shiny leaves, reddish bark given to peeling, and gnarled, twisted, multiple trunks. Unlike them, it bears dense, opulent foliage and the round, soft, rough-surfaced fruits for which it is named.

Clockwise from left: Oregon grapes (*Mahonia aquifolium*); Kousa dogwood (*Cornus kousa*) in autumn; a Kousa ball.

Clockwise from left: Love-lies-bleeding (*Amaranthus caudatus*), a common ornamental amaranth; Juniper berries (genus *Juniperus*); new growth of Douglas-fir (*Pseudotsuga menziesii*).

Clockwise from right: Barberries (*Berberis vulgaris*) in autumn; the tempting berries and lovely flowers of poisonous bittersweet (*Solanum dulcamara*); ripe crabapples (genus *Malus*).

Clockwise from above: Salmonberry (*Rubus spectabilis*) canes in flower; a salmonberry flower; Oxeye daisies (*Chrysanthemum leucanthemum*).

Clockwise from left: Saucer magnolia (*Magnolia soulangiana*) flower bud; Nasturtium (*Tropaeolum majus*); Johnny-jump-up (*Viola tricolor*); Viola (*Viola wittrockiana*).

Clockwise from top left: Highbush cranberries (*Viburnum edule*); European gooseberries (*Ribes uva-crispa*); a knotweed (*Polygonum cuspidatum*) shoot.

Clockwise from top left:
Dandelions (genus *Taraxacum*)
flourish on the margins of a city
park; Arbouses (*Arbutus unedo*)
in various stages of ripeness;
Squawbush (*Rhus trilobata*)
berry clusters.

Oxeye daisy (*Chrysanthemum leucanthemum*) growing near strawberries (genus *Fragaria*).

While some strawberry tree varieties can be trained very low (one of the Olympia plantings was a hedge), most are high, full shrubs or small trees.

The Romans considered the arbouse exclusively rural fare, perhaps because it doesn't keep or ship well, and was consequently only to be had in the vicinity of an arbousier. Even today, country people all along the Mediterranean appreciate arbouse preserves, sauces, pies, and liqueurs. I've even caught references to arbouse ice cream. But since none of these products are sold commercially, foragers are the only city people who can enjoy them.

Some fans eat strawberry tree fruit raw, but I find them seedy and insipid unless cooked. Fruit destined for jam, sauces, or pies should be sieved or milled to remove the seeds. A tablespoon or two of lemon or sumac juice per four to five cups of pulp or juice generally raises acidity to workable levels for preserves. Arbouse also mixes well with tarter fruits.

> **Peeling red and yellow arbutus** trunks often lean far over rocky West Coast shores, where they may be visible for miles. In late autumn, arbutus bears grape-like bunches of grainy, yellow-orange, marble-sized berries, usually high above the ground. These little fruits are even blander and seedier than arbouses, but preserves can reportedly be made from them. West Coast residents may encounter these fruits among windfall following a storm, or a felled tree may bring the clusters within reach. Texas and Arizona madroña, found in the southern reaches of their namesake states, are said to bear similar fruits.

Bamboo

Combining high strength-to-weight ratio, incredible diversity, and rapid growth, bamboo is the most useful plant on earth. Various species are used to make musical instruments, furniture, and other household goods, as well as rope, fabric, writing implements, plumbing, fishing rods, basketry—even the scaffolds erected around skyscrapers. The list goes on, encompassing literally thousands of applications, but the one most interesting to foragers is the fact that tender young bamboo shoots are a delicious vegetable.

Contrary to popular misconception, bamboo can be raised successfully in North America as far north as southern Canada. Bamboo's exotic appearance, dense vertical profile, and myriad practical applications contribute to its increasing popularity as a screen plant. By happy coincidence, many common ornamental varieties also bear choice shoots. Inasmuch as connoisseurs agree that fresh bamboo shoots beat the canned kind hands down, they are worthy quarry for foragers.

Cane (*Arundinaria gigantea*) is the only bamboo native to North America. Forests of it, called canebrakes, once stretched for miles as far north as the Ohio

Golden bamboo
(*Phyllostachys aurea*).

River valley. First Nations used canes of this species, which can attain a length of fourteen feet and measure two inches in diameter, to make mats, traps, weirs, baskets, and a broad assortment of other implements. Settler cultures followed suit, using it in trellises, fences, and furniture. When Mark Twain placed a cane pole in Huckleberry Finn's hands, he made this classic Southern fishing gear an internationally recognized symbol of freedom and leisure. But the introduction of grazing stock spelled the end of the great canebrakes. Cattle, pigs, and other farm animals relish the succulent cane shoots, chomping off every last one for acres around. Loss of wetlands finished the job. Efforts are now afoot to restore cane to protected areas, but fortunate indeed is the forager who finds a wild canebrake healthy enough to permit the cutting of shoots.

Carefully cultivated, cane can withstand temperatures down to −10°F, and it is now found in yards over much of the continent. Cane is unique in that its shoots remain palatable to two feet in height. As long as they snap cleanly, as opposed to a "green-stick" break that requires twisting and pulling, the cane is edible. Peel away the tough sheath to expose the clean, white pith. This may be thin-sliced and crunched raw with thick homemade mayonnaise or dip. Slices may also be tossed briefly in a wok, steamed, simmered in clear soups, or just boiled for fifteen minutes and eaten as a mild, pleasantly crunchy vegetable. Some consider this down-home North American bamboo the finest of all.

More common in suburbia is genus *Phyllostachys*: hardy, ornamental bamboos that often bear edible shoots. Native to northern Asia, these "running" bamboos aggressively colonize any soil their persistent rhizomes can penetrate, and the many shoots that pop up outside the gardener's approved bamboo zone are usually free for the asking.

Golden bamboo (*P. aurea*) is a typical garden variety that produces tasty shoots. Its yellow culms, or canes, can reach twenty feet in height. Compressed joints at the base suggest that they were pressed together by the weight of the long, stout cane. Golden bamboo shoots are often sweet enough to eat raw, or to stir-fry without preliminary boiling. Another *Phyllostachys* species, *P. dulcis*, boasts the provocative common name sweet-shoot bamboo. It must be tempting indeed, as dogs, not normally known for their vegetarian leanings, sometimes wipe out whole beds of this species by munching the tender young shoots. Moso, another common suburban species, is a large, dark green bamboo whose botanical name, *P. edulis*, reflects its use as a vegetable in Asia. Other potential foraging opportunities include waxy blue bamboo (*P. nigra "Henon"*) and crooked, supple zigzag bamboo (*P. flexuosa*).

Conical in shape, with a stout, woody bottom, bamboo shoots resemble giant fangs tightly wrapped in translucent leaves. Shoots up to six inches (a foot in some species) are generally edible, but they can surpass this height in just one day. Once they break into the sunlight, bamboo shoots quickly become tough and bitter, so timing is important.

Bamboo shoots often announce their intentions by cracking the ground above, warning foragers that the collecting season has begun and allowing surgical techniques that help ensure shoot-cutting privileges in the future. First, carefully enlarge the crack with a fiddling shovel and pry back the sod or humus. Then push aside the soil just enough to cut the shoot from its woody, horizontal rhizome with a greens knife. (See chapter 6 for a description of these tools.) With the soil scooped back into the cavity and the upper layer tamped back in place, little trace of the operation remains.

Freshly gathered bamboo shoots have a fibrous rind that must be peeled away before use. (Large ones are best blanched beforehand.) Once peeled, they resemble a raw potato in appearance and texture. Split down the middle, they reveal interior chambers destined to become nodes, or joints, in the mature cane. The shoots should be sliced thinly, after which most require at least one boiling before eating or stir-frying to sweeten and tenderize them, though some may be used raw, as noted above. Old or dark shoots often have a strong, unpleasant flavor, and must be boiled in multiple changes of water to leach out the bitter toxins. Whether this is worth the effort is a personal choice.

Bamboo shoots spoil quickly in the refrigerator, and should be used as soon as possible after cutting. (Not peeling them until use extends their shelf life a few days.) They can also be dried after boiling, using the rack method or a commercial food dryer. Dried shoots are very woody, however, and must be thoroughly rehydrated in warm water before eating.

> **Be sure to remove all of the rind,** including the inner bark, from fresh bamboo shoots. In some species, this rind contains tiny slivers that can damage the digestive tract. A thorough scrape with the edge of a sharp knife usually does the job. Shoots that contain bitter hydrocyanic acid poison grazing animals within their natural range. As a result, some sources list bamboo shoots as toxic. However, the boiling required to render such shoots palatable leaches out these toxins. Bamboo shoots that don't require boiling to become palatable are not toxic.

Asians consider the chewy, flavorful shoots of winter-sprouting bamboos a different vegetable from the milder, more delicate shoots that appear in spring. Either way, fresh bamboo shoots are crisper and sweeter than the canned variety, with no tinny aftertaste. The flavor is often compared to sweet corn, another giant edible grass. Bamboo is a short-lived plant that relies on production of new canes for survival. While running varieties rarely want for shoots, foragers should be careful to leave a healthy number of them behind to replenish the colony. This is especially important when cutting shoots within the approved zone.

It will come as no surprise that bamboo shoots are high in fiber. This is no doubt the reason that traditional Asian doctors prescribe them for digestive problems. Winter-sprouting species are an important off-season source of vitamin C. Scientists have isolated effective antibacterial chemicals in mature bamboo, justifying its long use in food preservation in the Orient.

Cornus

Dogwoods (genus *Cornus*) thrive in suburbs all over the continent, from chilly boreal climes to the balmy south. Many are native, and many more have been introduced from overseas. Some dogwoods are large trees, but those that bear the tastiest fruit are small trees or shrubs.

Kousa dogwood (*Cornus kousa*).

No dogwood fruits are toxic, but most are mealy, astringent, and seedy. Pacific dogwood (*C. nuttallii*), a common North Pacific tree and the emblem of British Columbia, is a case in point. Its tight, ruddy clusters, which appear to be one spiky berry, are uninteresting alone, but a handful of them lends character to preserves of overly sweet fruit. (Eastern dogwood [*C. florida*] fruits are similar, except that the clusters are smaller.)

Cornelian cherry (*C. mas*), on the other hand, is much more valuable. This shrub or small tree from eastern Europe and western Asia bears clusters of yellow flowers prior to leafing out in early spring. Some cultivars have striking, variegated (two-toned) leaves reminiscent of box elder (*Acer negundo*). In autumn its oblong "cherries" ripen crimson red.

Cornelian cherry is an important herb in the Near East, and is a common symbol in Greek and Muslim literature. Valued for its tart fruit and dye-rich bark (see Dyers' Notes), humans carried cornelian cherry across Europe and Asia, where it would ultimately play a prominent role in the most influential cultures in the Northern Hemisphere. Though unappetizing raw, cornelian cherries are the central ingredient of a syrup commonly used in Near Eastern cuisines (see Recipes, page 134). Cornelian cherry pie was widely celebrated in Europe before the twentieth century and "cornoulle" wine was a fad among the medieval aristocracy. Scarlet cornelian cherry juice sharpens and colors cider, and is a popular soft-drink flavoring in Slavic countries. Like green plums, green cornelian cherries have been pickled as an olive substitute.

Beauty and hardiness contribute to cornelian cherry's popularity in landscaping. Cultivated primarily for appearance today, the fruit of suburban trees varies in quality according to variety and location. Some are said to be palatable raw when completely ripe, but most are best appreciated in pies, preserves, or beverages.

Landscapers prize kousa dogwood (*C. kousa*), another immigrant, for its large, four-petalled, white or yellow flowers, sometimes tipped with red, as well as its blazing autumn foliage. But they grumble about kousa's golfball-sized, strawberry-like fruits (not to be confused with strawberry tree; see Arbutus entry above) which litter the ground and squish underfoot in autumn. Kousa balls are sweetish and marshmallow-soft when ripe, with a tender, pocked pink skin enclosing orange pulp in which small stones are embedded. Some people enjoy eating this fruit raw, though I find the texture a bit off-putting. Kousa balls make nice sauces and preserves, particularly in company with tart, highly flavored fruits, though some fruits don't take well to cooking and should be used raw. A bit of experimentation will determine how best to use local fruit.

> **Bloodtwig dogwood (*C. sanguinea*)** is a brushy Old World shrub whose scarlet bark and autumn foliage have earned it a place in suburban yards. Bloodtwig's cranberry-sized, glossy black drupes hang in loose clusters. I have yet to try these, but they look like they would add interesting color to preserves.

Kousa dogwood can be a multitrunked bush or a tree reaching twenty feet. It's happiest in mild, moist climates such as the Pacific Northwest and the Deep South, but occurs sporadically in other regions. Unlike most dogwoods, which flower in early spring, kousa is a midsummer bloomer. In fall its leaves turn striking red and gold. Like cornelian cherry, North American kousas are primarily planted for looks, so fruit quality varies.

Baskets of kousa balls can often be had for the asking. Enterprising foragers might even offer to "dispose" of these nuisances for a nominal fee. Because they are so soft, kousa balls shouldn't be gathered in a sack, and tend to crush under their own weight if too many are carried in a bucket. They don't keep well, and must be used soon after picking.

Dogwood berry tea is a traditional cold remedy in First Nations cultures. The Chinese and Japanese join them in using the same infusion as a blood-purifying tonic and diuretic, prescribed for a host of urogenital complaints. Traditional healers in Asia and the New World also consider dogwood berry effective against diarrhea. Species seem more or less interchangeable for all these purposes, as folk healers rely on local varieties to produce the same effects on both continents.

Cornelian cherries are rich in vitamin C and are a traditional treatment for joint and digestive disorders. Researchers in the Commonwealth of Independent States (the former Soviet Union), where cases of gross overexposure to radiation are sadly common, have isolated chemicals in cornelian cherry juice that help the body recover from radiation poisoning.

Elaeagnus

Respected for its ability to form handsome hedges under the least promising circumstances, genus *Elaeagnus* also bears unusual, edible fruits. Though their
"olives" (or gumis) frequently fall victim to rumors of toxicity, I have found no
reliable warnings about them anywhere. This total lack of negative press suggests
that *Elaeagnus* fruits are arguably safer than apples, cherries, peaches, and any
number of other common domesticated fruits, all of which are listed as toxic
under certain circumstances.

Russian olive (*E. angustifolia*) is probably North America's most widely
distributed *Elaeagnus* species. Indigenous to the Middle East and Central Asia,
on this continent Russian olive is either a godsend or a pest, depending on your
point of view. While land managers value its ability to stabilize soil under problematic conditions, Russian olive out-competes local plants and offers little to
sustain wildlife. This drawback is less critical in urbanized areas, however, where
Russian olive is used as a popular hedge and windbreak, prospering even in high-
traffic sites.

Cherry elaeagnus, or gumi
(*Elaeagnus multiflora*).

A deciduous shrub topping out at about twenty feet, Russian olive can also be trained into low hedges. Its multiple trunks are sheathed in dark, shreddy bark, and its narrowly oval, silver-green leaves, reaching two inches in length, are silver-grey underneath. Many cultivars bear thorns as well. Small, yellow-green flowers, famous for their musky perfume, droop from the leaf attachments. The fruits do indeed resemble small olives, though *E. angustifolia* is not related to true olives (genus *Olea*). They ripen greenish yellow, sometimes reddish, with shiny, silvery overtones.

Most *Elaeagnus* shrubs have characteristic brown or silver dots on the leaves and branches. Some have variegated foliage. Among the more popular species are:

- Silverberry (*E. commutata*). A small, silvery, thornless *Elaeagnus* native to the northern half of the continent, silverberry fruits resemble those of Russian olive.
- Autumn olive (*E. umbellata*). A thorny, silvery Asian species reaching as high as twenty-five feet, autumn olive bears juicy, flavorful fruits. Pea-sized autumn olives ripen red and silver in late autumn.
- Cherry elaeagnus, or gumi (*E. multiflora*). A respected edible native to northeast Asia, cherry elaeagnus resembles a low-growing autumn olive. Its marble-sized "cherries" or gumis are vivid red, flecked with silver. Juicy and somewhat astringent, they are not as tart as autumn olives.
- Evergreen cherry elaeagnus (*E. philippinensis*) fruit is very similar to that of the deciduous sort and can be used interchangeably. The leaves are light green and narrowly oval, with silver spots on the undersides that flash in the sun when the leaves flutter in the wind.

> **Foragers must be careful not to** confuse *Elaeagnus* with English laurel or privet, both of which bear toxic fruit (see Foraging Advisory).

Dry, mealy, and astringent when fresh, Russian olives can be cooked and sieved to make preserves. They may reach their highest expression when mixed with sweeter, tarter, or juicier fruits. Autumn olives and the fruits of the two cherry elaeagnuses can be used alone to make vibrantly colored sauces, syrups, and jellies that complement poultry, as well as desserts and baked goods. Unlike Russian olives, they can also be eaten fresh.

Elaeagnus figures highly in traditional Asian and Middle Eastern medicine, where elaeagnus fruit syrups and teas are considered effective against cough and catarrh. Mildly astringent elaeagnus infusions are used in dermal preparations and to counter diarrhea.

Mahonia/Berberis

In the Pacific Northwest, where I grew up, autumn is something of an anticlimax. While eastern Canada and New England revel in their fiery fall foliage, the North Pacific coast, dominated by evergreens, settles for the odd scarlet vine maple and a few banks of blotchy red Oregon grape (*Mahonia aquifolium*). This isn't the only time that Oregon grape relieves the green tyranny, either. In spring its dense sprays of tiny yellow flowers blaze like torches in the underbrush, to give way to equally dense clusters of neon blue berries. But in spite of the fact that Oregon grape bears such a weight of useful, eye-catching fruit, hardly anyone notices it. The berries drop to the ground or are eaten by birds. Many even believe Oregon grapes to be poisonous.

Oregon grape
(*Mahonia aquifolum*).

Official flower of its namesake state, Oregon grape strongly resembles holly (genus *Ilex;* see Foraging Advisory), giving rise to another common name, holly grape. Its spiny leaves are flatter, more flexible, and less glossy than those of true holly, and are only partially evergreen; some remain through the winter, while others turn red and drop in the fall. But the most telling distinction between holly and Oregon grape is the latter's vibrant blue berries. Borne in large clumps from late summer through late autumn, they positively glow against the glossy green foliage.

Some taxonomists lump the *Mahonia* species into genus *Berberis,* the barberries. Both genera have substantially the same botanical and herbal attributes, and for foraging purposes are essentially one. *Mahonia* is native to the West Coast, although it has been widely introduced elsewhere, while *Berberis,* an Old World genus, has been naturalized in the Northeast, South, and Midwest. Most bear clusters of waxy yellow flowers in spring. Many barberries have spiny, plastic-looking leaves recalling *Mahonia,* though others have narrow, oblong

Yeast from a Berry

Blue elderberries, Oregon grapes, and many other fruits are coated with a powdery, frostlike "bloom" that makes them appear lighter in color than they really are. This powder is a symbiotic yeast, a microscopic organism harmful to neither plant nor forager. When mashed, such fruits deliver a hefty shot of sugar to this yeast, causing it to multiply exponentially. Eventually the yeast outgrows its food supply and poisons itself on its own secretions. This waste product (alcohol) is also a powerful preservative. The resulting beverage (wine) has been known to keep for a thousand years when properly stored. Historians speculate that wine invented itself in an amphora of improperly processed grape juice somewhere in the Middle East, since wine grapes are uncommonly high in sugar and have a symbiotic yeast bloom. Elderberries, blueberries, and plums also anchor prestigious wine traditions in various parts of the world, no doubt because they too are high in sugar and have a yeast bloom. Today, these fruits contribute yeast, color, and flavor to wines of other fruits, too.

Berry yeast makes an interesting sourdough starter for baked goods. Just pour a cup of lukewarm water into a nonreactive bowl or jar and whisk in half a cup of flour. Dump in half a cup of unwashed, yeasty fruit such as blue elderberries or Oregon grapes, stir well, cover, and leave the batter in a warm place for about twelve hours to allow the yeast to start fermenting. By the following day, the starter will have started to bubble and will have a sweet, yeasty-winey smell. Strain the berries out, whisk in enough flour to bring the mixture to the consistency of pancake batter, and allow it to work for another day or so. The starter is then ready for use, and, if fed, will reproduce indefinitely.

Berry yeast sourdough has a sweet flavor well suited to scones, coffee-cakes, and sweet breads. It isn't as aggressive as the yeasts in ordinary sourdough starters, so it takes longer to rise and makes denser baked goods. Berry yeast starter can be mixed with ordinary starters to improve its performance, but such hybrid starters eventually become entirely "ordinary" as the more aggressive ordinary starter yeasts outcompete the fruit yeasts.

leaves that bear little obvious resemblance. Most barberries also have long, slender thorns, unlike *Mahonia,* which only has spiny leaves.

Common barberry (*B. vulgaris*) fruits in clusters of half-inch-long, bright red lozenges that have the remnants of a calyx on the blossom end, making them look like cartoon wieners. Oregon grapes and some barberries are round, and may be blue, black, purple, or pink, often with a yeast bloom that lightens their color considerably. All are seedy and extremely tart, but once the seeds are screened or milled out and sugar added, they become quite tasty. Rich in natural pectin, Oregon grapes and barberries make delicious jelly in lovely, stained-glass colors. They are also excellent companions for bland, sweet, or pectin-deficient fruits, and boast a long folk tradition as a beverage flavoring. Tart barberry wine was once a staple on European farms. Darker, yeast-covered fruits such as Oregon grape seem particularly well suited to fermentation, though they require unusually high quantities of sugar. Diluted with water and sugared to taste, fresh *Mahonia* or *Berberis* juice is an effective Indian summer thirst-quencher not unlike grape juice.

Picking barberries and high-growing Oregon grapes is fairly easy, as they carry their fruit at the top of the plant. Low-growing *Mahonias* are bothersome, since they require stooping to pick their sparser fruits. In any case, it's a good idea to wear long sleeves when picking *Mahonia* or *Berberis* berries, as a defense against the thousands of tiny needles that arm the leaves of many species. In addition, the ground underneath is usually littered with prickly dead leaves that make for very unpleasant strolling in sandals or bare feet, so good shoes are also a must.

The just-opened leaves of the Oregon grape are a surprising early-spring salad green. Translucent and nominally defended by rubbery, inoffensive spines, the tart, clean flavor and al dente texture of these unusual edibles complement other greens. But only brand-new leaves are edible. After a day or two, the spines harden, the flavor turns bitter, and the texture begins to resemble plastic.

Mahonia and *Berberis* root bark is a source of berberine, a potent external antibacterial indicated for psoriasis, acne, and other skin ailments. The fruit has an antiseptic effect on the digestive tract, and is used to combat intestinal infections such as giardiasis and amoebic dysentery. Both the fruit and infusions of the bark promote bile flow, and are taken against gallstones and other bladder-related problems. Studies also support their use against liver ailments. Berberine may be dangerous to unborn children, and pregnant women should consult their doctor before ingesting medicinal *Mahonia* or *Berberis* preparations.

Rhus

Native to Asia, Africa, the Mediterranean, and all of subarctic North America except the Pacific coast, sumac (genus *Rhus*) is a foraging standby. The extremely sour fruits of this genus provided pioneers with an easily made lemon juice or vinegar substitute, one that definitely deserves to be used more widely than it is today. In fact, sumac is actually better than lemon or vinegar for many applications, and once you have introduced it into your kitchen, it's hard to imagine doing without it.

Hardy, exuberant growth, vaguely exotic appearance, and fiery autumn foliage conspire to make sumac a favorite suburban ornamental. Like wild rose, it excels in hard-duty areas and is inevitably introduced to the few areas where it is not native. Hardy in most climates, rooting in poor soil as well as fertile, these attractive shrubs integrate well wherever they are planted.

Staghorn sumac
(*Rhus typhina*).

Squawbush
(*Rhus trilobata*).

The most popular ornamental *Rhus* species is staghorn sumac (*R. typhina*). Native from the Eastern Seaboard to the Rockies, it has been introduced almost everywhere in the Far West as well. Staghorn sumac's fuzzy branches reminded early settlers of a deer's velvety spring antlers, thus its common name. Erect clusters of dense, woolly, maroon berries, called "cones," appear in midsummer and persist through winter to the next growing season. Staghorn is generally a spreading shrub about twelve feet high. Where several occur, as in the sumac jungles that line highways, they combine to form a low canopy that shades out competing plants. Solitary staghorns growing in the open may grow to become tall trees, often going undetected by casual passers-by, who expect sumac to be a shrub.

Staghorn leaves reach about about six inches in length and are narrow, pointed, and finely serrated. They line the branch tips in opposing pairs with a final leaf growing straight out of the tip. The foliage turns brilliant red in autumn, with yellow or orange streaks. When the leaves drop, they leave stark, candelabra-like branches incongruously decorated with persistent fruit clusters.

Smooth sumac (*Rhus glabra*) is slightly smaller and the fruits and branch tips less hairy than those of staghorn sumac. But it readily crosspollinates with staghorn, making positive identification of individual plants difficult. Fortunately, staghorn and smooth sumac are largely interchangeable, so foragers need only identify plants as one (or both) of the two. Staghorn sumac is considered the best source of juice, though other sumacs, such as Southern California's lemonade berry (*R. integrifolia*), an evergreen with leathery leaves, also make good juice. Sugar bush (*R. ovata*), a smaller version of lemonade berry, has pointier leaves and berries encrusted with natural sugar. It is especially typical of arid climates, and can be used like other sumacs.

I use pruning shears to cut fruit cones or clusters from sumac branches. Gloves are also handy, as the berries quickly coat the hands with their sticky film. Staghorn cones reach optimum color and flavor in late summer, and are best harvested before autumn rains sluice away their flavor. Others ripen at different points in the summer and fall. Sumac fruit clusters can be gathered and stored in a paper sack, where they will dry readily. If picked into a plastic bag, they should be removed as soon as possible to prevent spoiling.

To make sumac juice, pick the berries from the cluster (or clip off the small bracts of staghorn cones with pruning shears) and place them in a blender with twice as much cold water. (Some authorities suggest using hot water, but hot water infuses no more efficiently than cold; what's more, the hot water leaches out certain bitter constituents from the bracts and dramatically reduces sumac's rich vitamin C content.) Blend them for about three minutes, then wring the burgundy-colored infusion through wet muslin and discard the seeds and bracts. Sumac juice is extremely corrosive, and only nonreactive implements should be used to process it.

I prefer sumac juice over lemon juice for almost everything. Sumac's malic acid adds a hint of wine to its flavor, and its vibrant color enhances the visual appeal of beverages, salad dressings, and desserts. Having tasted sumac meringue pie (just substitute sumac juice for lemon in a lemon meringue pie recipe and proceed as usual), I can't go back. Sumac juice also brings a taste of the Middle East to marinades for chicken, fish, and lamb. It makes a tasty jelly all by itself, and adds acid and flavor to preserves of other fruits.

Freeze sumac juice if you expect to keep it more than a week. The berry clusters dry readily, so I stock up cones or clusters in August and process juice throughout the year as I need it.

The tart Middle Eastern spice blend known as zattar is made from the ground berries of a Mediterranean sumac (*R. coriaria*), but staghorn cone bracts can be used to create a North American version. Warm an oven at its lowest temperature setting, then turn it off. Place well-dried staghorn bracts in a pan and pop them in the oven for about ten minutes, until the sour little hairs become brittle. Seal the crisped bracts in a plastic bag and whack it several times against a table or counter top to break the hairs free. The seeds and bract bits can then be sifted out, leaving a quantity of bright red hairs. To make zattar, mix these with thyme, savory, sesame seeds, and salt. Dredge poultry, lamb, or fish in this mixture before broiling or grilling, or sprinkle it over salads or oven loaves of flat bread before baking.

Sumac, one of the richest sources of vitamin C, is useful in combating nutritional

Backyard Mangoes

As a member of Anacardiaceae, the Cashew family, sumac is kin to mango (*Mangifera indica*). Squawbush (*Rhus trilobata*) and fragrant sumac (*R. aromatica*) bring this pedigree home with a jolt.

Both these rather homely sumacs resemble poison oak (see Foraging Advisory) more closely than the graceful, long-leaved, tropical-looking staghorn and smooth sumacs. Both are dense, twiggy shrubs with oak-shaped leaves and a tendency to form low banks or hedges. Their foliage releases a strong odor when crushed. The smell of fragrant sumac is fairly pleasant, while that of squawbush (also known as skunkbush or stinking sumac) is less so. Both set small, irregular clumps of bean-sized, minutely bristly, orange-red berries. These fruits are sort of an evolutionary practical joke. In spite of the fact that they grow thousands of miles from the tropics, they look like tiny mangoes. And they smell like mangoes. Best of all, they *taste* like mangoes.

Taken straight from the bush, these berries are tacky, painfully tart, and mostly pit. But 3/4 cup of them, whirled in a blender with 1 1/2 cups cold water, then wrung through muslin, yields a startling fluorescent orange concentrate. (Muslin and hands must both be washed immediately afterward with soap and water, as they will be coated with sticky, roadcrew-orange oil.) Diluted with 5 cups of iced water and sweetened with 2/3 to 3/4 cup of sugar, this concentrate makes a drink that tastes remarkably like mango juice.

For a tropical apéritif, whirl the berries in rum or vodka instead of water. Allow the pulp and liquor to infuse in a tightly covered jar for an hour or so, then wring it through muslin. Sweeten, dilute to taste, and enjoy.

Like strawberries, tomatoes, and other high-acid foods, sumac has a high incidence of allergic reaction. Foragers should observe strict first-try protocol (see chapter 1) until they become accustomed to sumac. Excessive consumption may prompt mild reactions even in nonallergic individuals. Sumac is also a high-tannin food, another reason to treat it with respect. Having said that, I guzzle icy sumac lemonade (see Recipes, 135) by the quart in the dog days of summer, and have yet to experience any discomfort.

deficiencies and colds. High tannin content means that sumac juice is useful as an astringent wash for wounds, and it is said to slow bleeding and promote clotting, though it must sting incredibly.

Sumac sap was a frontier antiseptic used on cuts and wounds. Sumac bark tea was taken for internal bleeding. Squawbush (*Rhus trilobata*), also called crampbark, derives its common names from native women's practice of drinking tea made from its bark to ease menstrual difficulties.

Ribes

Currants and gooseberries (genus *Ribes*) are classic European hedgerow shrubs, and maintain a high profile in northern cultures on that continent. *Ribes'* iconic status in the United Kingdom even inspired the makers of Ribena, a beverage made from the juice of English black currant (*R. nigrum*), to bill their product as "quite possibly the world's most civilised fruit drink." Scientists would be hard-pressed to verify this claim, but it points to the deep respect currants and gooseberries command in the British Isles. *Ribes* enjoyed similar admiration among North American settlers and First Nations cultures, who have gathered *Ribes* fruits since prehistoric times.

Black gooseberry (*Ribes lacustre*).

Ribes shrubs are multistemmed and weedy, seldom growing higher than ten feet. Some, particularly gooseberry bushes, bristle with needle-fine thorns. Their small, dark green leaves, which resemble those of hawthorn, are generally lobed, serrated, coarsely veined, and somewhat fuzzy. In color, *Ribes* fruits and flowers span the spectrum, from red to orange, yellow, blue, green, and black.

Many *Ribes* species are carriers of white pine blister rust, a disease that attacks valuable timber trees, and have been the subject of eradication campaigns in some areas. Rust-resistant hybrids have been developed in recent years, and with luck this valuable resource will slowly return to its former haunts.

Currants and gooseberries are round, pea- to marble-sized, and sometimes translucent. Gooseberries are often armed with fine spines. Picking takes patience (and leather gloves, in the case of gooseberries), but it's worth the effort. Traditionally, *Ribes* fruits are dried, juiced, or cooked before eating. They bring a vaguely grapelike quality to

> While tannins in raw *Ribes* berries can cause gastric disturbances if eaten in excessive amounts, a handful or so makes a tasty and refreshing snack. Tiny bristles on fresh sticky currants (*R. viscosissimum*), a gooey Western native, may cause nausea even in moderation, so they are best cooked before eating.

sauces and preserves. Naturally high in pectin, currant preserves set without the addition of apples or store-bought pectin. Like apples, currant juice can be used to jell preserves of low-pectin fruits.

In times past, diluted currant juice stood in for wine in nonalcoholic beverages and sauces. It was also fermented into wine and brandy in its own right. *Crème de cassis* ("cream of currant") is a popular liqueur in its native France. For their part, gooseberries are a popular jelly fruit across Northern Europe. Gooseberry fool, a smooth, iced purée of fresh gooseberries and cream, is as necessary to an English summer as watermelon is in North America.

Currants are an important foodstuff in circumpolar cultures, thanks to their long shelf life and high vitamin C content. In the past, the harvest would be spread on mats or tarpaulins and sun-dried until the currants were fit for long-term storage. Today, a hot car interior makes short work of drying them (see page 21). In a matter of hours, raisin-like dried currants are ready to be stored in airtight containers for later use. (Incidentally, the supermarket's Zante "currants," which actually are raisins, cannot stand in for the real thing in medicinal preparations. Since they are dried grapes, Zante currants lack *Ribes'* chemical properties.)

Dried currants adorn the scones, cakes, and other baked goods for which Britain's afternoon teas are justly famous. As a rule, any recipe calling for raisins profits from the substitution of dried currants. Northern Europeans stew dried currants with meat, and while geographically out of place in couscous and curry, I find them less obtrusive and of better texture than the traditional raisins in these dishes. In Sweden, young black currant leaves are used in herbed butters and vinegars and to flavor pickles.

Tea made from young *Ribes* leaves is a diuretic, helping patients pass kidney stones, whereas the seedy fruits provide dietary fiber for clearing slow-moving bowels. Currant juice is a traditional stomachic, said to improve weak appetites and rehydrate feverish patients. Currant jelly dissolved in whiskey combated cold symptoms in pioneer households, while folk healers consider black currant juice and honey effective against sore throats. In some First Nations cultures, pregnant women are said to crave fresh gooseberries.

Rosa

Genus *Rosa* includes around 250 species—as well as innumerable hybrids and cultivars—of humanity's most honored flower. Roses are an important symbol in many cultures, and have figured highly in world literature since the advent of the written word. The Song of Solomon refers to "the rose of Sharon," while here in the New World, the Canadian province of Alberta and five American states have chosen a rose as their official flower. (In four American states plus New Brunswick, genus *Viola* [see chapter 4] is the only other blossom in *Rosa's* league.) Roses were once ascribed tremendous healing powers. Dog rose (*R. canina*) received both its common and species name from the Roman belief that it cured rabies, while doctors in the Middle Ages washed patients' faces with rose water to break fevers and calm the insane. Though modern medicine has debunked these applications, roses

Ramana rose (*Rosa rugosa*).

are in fact one of the richest sources of vitamin C, a nutrient known to boost dramatically the body's ability to heal itself.

In the days when roses were widely used in medicine and cooking, wild rose species and proto-domesticated varieties were the norm. By contrast, modern hydrid roses, bred for appearance, are often tasteless or bitter, and their medicinal properties may be compromised as well. Garden roses are more regularly and more heavily treated with pesticides than any other suburban plant, making them dubious foraging resources. Then too, rose gardeners are a gung-ho crowd, and have been known to greet browsing life forms with gunfire. For all of these reasons, foragers usually have better luck with the fragrant, unpretentious wild species that made the genus famous. These are rarely sprayed, or even tended, though they are often planted as hedges and barriers in parks and other public places. I have collected wild rose hips, petals, and leaves in full view of polite society without provoking so much as a frown, let alone armed confrontation. (I have, however, had many pleasant conversations with passersby who were curious about what I was doing.)

Wild roses bear little resemblance to most modern garden varieties. Whereas the latter tend to be leggy, with large, sparse thorns and leaves, wild rose briars are bushy and leafy. Completely sheathed in tiny, incredibly sharp spines, wild rose thickets are as impassable as an electric fence. Their blossoms are simple and open, distinct from the cabbagelike flowers of most garden varieties. Wild rose blossoms are most frequently soft pink, less often white, yellow, or lavender, but rarely boldly colored like bouquet roses. In fact, since their petals drop immediately after picking, wild roses are worthless as cut flowers.

Unlike garden roses, which quickly die unless cared for, wild rose banks renew themselves indefinitely and are extremely disease-resistant. Highway departments and commercial developers are especially fond of them, which is the reason they are so common in residential areas. This is good news for foragers, since the roots, stems, bark, leaves, blossoms, and fruit of these plants are all herbal resources. Historically, the entire bush, from the roots to the flowers and all parts in between, was infused for serious diseases. However, for suburban foraging, the petals, leaves, and fruits are most valuable.

Rose petals make a delicate, fragrant wine and are infused in tea and syrup. Sweet, fragrant rose petal jams and sauces were medieval luxury items, and rose water, a distilled infusion, was fundamental to medicine and perfumery until the twentieth century. Since most of these preparations call for quarts of rose petals, suburbanites have little chance to try making them at home. Also, removing the bitter white heel from so many petals is a substantial task. However, smaller quantities of petals can be candied like violets (see page 96) or baked in cakes, sweet breads, and scones. They dry readily in a paper sack, after which they may be sealed in an airtight container for use in cooking or potpourri.

Rose leaves require less processing than petals and are easier to gather. They make surprisingly flavorful tea and herbed vinegar, imparting a subtle "rosy" taste with a slightly green edge. They may be gathered any time, but taste best if picked before the plant

flowers. Rose leaves can be dried for year-round use using the paper-bag method.

During World War II, when German U-boats pinched off citrus shipments from overseas, the British government fell back on England's vast rose hedges to provide the populace with vitamin C. Fiery red and orange rose hips are in fact an extremely rich source of vitamin C when fresh, on the order of 1,500 milligrams per 100 grams of seeded pulp by one estimate. This has led some to claim that drinking rose hip tea prevents the common cold. Unfortunately, while studies do suggest that megadoses of vitamin C may suppress colds, dried rose hips contain only one-fifth the vitamin C of fresh ones, of which maybe one-tenth infuses in tea. Given these figures, it would seem that tea made from dried rose hips is more flavorful than nutritious or medicinal.

Rose hips are a versatile, plentiful fruit. Briars fairly droop with them from autumn well into winter, when the bright red orbs are especially conspicuous among the bare branches. Most taste best cooked, though some may be eaten raw. People of the First Nations used raw rose hips as a breath freshener and trail food, but warned their children not to swallow the white seeds, because the tiny bristles with which they are studded pass through the digestive tract unaltered, to irritate the colon on the way out. The end result, so to speak, is reflected in the French word for rose hip, *gratte-cul,* which is a vulgar term in every sense of the word.

In my estimation, ramanas rose (*Rosa rugosa*) bears the best hips in the world. Common in landscaping and along roadsides, ramanas rose is occasionally cultivated in gardens. (Gardeners call it rugosa.) The luscious fruits, soft, bright red, and walnut-sized, ripen in late summer. This, together with ramanas' shoreside origins, give rise to another common name, sea tomato. Ramanas rose can be identified out of season by its glossy, oval leaves and its very pale, almost white stems, fearsomely defended by dense, lacerating spines. Ramanas hips are delicious raw as well as in tea, preserves, and sauces. Fresh ones don't keep long, but they dry well if split and seeded.

The hard, waxy hips of most other roses are unappetizing fresh, but soften and become tangy and sweet when simmered in liquid. The odd white worm found in some hips is actually after the seeds, not the fruit. A few inevitably appear whenever fresh, whole hips are infused, as for jelly or tea. They are tiny, tasteless, and strain out in processing, so most foragers just ignore them. Since they live among the seeds and not in the rind, exceptionally squeamish people can avoid them entirely by seeding all hips before use.

To clean rose hips, remove the blossom end, split open the hip, and push the hairy white seeds out of each half with a teaspoon or thumbnail. The rinds can then be pulped in jam or stewed with tomato sauces to enhance flavor and body. Jelly (see Recipes, page 133) and tea require only removal of the blossom end before covering whole hips with boiling water, mashing, and infusing.

> In *Wild Coffee and Tea Substitutes* of Canada (see Further Reading), Adam F. Szczawinski and Nancy J. Turner suggest stringing rose hips with needle and thread and using the garlands to decorate the Christmas tree. The dried hips can then be stored for use in tea. Although there are more efficient ways to dry rose hips, there are certainly none more charming.

Apples, which ripen about the same time, are traditionally paired with rose hips in recipes. Apples jell rose hip preserves, while chopped and seeded rose hips contribute color and flavor to apple pie and applesauce. Substituting rose hips for half the sorbs in the rowan jelly on page 72 gives a mellower, tangier product. The color and flavor of strong liquors such as brandy or rum can be influenced for the better by infusing them with rose hips in the ratio of one part liquid to one part cleaned, crushed rose hips.

Rose hips can be dried either seeded and chopped or whole using a rack, commercial food dryer, or hot car. Properly dried rose hips may keep for years, though, as noted above, the drying process destroys much of the nutritional value.

In addition to vitamin C, rose hips contain vitamin A and several B complex vitamins, and the fuzzy pips are a source of vitamin E. Rose leaves also contain vitamin C, though not as much as fresh hips. The leaves are reputed to be good for bee stings, either as a poultice or in ointment, while rose leaf tea is a spring tonic. The blossoms are being investigated for possible cholesterol-reducing properties. Rose petals, leaves, roots, and hips have all been used to treat wounds, as they are believed to staunch blood flow and disinfect.

Rubus

The thorn-bearing, berry-producing brambles of genus *Rubus* are found on all continents except Antarctica, and bear some of the world's best-loved fruits. *Rubus* plants produce lustily with little human interference, and so are an important resource everywhere they occur. Blackberry is the most common suburban *Rubus*. This includes blackberry hybrids, such as boysenberry and loganberry, that have escaped cultivation or persist on former farmland. Wild and feral raspberries run a close second.

Himalayan blackberry (*Rubus procerus*).

Prolific growth on unmanaged land accounts for blackberry's historical association with the rural poor. Blackberry canes or vines sprout from perennial root systems in their first year, flower and fruit in their second, then die. In many cases, dead canes form a trellis for new ones, which in turn block the sunlight and squelch any competition. In this fashion, blackberries often establish a virtual monoculture if left to their own devices.

Blackberries grow with such riotous abandon, and their luscious fruits set so heavily, that they can hardly be overlooked. Yet most suburbanites don't take advantage of them, and many even hate the plant as invasive and ugly. Their contempt is misplaced, since the huge size of the two most common varieties means that bucketfuls can be picked in no time. A minimum of processing bends them to myriad uses.

Himalayan (*R. procerus*) and lace-leaf blackberry (*R. laciniatus*), both Old World immigrants, have become the most widespread wild blackberries in North America. Himalayan leaves are widely oval, serrated, and pointed, while those of lace-leaf, as the common and botanical names imply, are deeply lobed and serrated, resembling Japanese maple leaves. Both are evergreens, and in the absence of interference, will readily form huge, dome-shaped bramble patches.

Trailing natives persist in some areas, crisscrossing the ground like trip wires. Trailing wild blackberry (*R. ursinus*), also known as Pacific dewberry, is a Western variety, while swamp blackberry (*Rubus hispidus*) and Allegheny

Blackberry Precautions

Few fruits defend themselves as ferociously as blackberries. The canes' needle-sharp thorns accept any opportunity to pierce and hold pickers' skin and clothing like fish hooks. Even the leaves are heavily armed, an extreme measure in the plant kingdom. And blackberries aren't just vigilant, they're downright vindictive; their thorns curve toward the plant's center. This allows raiders to push deep into the brambles without encountering much resistance, but when they try to withdraw with the spoils, the thorns bite down, trapping the victim. A painful, difficult extrication process ensues. A few precautions will minimize such mishaps.

· A berry hook is indispensable for working large patches, since the best clusters are often out of reach, or lure ill-equipped pickers into the tangle, usually with unfortunate results.

· I keep my pruning shears in my back pocket and nip off exploratory tendrils, dead canes, and other annoyances as I pick. Patches consistently groomed in this fashion grow friendlier and more productive with the passing seasons.

· Blackberry vines devour knit fabrics like candy. They are especially fond of sweaters and sweatshirts. Thorns snagging in the stretchy material can ruin such garments in short order. Flat weaves catch less frequently and are easier to untangle.

· Once snared, the uninitiated instinctively pull away. This is exactly what the bramble wants, since its thorns are perversely positioned to penetrate on retreat rather than attack. Entangled limbs should be pushed slightly *into* the plant and the tendrils carefully picked off with a free hand.

· Bramble thorns slash the forager's trusty plastic shopping bag, lacerating the harvest. The berries also get mashed as the bag bangs around during picking. The result is a dripping, staining mess. A plastic pail with bale and lid, such as ice cream is sold in, solves these problems. The rigid sides fend off thorns and blows, and the bucket can be set on the ground or among the brambles to free both hands for picking. Hands usually get pretty messy during picking, and a container that can sit open on the ground eliminates the unpleasantness of clutching gooey plastic while gathering.

· Sharp thorns on the underside of dried blackberry leaves make it impossible to crumble them with bare fingers to make tea. A better approach is to crisp the dried leaves in an oven that has been warmed at the lowest setting, then turned off. Then shake the brittle leaves into a coffee can and pulverize them quickly and painlessly with a potato masher.

blackberry (*R. allegheniensis*) occur east of the Rockies. Most natives bear tiny, infrequent berries, which foragers must stoop or kneel to pick. Naturally, they are also the best-tasting.

Wild blackberries are seedy, which is why hurried modern folk prefer larger and juicier farm-grown loganberries or boysenberries. But wild ones require only cursory processing before use. I dump them into a basin of water, turn lightly with my hands to wash, then drain. Then I crank them through a food mill to remove the seeds. In short order I have a quart or more of pulpy juice, ready to be turned into jam, syrup, or pies, or blended into ice cream and milkshakes.

Rich purple blackberry syrup (see Recipes, page 133) was once a universal household flavoring and medicinal preparation. Bramble (blackberry) jam traditionally accompanies the Scottish crofter's oatmeal scones, partly because blackberries are plentiful in rural Scotland, and partly because the red ones are loaded with free pectin. A ratio of about one part red berries to three parts ripe will jell blackberry (or other) preserves without the expense of commercial pectin or the added effort of finding and processing apples. The red berries can be cooked whole in the milled pulp of ripe ones, then mashed in the pot. Their relatively few seeds will not spoil the finished product. Ratios may vary according to the age of the red berries (they're best just before they ripen), the species used, and local conditions.

Blackberries are also highly esteemed as a beverage flavoring. The deep, portlike excellence of blackberry wine, crafted by experienced country folk, sweetens many a special occasion in rural societies around the globe, proving once again that the wealthy have no idea how to live. Some of these home blackberry wine recipes are as sensitive and complex as any grape-based tradition, and yield a product comparable to the finest French vintages. Others are more straightforward; some of the Appalachian recipes recorded in Foxfire (see Further Reading) produce worthwhile results without any specialized equipment or techniques.

Strained through wet muslin, raw blackberry juice makes refreshing beverages such as blackberry shrub (see Recipes, page 134), a tart drink that has slaked farm hands' thirst for centuries. Unsugared, it makes an unusual stewing liquid for meats. My wife makes mellow, exotic blackberry vinegar by crushing ripe berries in a nonreactive saucepan and stirring in an equal amount of cider vinegar. Then she covers the pan and warms it gently over medium-low heat, without boiling, for half an hour. Finally she strains, bottles, and cellars the liquid for at least a month before she lets me use it. The result is a refreshing change in salads and marinades, and a winelike cooking seasoning. Hill cultures in the mountains of the American South dilute this vinegar with iced water, add sugar to taste, and savor it as "blackberry nectar."

Drying blackberries is hardly worth the effort, since they have to be reconstituted and screened before use. If they must be dried, it's better to process them into fruit leather. The leather can later be rehydrated into syrup or eaten as is. I prefer to can the syrup in the first place, then use it as is or make jelly, shrub, or vinegar as needed.

Blackberry leaves are as famous as the berries themselves in European and North American folk cultures. Farmers in Ontario once made a delicate wine from them, and in the days when black tea was both rare and expensive in rural Canada, farmers, prospectors, and Hudson's Bay Company employees infused dried blackberry leaves instead. Blackberry leaf tea tastes something like Japanese green tea, and is taken both medicinally and as a beverage. I used to rely on Himalayan blackberry for tea, until local First Nations herbalists advised me that the scarlet winter leaves of native trailing blackberry make better tea. They know their stuff. Tea made from these leaves is a delicate pink color, with a subtle but distinct fragrance and flavor of rose.

First Nations peoples value blackberry leaf tea as a treatment for joint pain. Infusions of blackberry rhizome serve as an eyewash, cold remedy, and general tonic, and a powerful treatment for loose bowels. In *Field Guide to Medicinal Wild Plants* (see Further Reading), Bradford Angiers reports that the Oneida met a dysentery epidemic with blackberry root tea and suffered no casualties, while white settlers in the area, unwilling to trust the "heathen" medicine, dropped like flies.

> **First Nations cultures cut young** blackberry and raspberry shoots, as well as those of salmonberry (*R. spectabilis*), when tender and new, for use as a vegetable. Peeled and steamed, they make an excellent side dish for fish or poultry.

Blackberry juice, wine, and cordials are recognized worldwide as a remedy for diarrhea, nausea, and other digestive problems. Mild and pleasant-tasting, these preparations are particularly effective for children. Since blackberries are chock-full of vitamin C and natural sugars, they serve as both medicine and food for patients who have difficulty keeping things down.

The best raspberries for foraging are domestic varieties (*R. idaeus*) that have gone feral. Raspberry canes are studded with small, inoffensive spines that only "rasp" the skin, rather than puncturing or tearing it. This makes them much more agreeable to pick than blackberries. They also aren't as seedy as blackberries, so they don't need to be screened before making jam. Raspberry canes aren't as hardy as blackberries, but under the right conditions, feral raspberries can provide a respectable harvest. In most other respects they are interchangeable with blackberries.

Wild species, including thimbleberry (*R. parviflorus*) and blackcap (*R. leucodermis* and *R. occidentalis*) sometimes crop up in parks and other greenbelt areas. Most are thornless, low-growing canes or shrubs. Some have fine spines. Wild raspberries are typically mealy, seedy, and hard to pick since the thin-walled fruit falls apart in the fingers. Still, a cup of wild raspberries, whirled in a blender with water, then strained through wet muslin and sugared to taste, makes a superior shrub.

Raspberry juice is said to be an excellent oral antiseptic and gargle, while raspberry leaf infusions, decoctions, creams, and ointments are a famous topical treatment for hemorrhoids, acne, cold sores, and other skin disorders. Expecting women all over the world take infusions of raspberry leaf or bark to prevent miscarriage and ease morning sickness. Recent scientific studies suggest that raspberry leaf tea stimulates production of balance-promoting hormones that bring a measure of stability to a woman's body chemistry during this tumultuous time. (As always, pregnant women should consult their doctor before taking this or any other medication.)

Sambucus

Elder (genus *Sambucus*) is a case study in the dramatic conversion of North Americans from largely self-sufficient peoples to consumers. Present over most of the continent, elder was once central to North American gastronomy, so central that Eliot Wigginton's kids were able to collect three pages of Appalachian elderberry lore for *Foxfire*. Their informants' generation has since passed on, and in their absence the bulk of North America's elderberries go unpicked. The good news is, modern foragers face little competition for this beautiful, versatile resource.

More than a dozen *Sambucus* species occur in North America. Most are native to some part of the continent, though one common suburban variety, European red elder (*S. racemosa*), is an immigrant. Several native species have migrated beyond their natural ranges as well, so it's not uncommon for a single neighborhood to boast several different elders. Usual suspects include Pacific or American red elder (*S. pubens*), whose ruby red fruit blazes among the greens of

Red elder (*Sambucus pubens*), in flower.

the Pacific Northwest in early summer, and blue elder (*S. caerulea*), with flat, powder-blue berry sprays that ripen from mid to late autumn. American elder (*S. canadensis*), the species most often introduced beyond its natural range, bears umbrella-like clusters of translucent black berries in late autumn.

The elders are weedy, multitrunked shrubs whose narrow, pointed leaves suggest sumac, for which they are sometimes mistaken. Unlike sumac, elder branches are hollow and pithy and covered with smooth bark easily torn with a thumbnail. Some reach fifty feet under ideal conditions, but the average elder is between six and fifteen feet tall. An avid opportunist, elder readily colonizes vacant lots and cleared land and is common in yards and parks and along embankments.

Flat or domed umbels of tiny, fragrant, cream-white blossoms flare like sparklers from mid-spring to mid-summer, depending on variety. These flowers, also called elderblow, are an important culinary herb in Appalachia, where lacy, delicate elderblow fritters are a sought-after delicacy. Clip the umbels from the bush when fully "blown," coat with a thin egg batter (crêpe batter works well), then dip briefly in hot oil, until delicately crisp and golden. Serve piping hot, with powdered sugar, lemon juice, or syrup. Take the umbels by the stem to nibble off the pastry-encrusted blossoms, which taste something like a crisp, fruity doughnut.

When the blossoms begin to drop, the umbels can be enclosed in a sack while still on the bush and shaken vigor-

While elderflowers and the juice and flesh of ripe berries are edible, every other part, including seeds and unripe fruit, contains dangerous levels of cyanic glucosides. Only thoroughly ripe elderberries, soft and not a bit green, should be eaten. Ripe clusters usually include a few green berries, which should be removed and discarded. Pits should not be swallowed in quantity, though I've eaten up to a cup of whole cooked fruit without experiencing problems. Elderberries destined for wine or tea are used seed-in without negative result, because the hulls are not broken in processing.

The portion of the branch that forms the flower stem is not especially toxic, but it's still a good idea to avoid swallowing much of it while enjoying elderblow fritters. And though elder's hollow branches have a long record of service as whistles, flutes, snorkels, taps, and pipes, it's best to use bamboo for such implements and avoid putting elder wood in the mouth. Children sometimes poison themselves while playing with blowguns or pea shooters made from green elder branches.

Elderberries of all varieties should be cooked before eating to minimize allergic reactions and toxins, but most can be safely tasted for quality before picking. Contrary to some reports, red elderberries are not poisonous, though they often cause nausea when raw. Foragers should avoid even tasting raw red elderberries, and wine should not be made from uncooked red elderberries or their juice. According to the most reliable sources, cooked red elderberries are as safe as any other, in spite of the fact that they cause nausea when raw.

ously. Petals so collected can be stirred into pancake or muffin batter, or infused in tea. They can also be dried using the paper bag method.

Elderblow makes a rare white wine, rare because of its dainty dryness and the difficulty of collecting enough little petals for a whole batch. Much easier is elderflower champagne (see Recipes, page 136), a refined beverage made all the finer for the fact that, like the gentle sunshine it captures, this sparkling, lightly alcoholic libation is only available a few weeks of the year.

The BB-sized berries ripen blue, black, red, purple, or (rarely) yellow at various points in the summer and fall, depending upon species. Foragers who have access to more than one variety enjoy multiple harvests as each comes successively into flower, then fruit. Raw elderberries are seedy, have a greenish flavor, and may be toxic if improperly handled. But gathered ripe and processed as required, they yield wonderful preserves, syrups, pies, wines, and cordials. Elderberries are also famous companion fruits, lending color, flavor, and even yeast (see Yeast from a Berry, page 110) to recipes made with other fruits. In Appalachia, a handful of elderberries makes the difference between a merely good apple pie and a great one.

If not for elder's habit of setting in dense clusters, the bother of picking such tiny berries would severely dampen foragers' enthusiasm for them. As it is, several pounds can be gathered in short order by gently pulling down the branches with a berry hook and clipping the clusters off with pruning shears. The berries can then be stemmed later on at home while watching TV or chatting with friends.

Fresh elderberries should be milled before use to remove the seeds, which are large and slightly bitter due to their cyanide content. (That's right, cyanide; see Special Note, page 125.) Elderberries destined to become tea should be dried whole using the hot-car method. Otherwise, they freeze famously. Just wash, drain, and seal in an airtight bag or container. Elderberries should never be eaten raw, as some cause nausea unless cooked. And anyway, they don't taste very good fresh. Processed into preserves or other dishes, they taste great, and, barring allergy, cause no health problems. The juice of most elderberries can be used raw in wines and beverages, but juice from red ones is mildly toxic unless it is cooked before fermenting.

Scientific tests confirm that the potent antiviral constituents in elderberries counter colds, vindicating folk healers in Europe, Asia, and the Americas. Sambucol, an elderberry extract available in health-food stores, has proven effective against influenza, herpes, and the human immunodeficiency virus, or HIV.

A traditional and appealing response to flu is a heartwarming mug of mulled elderberry wine or elderberry tea. To make the latter, stew two tablespoons of dried elderberries in a cup and a half of water, crushing the berries as they simmer, then strain and drink. (A tablespoon of elderberry syrup per cup of hot water will do in a pinch.) With honey and lemon or sumac juice, elderberry tea is a pleasant, effective physic against cold and flu.

Succulents

Most people know that the sap of aloe (genus *Aloe*), a common houseplant and Southwestern ornamental, is an effective treatment for burns, scrapes, and other skin problems. Fewer know that other common succulents are also valuable herbs.

Houseleek (*Sempervivum tectorum*), or hen-and-chicks, is a ubiquitous and prolific ground cover. Europeans root this odd little plant, which looks like a cactus doing an impression of a rose, on tile roofs, ostensibly to fend off malevolent spirits. By happy coincidence, the plant's rubbery runners also anchor the tiles in place. While the Dutch reportedly eat young houseleek leaves raw, they are more commonly used like aloe for skin problems. The stubby, pointed leaves are broken off and the sap squeezed onto the affected area. Failing that, a poultice of mashed leaf pulp can be applied.

Houseleek or hen-and-chicks (*Sempervivum tectorum*).

Yucca (genus *Yucca*) is high in saponins and is widely used as a lathering agent in laundry and bathing in traditional Southwestern and Latin American cultures. In the 1970s, North American corporations exploited yucca as a gentle shampoo additive. Yucca bears palmlike clumps of sword-shaped leaves, and frequently a high stalk covered with fragrant white or yellow blossoms. Most yuccas are limited to desert climates. Some, such as soap tree (*Y. elata*), reach tree size. As the common name suggests, Hispanic settlers in Mexico and the American Southwest used soap tree for washing clothes and hair. Plains tribes use soapwell or soapweed (*Y. glauca*), whose natural range extends as far north as Montana, the same way.

While living in Costa Rica, I was served the sautéed, slightly bitter fruits of a huge, ground-dwelling forest yucca, a delicacy which Central American chefs depend on sharp-eyed foragers to keep them supplied with. Southwestern First Peoples similarly prepared the fruits of datil yucca (*Y. baccata*), also called Spanish-bayonet, and young yucca flower stalks are sometimes peeled, sliced, and eaten raw.

Agave (genus *Agave*), an arid-zone ornamental, looks like an aloe that grew up on the wrong side of the tracks. Lean and scrappy, resembling the top of a

> **Throughout its approximately** ten-year lifespan, agave neither flowers nor fruits. In its final season it sends up a clublike flower stalk, reaching twenty feet in some species, upon which the plant sets fruit. Then the agave dies, scattering seeds across the desert floor to create a new generation.

giant pineapple, many agaves sport spines that cause the sort of wounds their sap helps heal. (But agave sap itself may irritate skin in particularly sensitive individuals.)

Prickly personality aside, agave is an important Latin American herb. Most species contain saponins and are pulped like yucca for use in laundry. The coarse fibers of sisal agave (*Agave sisalana*) are spun into household twine, while folk healers prescribe agave juice as an internal treatment for gastric ulcers. Agave juice is also the primary ingredient in pulque, tequila, and other strong Mexican drinks. Recent studies suggest that enzymes in agave slow the aging process, and may relax the vascular constriction that causes impotence in older men.

Viburnum

Though most suburban viburnums (genus *Viburnum*) owe their existence to showy flowers and attractive foliage, they share the same genus as the wild viburnums that are a First Nations and Northern European staple. The fruits of many are just as edible.

> **Salicylates in viburnum bark closely** resemble aspirin, so infusions of it should not be taken by children, people who are allergic to aspirin, or pregnant women.

Viburnums generally have wrinkled, spade-shaped leaves, waxy white or pinkish flowers, and colorful, clustered fruit. They vary tremendously in appearance and habit, so identifying individual species requires a good guidebook. Korean spice viburnum (*V. carlesii*) and linden viburnum (*V. dilatatum*) are among the many introduced varieties that bear edible fruit. Blackhaw (*V. prunifolium*) and possum haw (*V. nudum*), native to the eastern part of the continent, are common landscaping shrubs across North America. Though not related to the hawthorns of genus *Crataegus* (see chapter 3), both are important resources to First Nations peoples who live within their natural range.

The red, black, or blue fruit of ornamental viburnums may or may not be valuable food, depending on variety and location. In general, bitter-sour, cranberry-like viburnum berries, regardless of color, are worth cooking or blending with other fruits, and those that are merely bitter are not. All tend to be seedy, but can be milled or used in jelly.

Highbush cranberry (*V. trilobum*), also called wild guelder-rose, is riding

American highbush cranberry (*Viburnum trilobum*).

the native gardening movement into landscaping across the northern part of the continent. Unrelated to the bog cranberries of Thanksgiving fame (*Vaccinium oxycoccos* and *V. macrocarpon*), highbush cranberry is virtually indistinguishable from its namesake when cooked. It is also much easier to pick, since it grows on dry, firm ground and requires little stooping.

Highbush cranberry has wrinkly, tulip-shaped leaves that turn scarlet in fall, and round, showy clusters of white blossoms in the spring. Its drupes, or berries, set in hanging clusters and may remain through the winter in hard winter climates. The fruit is mostly pit, and, like bog cranberries, intensely bitter-tart when raw. However, they make fine preserves, both alone and in conjunction with less-acidic fruits. Other edible wild viburnums that persist in and around residential areas

Dyers' Notes

Cornelian cherry root bark is the reason Turkish fezzes are red. That of some native North American *Cornus* species, notably Eastern dogwood, gives similar results on unmordanted or alum-treated wool.

Though blackberries and raspberries seem promising dyestuffs, shades taken from the berries are unfortunately unstable and of inferior quality. Young *Rubus* shoots, on the other hand, dye wool grey with an alum mordant, blackish with an iron mordant, and a range of greens and blues with copper sulfate.

Holly twigs (genus *Ilex*) give shades of brown with no mordant.

Sumac is said to give a range of earth tones with various mordants, but the reviews are less than enthusiastic. Sumac's real value to dyers is as a source of tannin. Found in the leaves, bark, twigs, and fruit, sumac tannins effectively mordant both plant and animal fibers.

Barberry is a source of yellow dye in traditional Old World cultures. The root bark gives the strongest results. The dye is said to be particularly effective on silk. It is used without mordants, though alum and tin vary the shade.

Oregon grape is an essential part of the textile technology of Northwest coastal First Nations peoples. The berries color ceremonial robes dark blue. Traditionally used without a mordant, Oregon grape dye is more durable when paired with alum. Mashed roots yield gold or tan on alum- or chrome-mordanted wool.

include nannyberry (*Viburnum lentago*), mooseberry viburnum or squashbush (*V. edule*), and hobblebush (*V. alnifolium*), also called moosewood. All are splendid jelly and sauce resources.

Viburnum berries were an integral part of Northwest coastal First Nations cultures before European contact. Backwoodsmen in the Big North Woods learned to relish fresh viburnum berries sweetened with maple syrup. Scandinavians, famous for their appreciation of bitter-sour fruits, bake them in breads and pastries and ferment viburnum berries into tangy wine.

Viburnum berries are high in vitamin C and are a traditional antiscorbutic. Viburnum bark is known to First Nations healers as a muscle relaxant, hence its alternate common name, crampbark. All are considered effective against menstrual cramps, especially blackhaw. Scientific studies reveal that viburnum bark does indeed contain several known antispasmodics, including some that specifically target the abdominal muscles.

Foraging Advisory

Few would be tempted to taste the prickly, plastic-looking leaves of English holly (*Ilex aquifolium*), which is just as well since they're probably toxic. However, the bright berries sometimes tempt children, as well as adults who believe them edible because birds eat them. The violent nausea that follows re-educates experimenters. Other *Ilex*es that suburban foragers may encounter include winterberry (*I. verticillata*), inkberry (*I. glabra*), and the yellow-berried yaupon (*I. vomitoria*), whose botanical name is a timely warning.

English laurel (*Prunus laurocerasus*), also called cherry laurel, is probably the most common ornamental in North America. Though a member of the cherry genus, all parts, including the olivelike berries, are toxic. Though nausea is the most typical reaction, English laurel bark, foliage, or fruit has been known to kill people who ingest them, particularly children. English laurel's glossy, greenish yellow leaves are oval and about six inches long in the most popular variety. Others may have narrow or pointed leaves. Laurel berries set in sparse clusters that ripen from red to black or deep purple. A bird favorite, laurel berries frequently sicken humans who think they can eat bird food.

Many ivies (genus *Hedera*) bear grapelike bunches of juicy, tempting black or dark blue berries. These cause a variety of unpleasant symptoms when ingested—the most common of which is gastrointestinal distress—and are best left to the blue jays.

Poison ivy, poison oak, and poison sumac are more or less interchangeable common names for the toxic *Rhus radicans, R. diversiloba,* and *R. vernix.* (Some taxonomists place these species in a separate genus, *Toxicodendron.*) The foliage of all contains urushiol, an irritating oil that causes severe contact dermatitis in most people. Poisonous *Rhus* species vary greatly from region to region, and even from site to site. A single species may be a low-growing bush in one situation, a climbing vine in another, and a tree in yet another. All toxic *Rhus*es bear smooth white or grey berries. By contrast, the edible sumacs bear more or less hairy red fruit, and their foliage can safely be touched by all but a minority of allergic individuals. Foragers should consult a reliable local guidebook and learn to recognize local poison ivy, poison oak, or poison sumac varieties *before* they encounter them.

As a hedge shrub, privet (genus *Ligustrum*) is second only to English laurel in popularity. Unfortunately, thanks to the tempting appearance, longevity, and toxicity of its fruits, it's the most dangerous peripheral in suburbia. Privet is a twiggy, compact bush with small, oval leaves. In some varieties the leaves are pointed at both ends, in others rounded. Its tiny yellow flowers are fairly nondescript, but the round, translucent black berries set in dense clusters all over the plant, and may persist well into winter. These berries cause intense gastrointestinal distress in those who ingest them, and have even killed some people. Sap from broken branches causes severe contact dermatitis in many individuals. Since privet takes readily to pruning, it is frequently used in hedges. Freestanding bushes occur as well. Because it grows low and bears its tempting but significantly toxic berries for many months, privet is especially dangerous to children.

Sassafras (*Sassafras albidum*) root bark is spicy and highly flavored, and the source of the quintessential Southern tea. Now experts tell us sassafras is a carcinogen. In opposition to them are untold generations of sassafras tea drinkers who died at an advanced age of something other than cancer. The Southern foragers in my acquaintance spit at the very suggestion that sassafras tea is harmful. Ultimately, it's up to the individual to decide whom to believe, and if the pleasure is worth the risk. Sassafras is distinguished by its large, usually two- or three-lobed leaves, the spicy aroma of its broken foliage, its thicket- or hedge-forming growth habits, and its black, berrylike fruits, held erect on stalks. Aficionados pull up a few roots along the drip line of the plant, clip them off with pruning shears, and peel and dry the aromatic bark for use in tea.

Recipes

Sumac Chicken

SERVES 6.

Sumac makes this melt-in-your-mouth chicken smell and taste exotic. The dish is even fancier if made with boneless chicken breasts. This method also suits lamb, turkey, and lean pork cuts.

> 1 cup dry white wine
> 1 cup sumac juice
> $1/2$ teaspoon dried thyme
> $1/4$ teaspoon dried sage
> Salt and pepper to taste
> 1 tablespoon olive oil
> 1 large clove garlic, chopped
> 1 medium onion, chopped
> 2 to $2^{1}/_{2}$ lbs chicken pieces, skinned
> 1 cup chicken stock
> 3 tablespoons flour mixed with $1/4$ cup cold water

Mix the wine, sumac juice, and seasonings together and set aside to infuse.

Swirl the olive oil into a frying pan and place over medium heat until a piece of onion sizzles when dropped into it. Add the garlic and onion and sauté briefly, until the onion is translucent. Add the chicken and turn the pieces until they are evenly seared.

Add the wine, sumac juice, and seasonings, cover the pan, reduce heat, and simmer until the liquid is reduced by half.

Uncover the pan, add the chicken stock, and raise the heat to medium-high. Keep turning the chicken until it has cooked through, then remove it to a warm plate.

Whisk the flour and water mixture into the leftover liquid and simmer over medium heat, stirring constantly, until it becomes a thick gravy. Pour this over the chicken and serve.

Rose Hip Jelly

MAKES ABOUT 3 PINTS.

The flavor and color of this jelly varies with the species of rose used. The hard, orange-red hips of most wild roses yield a fairly tart, orange jelly. Rugosa hips give sweeter, redder preserves. A box of high-quality commercial pectin will jell this recipe if apples are unavailable.

3 cups fresh rose hips, washed and blossom ends removed
1/2 pound underripe cooking apples, chopped. (About 4 medium-sized
pie apples, or 12 crabapples)
2 cups sugar

Place the rose hips and apples in a nonreactive pan and cover them with water. Bring to a boil, then reduce heat and simmer, covered, for about half an hour, until the fruit is soft. Allow the fruit to cool to handling temperature, then mash it in the water. Cover the pan and allow the pulp to steep 6 hours or overnight.

Strain the juice through a square of wet muslin, then tie the pulp up inside and allow it to drip for several hours.

Return the juice to the pan, bring it to a boil and add the sugar. Reduce heat until a vigorous simmer can be maintained without boiling over. Cook, stirring constantly, until a spoon test indicates the juice is ready to jell.

Skim off the foam that forms on the top, pour the syrup into hot, sterilized jars, and seal.

R
E
C
I
P
E
S

Blackberry Syrup

MAKES ABOUT 3 PINTS.

Blackberry syrup is easy to make and cans well. It's delicious on pancakes and ice cream, as well as in milkshakes and other drinks. Blackberry syrup can be further processed into jelly, vinegar, wine, or cordials at a later date if stocks of those items run low. It's also a handy stomachic.

4 cups whole blackberries, washed
1 3/4 cups sugar

Run the blackberries through a food mill, or juice them in a blender and strain the seeds out with a sieve. Pour the slurry into a large, nonreactive saucepan and stir in the sugar.

Bring the syrup briefly to a boil, then reduce the heat until a vigorous simmer can be maintained without boiling over. Continue cooking until the liquid thickens perceptibly, bearing in mind that the syrup will be considerably thicker when cooled.

Skim off the foam that forms on the top, pour the syrup into hot, sterilized jars and seal. It will keep at least a year if stored in a cool, dark place. Refrigerate after opening.

Cornelian Cherry Sauce

MAKES ABOUT 3 PINTS.

This ancient dessert topping was the special privilege of European and Asian aristocrats before the dawn of the twentieth century. Sour pie cherries can stand in where cornelian cherries are unavailable, but the color and flavor of the result are disappointing by comparison.

5 cups whole cornelian cherries, washed
5 cups water
3³/4 cups sugar

Place the fruit and water in a nonreactive saucepan and bring them just to a boil. Remove the pan from the heat and strain the liquid into a second nonreactive saucepan, reserving the fruit. Stir in the sugar and simmer over medium heat, stirring constantly, until it dissolves. Reduce the heat to its lowest point.

Put the cornelian cherries back in and mash well. Cover the pan and warm the mixture over lowest heat for 2 hours.

Bring the mixture to a boil again, then turn off the heat, cover, and let it steep from 8 hours to overnight.

Bring the syrup to a boil one final time, then reduce the heat until it will sustain a vigorous simmer without boiling over. Cook, stirring constantly, until a spoon test indicates it has reached the consistency of hot honey. (Remember that the sauce will thicken as it cools.)

Heat a metal sieve in boiling water and strain the syrup through it. Pour the syrup into hot, sterilized jars and seal. (Bits of fruit that pass through the sieve and into the final product are an intended effect.)

Blackberry Shrub

MAKES 2 QUARTS.

"Shrub" is an eighteenth-century term for a cold, fruit-based drink. Shrub can be made with raspberries, currants, Oregon grapes—in fact almost any juicy fruit. This easy recipe is highly compatible with porch swings, patios, and lazy summer days.

2 quarts chilled water
1 cup fresh blackberry juice
¹/3 cup sugar (or substitute blackberry syrup to taste, generally about ¹/2 cup)
1 lemon, sliced thin, or 1 tablespoon lemon or sumac juice (see page 113)

Pour the chilled water into a pitcher. Stir in the blackberry juice and sugar, or syrup.

Float the lemon slices in the shrub, or add the sumac or lemon juice.

Chill for several hours to allow the flavors to mingle and serve over ice. (Ice cubes with a whole blackberry frozen inside add an artistic touch.)

Mulled Blackberry Punch

MAKES ABOUT FOUR PUNCH CUPS, OR TWO MUGFULS

"Punch" is another eighteenth-century term, this one referring to a hot, fruit-based beverage, often with rum in it. Either way, it infuses drinkers with summer's warmth. This virgin (nonalcoholic) version can be "punched up" by reducing the amount of water used to 2 1/2 cups and adding half a cup of rum to the pan 2 minutes before removing it from the heat.

3/4 cup blackberry syrup
3 cups water
One 2-inch cinnamon stick
4 whole cloves
1/4 teaspoon nutmeg
4 thin slices fresh ginger root
1 teaspoon dried lemon peel, or 2 teaspoons fresh

Mix all ingredients in a nonreactive saucepan and mull them gently over low heat for 20 to 30 minutes. Strain the punch through a tea strainer into small coffee cups and serve hot.

Sumac Lemonade

MAKES 1 1/2 QUARTS.

With its snappy taste and striking deep pink color, this traditional haying time thirst-buster competes head-to-head with frozen or powdered "artificial juice-type beverages." And it packs more vitamin C than fresh-squeezed orange juice.

3/4 cup staghorn sumac cone bracts, packed
1 1/2 cups plus 5 cups cold water
1/2 cup sugar

Place the sumac bracts and 1 1/2 cups cold water in a blender and whirl at low speed for 3 minutes. Strain and wring the concentrate immediately through wet muslin into a bowl. (Do not let the pulp soak in the infusion, as bitterness from the twigs will leach into it.)

Place the concentrate in a pitcher. Add the sugar and the rest of the water and stir. Serve over ice.

Elderflower Champagne

Makes about 1 gallon.

Natural yeasts in elder pollen cause the fermentation that creates this mildly alcoholic, carbonated cooler. Served well chilled, it is one of foraging's most memorable rewards. Elderflower champagne keeps only a few months. As a result, it is strictly a seasonal treat.

12 cups plus 4 cups water
3 cups sugar
6 or 7 average-sized elderflower clusters
2 tablespoons cider or berry vinegar
3 lemons, thinly sliced

Pour 12 cups of water into a large pot, cover, and bring to a rolling boil. Allow the water to cool to room temperature.

Meanwhile, bring 4 cups of water to a boil in a medium saucepan. Remove it from the heat and dissolve the sugar in it. Pour this syrup into a sterilized, nonreactive bucket or crock and allow it to cool to room temperature before adding the 12 cups boiled water (also cooled to room temperature) and the rest of the ingredients. Stir, then cover loosely. Allow the mixture to ferment undisturbed for four days in a slightly warm place, such as atop the refrigerator.

Strain the liquid through wet muslin into sterilized plastic soda bottles and screw the caps down firmly. (For the sterilization process, see "Marigold Vinegar," page 97.) Store the bottles in a cool, dark place for at least a week. Carbon dioxide produced by continuing fermentation causes pressure to build up in the bottles, which in turn causes the gas to dissolve in the liquid. Progress can be monitored by pressing on the bottles, which become harder as the pressure builds. When the bottles are rock-hard, they should be stored in the refrigerator until use.

Particulates may form in the champagne during fermentation, but they are both harmless and tasteless. Elderflower champagne should be kept cool and moved as little as possible to avoid stirring up sediment and interfering with the carbonation process.

— Detail: Nopal cactus, or Indian fig *(Opuntia ficus-indica)*.

The 1980s were a peculiar time for foragers. Young urban professionals (the infamous "Yuppies") hungered after exotic dining experiences, and their interest initiated a weekly cycle of food fads that kept restaurants and groceries in a constant state of flux. The frenzy dramatically broadened North America's notoriously narrow palate. Unfortunately, the 1980s penchant for pretence squelched farther-reaching changes that might have raised foragers in the public esteem. Rather than admit that the trendy new salad greens were in fact weeds, Yuppies disguised them behind elegant-sounding foreign names. Thus, diners in fashionable restaurants can now crunch endive, escarole, arugula, and radicchio, blissfully unaware that these greens, or near relatives, are growing through the cracks in the parking lot outside.

The fact is, most of North America's most hated weeds were intentionally introduced to this continent by our ancestors, who prized them as culinary and medicinal resources. Dandelion, that poster child of suburban angst, may be the most respected herb on the planet. The French have even founded a lucrative industry on agricultural production of dandelion. Chicory, plantain, chickweed, purslane, and several species of dock all arrived in the Americas as seeds lovingly tucked into the baggage of some long-vanished European settler. Appalachian hill peoples still enjoy mustard greens, lambs-quarters, and amaranth greens, as their ancestors did before them. I've even found canned versions of these greens in the supermarkets of northern cities with sizable Appalachian expatriate communities. Meanwhile, Jerusalem artichoke, a North American native sunflower, has been threatening to reclaim its rightful place in the produce section for decades.

There is a certain visceral resistance to wild vegetables, even though most of them were originally cultivated in gardens. The unspoken feeling is that the switch to modern produce must represent some kind of "progress," the dumping of an inferior product for a superior one. In fact, the change came about for reasons entirely unrelated to flavor or nutritional content. As the steam engine connected far-flung corners of the continent, long-distance transport of perishables became cost-effective for the first time. Farmers wanted to reach the new continental market, so their crops were re-engineered to warehouse well and stand up to shipping. Flavor was low on the list of priorities. These market forces squeezed highly flavored, locally grown produce off our plates. Succeeding generations, raised on insipid "railroad" vegetables, earned North American produce its reputation for rubbery blandness. Many a modern Canadian or American returns from Europe with lurid tales of "awful" salads served in cafés and restaurants on the far side of the pond. "Taste like weeds!" the tourists complain. They're not far wrong: European societies never abandoned locally grown produce, so their vegetables are similar to pre–Industrial Age strains that were in fact little more than weeds. Europeans still esteem strong-tasting greens because they were never "iceberged" into submission by mass-marketed vegetables.

And then there's radicchio. Italian visitors to North America must get quite a chuckle from this one. *Radicchio,* which literally means "root," is a synonym for weed in Italy. So much for pretence.

Collecting Greens and Roots

Digging roots was one of the first things humanity did with tools. Indeed, some scientists believe it even predates clubbing people, which would make it the oldest tool-assisted activity in existence. The techniques involved are correspondingly straightforward. A few simple tools optimize work-to-reward ratios and mitigate environmental impact, whether in a landscaped bed or a vacant lot.

A greens knife. Surprising as it may seem, stooping and ripping off leaves can be exhausting. A knife not only saves effort, it reduces trauma to the plant, allowing it to recover more quickly. The ideal greens knife cuts stems and roots without difficulty, but does not do likewise to fingers. A cheap paring knife or jackknife, infrequently sharpened, fits the bill. (A pair of scissors is equally effective on thin stems.)

If all the aerial parts of a plant are to be taken, grasp them together, gently pull back, and slice them cleanly from the taproot at ground level with the greens knife. This is infinitely easier than twisting them off, which mangles the harvest and makes it more difficult for the root to recover. Similarly, the force required to snap tender sprouts such as knotweed may crush them. A greens knife is the answer here, too.

Cutting greens is a fairly safe activity in suburbia, politically speaking, but digging can be a ticklish matter, especially if the venue is someone else's lawn or flower bed. Most gardeners are happy to part with their weeds, but may balk at having holes torn in their landscaping. Suburban foragers must therefore select their digging implements wisely and ply them with sensitivity. Options include the digging stick, the potato fork, and various species of shovel. Which to wield depends largely on the kind of root and its location.

The digging stick is probably mankind's oldest tool. At its most basic, it's just a sharpened branch. A digging stick scrapes out a small hole near the plant to pull the root into, and pries up tubers. It is a fairly low-impact device, and easy and cheap to make. The digging stick reached its ultimate expression in a Hudson's Bay Company design consisting of an iron rod about as long and heavy as a tire iron, but slightly curved along its length and oblong in cross section. One end was ground to a point, the other wrought into a loop into which a wooden T-handle could be driven for leverage. Since the handle was user-installed, the actual trade item resembled a huge, curved needle. Though Company blacksmiths turned out hundreds of these over a three-hundred-year period, the HBC digging stick is now found only in museums. But the design is straightforward, and poses little challenge to anyone with rudimentary metalworking skills.

For the rest of us, the best substitute is a long-handled weeder. This tool resembles the more familiar hand weeder but has a three-foot handle that affords leverage for digging out deep taproots.

The potato fork, a D-handled implement often incorrectly called a pitchfork, is the best choice for digging up a whole plot of roots, as when a homeowner wants to clear a large area. The fork's curved tines enter smoothly into most kinds of soil and provide excellent leverage, but, unlike a shovel, the fork does little damage to the harvest.

The fiddling shovel, however, represents the very latest in root-digging technology. In flower beds and lawns, a low-impact technique called "fiddling" keeps the gardener on our side. Sink the shovel into the ground an inch or so from the target root. (This usually means either cutting off part of the leaf crown with the shovel blade or holding the leaves clear.) Gather the plant's aerial parts firmly in one

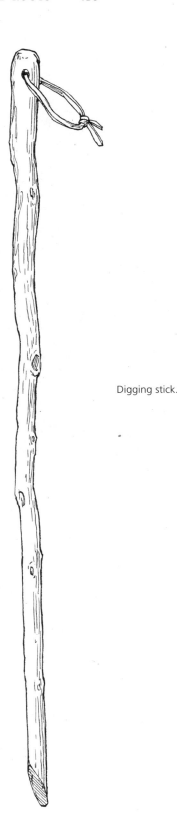

Digging stick.

How to "fiddle" a root.

Top left: A narrow-bladed transplanting shovel is the forager's tool for "fiddling" roots.

Bottom left: Sink the blade an inch or so from the target plant.

Below: Loosen the soil around the plant's root system.

Below: Gather the above-ground parts of the plant in one hand and gently lever the shovel back and forth as you wiggle the plant.

Top right: Given a little patience and practice the tap root should come cleanly out of the ground.

Bottom right: Replace and tamp down the sod.

Residents of the Pacific Northwest will find that a *clam gun,* the short-handled shovel used in razor clamming, makes a worthy fiddling instrument if a drain shovel is not available. However, since clam guns are only built for moving sand, repeated fiddling eventually breaks them.

hand and lever ("fiddle") the shovel back and forth while you wiggle, but do not tear, the plant. Given cooperative soil and a little practice, the taproot will come cleanly out of the ground, leaving only a root-sized hole and a plug of pried-up soil or sod. Tamp down the sod afterward, leaving little trace of the operation. (You may have to fiddle stubborn roots on more than one side.)

Because ordinary shovels are too wide and shallow for world-class fiddling, the forager's Stradivarius is a long, narrow spade called a drain shovel. This D-handled instrument, available from any serious gardening center or hardware store, has a narrow, rounded blade about eight inches wide by eighteen inches long. In most cases, the long blade need only be driven about halfway into the soil. More, and it may break.

Amaranthus

When Hernando Cortez arrived in Mexico in 1519, he encountered a society unlike any imagined in Europe. The Aztecs knew neither the horse nor the wheel. The highest sacrament in their state religion was gory human sacrifice, while warfare was ritualized to the point of sport.

Even the Aztec diet bore no resemblance to that of Old World cultures. Potatoes, corn, and pumpkins, unknown in Europe, were staple crops. And the cereal upon which the entire civilization rested was a six-foot-tall version of a common Mediterranean roadside weed.

A genuine evil genius, Cortez instantly deduced the connection between amaranth (genus *Amaranthus*) and Aztec survival. He ordered the fields burned, and anyone attempting to cultivate amaranth thereafter was severely punished. In this way Cortez broke the back of one of the world's great powers in a matter of weeks.

Amaranth is widely distributed across the continent, though for reasons cited above, the tall, grain-rich varieties are now rare. Most North American amaranths grow no more than waist-high. They have smooth, oval, light green leaves, coarsely veined and often with scalloped edges, and dense, fuzzy flower spikes full of tiny, glossy black seeds. Most have sparsely hairy stems as well. The lower stem of redroot (*A. retroflexus*), one of the most common species, is dark red. Amaranth is one of the three "pigweeds" once harvested for stock feed, because their monoculture-forming habit makes them as easy to harvest as sown crops and they provide a full range of nutrients. (See *Chenopodium* and *Portulaca.*)

Most North American amaranths seed themselves on roadsides and disturbed ground, but red-leaved species are actually planted as ornamentals in suburban gardens. Because they set a lot of seed, ornamental amaranths are often included in songbird-attracting seed mixes.

Amaranth is a respectable steamed herb, subtle of flavor and tender, yet not mushy or mucilaginous. *Hin choy-shien* (*A. aanoeticus*), or Chinese spinach, is a common ingredient of Asian soups and stir-fries. Hin choy-shien is also served as a side dish, with a sprinkling of lemon juice, soy sauce, or grated daikon. *Amaranthus crespus*, which may be the Aztec species, has found new life in East Africa as African spinach, or *mchicha* in Swahili. An important crop in the region, it is cultivated as a potherb only; evidently, its grain-producing potential has not been developed.

Redroot
(*Amaranthus retroflexus*).

Some foragers find amaranth so superior to domestic greens that they blanch and freeze great quantities of it for year-round enjoyment in omelettes and lasagna, for use as a bed or stuffing for baked fish, and as a side dish. Adding a handful of redroot to more bitter greens also tempers the overall flavor. (I have never tried red-leaved amaranth, but a fellow forager finds it without flavor or texture. Whether he tried it in season, I can't say.)

Amaranth seed is just as edible today as it was in pre-Columbian Mexico. The protein- and iron-rich grain substitute has recently drawn attention as a health food and agricultural crop in regions with little arable land. Curious or health-minded foragers might like to process small quantities of amaranth seed, which can be boiled with the morning oatmeal or kneaded into whole-grain breads and muffins. (See "Grist for the Mill.") Amaranth seed is said to pop like popcorn when tossed in a hot skillet. Sounds like a fun party alternative.

More than most plants, amaranth absorbs minerals from the soil in which it grows. This is a good thing if the minerals are beneficial, but harmful ones may render the plant toxic. Amaranth should not be collected from potentially polluted sites, such as industrial sites or parking lots, or near places where nitrate fertilizers are applied, such as golf courses and truck farms.

Grist for the Mill

Traditional peoples exploit the seeds of many wild plants, some of which may also be of interest to suburban foragers. Some, such as amaranth and dock, provide flour. Mustard seeds are ground for spices and condiments. Still others, such as plantain, have medical applications.

Though seed crops occur in residential areas, most suburban foragers don't have the skills, equipment, or time to process them. Should the opportunity present itself, or should readers want to process a few out of curiosity, the following approach is both easy and practical:

1. Cut several ripe seed stems or spikes and divide them into manageable bunches. Rubber-band a cloth sack, pillow case, or square of muslin over the seed heads.

2. Hang the bundles upside down in a dry place until thoroughly dry and brittle.

3. Take the bundles down and thresh (separate) the seed by grasping a bundle by the base and whacking the wrapped end several times against a table or counter top. Rubbing the still-wrapped seedheads between the palms of the hands helps to separate the seeds from the chaff (husks and stems).

4. Remove the cloth and shake the seeds and chaff into a platter or pizza plate. Remove any chaff large enough to pick out with the fingers.

5. Winnow (clean) the seeds by tossing them gently into the air in front of a fan or in a gentle breeze. This is a lost technology in Western society; maximizing chaff removal and minimizing seed loss takes a little practice.

6. Store clean seed in an airtight container in the freezer. (Many seeds are oil-rich and spoil quickly at room temperature.)

To use cereal-type seeds, such as amaranth and quinoa, simply boil and eat like rice, bulgur, or Scottish oatmeal. They may also be ground into flour with a mortar and pestle or grain mill. Mustard seeds are ground the same way, except that vinegar and sometimes oil and seasonings are added to make a thin, strongly flavored paste. Those low in natural oils are sometimes left dry and used as a spice.

Most of the nutritional information available for amaranth concerns the seeds, but amaranth foliage is high in minerals, especially potassium and calcium. Amaranth greens are also a source of astringent infusions that stanch bleeding, soothe vaginal infections, and treat swelling-related disorders such as hemorrhoids and boils. Amaranth infusions are taken internally for bronchitis, diarrhea, difficult menstruation, and blood in the stools. Infusions of the seeds are a wash for skin conditions such as acne and rashes.

Arctium

One day in 1948, a Swiss outdoorsman named George de Mestral picked up his gun, whistled for his dog, and headed out to tramp the Alps for game. He didn't find any, but on returning home he found several large, round burs tangled in his spaniel's coat. Removing them sorely tried Mestral's patience. Closer inspection showed that the burs' spines were really tiny hooks, engineered to grab at the slightest touch. Mestral smelled profit, and spent the next nine years trying to jump Mother Nature's patent.

Common burdock (*Arctium minor*).

Ultimately he discovered a way to fashion credible bur and spaniel hair knockoffs out of nylon. He quickly patented the miracle fastener, which consisted of a strip of loopy nylon nap, soft as velvet (*velours*), and a nylon "bur" bristling with tiny hooks (*crochets*). Mestral's "Velcro" made him a millionaire.

That story encapsulates the difference between a shrewd entrepreneur and me. I would have just found the plant the burs came from, and eaten it.

Burdock (genus *Arctium*), a common weed across North America, is an Asian immigrant. Common burdock (*A. minus*) and great burdock (*A. lappa*) account for most occurrences. Common burdock leaves may reach a foot in length, with reddish stems and burs, while giant burdock can reach rhubarb proportions with bluish-green stems and burs. First-year leaf rosettes of common burdock may escape casual notice, but a large great burdock always attracts attention. The leaves of both are mat green and arrowhead-shaped, with fuzzy white undersides.

In its second year, burdock sends up a tough, fibrous stalk with clusters of round, cherry-sized burs. These resemble thistle heads, particularly while the purplish flowers are in bloom, but they aren't prickly. Instead, their tiny hooks grapple at anything, even fingerprint ridges. This gives them a "sticky" feeling when handled.

Like other kids, I used to press burdock burs into a ball, then pull them off one at a time to pelt others with them. The flying burs cling to knit clothing at the slightest contact, yet readily come off with the familiar "rrrrrip" of Velcro. Those that land in the victim's hair are a different, and much uglier, matter.

If Georges de Mestral had been Japanese, Korean, or Hawaiian, he would have recognized the plant as gobo, a common root crop in northeast Asia and

Hawaii, where it is cultivated on a large scale. Like me, he might have been satisfied to eat the first-year roots, boiled or pickled, without further reflection. Or he might have grated and steamed them as a side dish for sushi.

Wild gobo root tastes at least as good as the imported ones sold in Japanese and Korean groceries, and is much more widely available. First-year burdock, which offers most of the edible rewards, can be a challenge to find and identify, lacking as it does the conspicuous bur-topped stalk. I generally look for first-year burdock in the vicinity of second-year plants. The huge leaves of great burdock are hard to miss.

Harvesting and preparing burdock root is simple in theory: Dig up first-year plants and cut off the leaves, then scrub thoroughly with a plastic scouring pad to render them ready for use. Reality, on the other hand, is a bit more problematic. Burdock roots may penetrate more than two feet into the ground, and, as luck would have it, the plant adores rocky, difficult soil. Although it occasionally occurs in soft or recently disturbed earth, in most cases a heavy iron pinch bar is the weapon to use. Thunk this blunt instrument into the ground a few inches from the root, prying out large rocks on the way down. When the hole is sufficiently deep, pull the rough, black root sideways into it.

Raw burdock root has all the culinary attraction of rope, but after slicing and boiling it assumes the manageably fibrous consistency of bamboo shoots, with a mild, earthy flavor few object to. While some sources report that burdock root is bitter, I've never met one that was anything but pleasant. Perhaps those writers ate second-

year roots. Some also recommend removing the roots' thick rind before cooking. I've eaten them with and without, and the only difference I can see is that a third of the harvest ends up on the compost pile when it is removed. Instead, I peel the dark skin from the roots with a potato peeler, then bias-slice them intact.

Unpeeled roots keep for weeks in the refrigerator if wrapped in plastic, but they taste best when used a few days after harvesting. Sliced burdock root will turn brown unless immersed in water, preferably with a few drops of lemon or sumac juice, or vinegar.

Burdock can be served by itself as a side dish, though it is somewhat bland. The ivory slices add texture to stir-fries if boiled first, and complement curries, mixed vegetables, or stews. The Japanese deep-fry them in tempura. Sliced or julienned burdock root is also an excellent substitute for bamboo shoots in recipes.

Very young burdock leaf stems and second-year flower stalks can be steamed as a green vegetable. Some even peel the bitter green rind from the stalk before the plant blossoms and candy the pith by boiling it in syrup.

Gobo is renowned as a body-building agent in Asia, though as Euell Gibbons speculated, yanking quantities of it out of the ground is probably what really makes burdock eaters muscular. Burdock is high in potassium, so folk medicine prescriptions against feminine problems are probably accurate. It is said to be good for skin conditions, taken internally and applied externally, and is indicated for joint disorders such as arthritis and lumbago as well as for building and maintaining healthy blood.

Capsella

Shepherd's purse (*Capsella bursa-pastoris*) owes its common name, its genus name (meaning "box" or "capsule"), and its species name (meaning "shepherd's purse") to the tiny, heart-shaped seed cases, each on its own little stem, that decorate the plant's twelve-inch flower spike. These make it one of the most readily recognized suburban wild edibles.

Shepherd's purse is yet another European herb originally planted in colonial gardens on the East Coast and now a free agent across North America. Its distinctive flower spike, lined with the eponymous seed cases, rises from the center of a rosette of somewhat hairy, four-inch leaves. Lying flat on the ground, they resemble deeply lobed dandelion leaves, without the milky sap. A wiry taproot secures the whole to the ground.

Sticky hairs in the plant's tiny flowers trap and digest insects much like the famous Venus flytrap (*Dionaea muscipula*) and sundew (genus *Drosera*). Unlike them, though, shepherd's purse's prey is nearly microscopic, which significantly reduces the coolness factor. But the ability to extract nutrients from such novel sources enables this plant to thrive almost anywhere, which in turn enhances its usefulness to foragers.

Young shepherd's purse leaves have the typical zing of the mustard family (see "The Mustards" entry, page 159) and can be used raw in salads until they become bitter, about the time the plant flowers. After that, they can be fried with other greens or used in spicy cooked dishes. When the leaves become too strong even for these uses, the

Burdock leaves resemble those of foxglove (see Foraging Advisory, chapter 4), a deadly poisonous plant that shares its habitat. They are wider and darker than foxglove, but the definitive test is to press the fuzzy underside of a leaf against the tongue. Burdock leaf fuzz is unmistakably bitter, while the foxglove fuzz (which is not toxic) has no particular taste. When doing this test, foragers should scrupulously avoid getting any juices from a torn leaf on the tongue. That much digitalis is unlikely to cause harm, but there's no sense taking chances.

Shepherd's purse (*Capsella bursa-pastoris*).

For foraging purposes, pepper-grass (genus *Lepidium*) and shepherd's purse are interchangeable. Two or three dozen species of peppergrass occur across subarctic North America. As the name suggests, the leaves and seeds of this mustard were used as a condiment in the Old World, and the plant was imported to North America for this use. Peppergrass strongly resembles shepherd's purse, but is taller and bears more seeds.

seedpods can be used as a spice, which is the origin of another folk name, "poor man's pepper." When minced with vinegar, the pods become a relish for meat and fish, something like hot mustard in flavor. In fact, European peasants once gathered shepherd's purse seeds, dried them, and ground them into mustard. (For collecting and processing tips, see "Grist for the Mill," page 144.)

Like all spicy herbs, shepherd's purse is considered a digestive. Folk healers in Europe and North America use poultices, tinctures, or infusions of the entire plant, all powerfully astringent, to stem both internal and external bleeding, a practice seconded by medical studies. Like other astringent plants, shepherd's purse combats diarrhea and dysentery, and is a traditional treatment for urinary tract disorders.

Chenopodium

Genus *Chenopodium* includes several weeds common to roadsides and disturbed soils, and its member species have a long, illustrious record of service to humanity as a source of vegetables, grains, and medicines. In the kitchen, Chenopodium is interchangeable with its fellow pigweed, *Amaranthus* (see page 142), and in some cultures they are considered a single resource.

Archaeologists have found *Chenopodium* seeds in fossilized human feces, suggesting that these plants have been an important food since prehistoric times. The greens are substantially more nutritious than cabbage or spinach, while the seeds of many species are used as grain. Quinoa (*C. quinoa*) seeds were the amaranth of the Incan Empire. The *conquistadores* somehow overlooked quinoa, and it remains a staple in the Andes to this day. One of the few crops that produces lustily in harsh alpine habitats, quinoa has recently attracted a following among health food enthusiasts and Third World agronomists.

The name *Chenopodium* means goosefoot, which is also a common name for several *Chenopodium* species. Both are references to the plants' leaves, which resemble a goose's webbed feet. Most species have more or less lance-shaped leaves with three or four large, rounded teeth per side. (Small leaves often have no teeth, or have embryonic bumps where teeth will develop.) The leaves grow in opposite pairs and possess the ability to make water bead up and roll off, leaving the surface completely dry. This is more than a little frustrating when they're being washed, but as the leaves seem to have much the same effect on dirt, the issue isn't as serious as it might appear. The underside of the leaves in many species has a grainy white coating that comes off on the fingers. Mature plants are topped with irregular clusters of white, mealy, BB-sized seedpods that feel gritty between the fingers. Most species reach a maximum height of about three feet.

Edible *Chenopodiums* are delicious steamed or fried if collected when no higher than about eight inches. After that they become stringy and develop an off taste. Slice off the plants at the base, leaving the root cluster in the soil to regenerate. Then immerse them in a bucket of water, shake vigorously to wash, and cook.

Dozens of *Chenopodium* species grow on this continent, most of them edible. Here are a few of the most widespread:

Lambs-quarters
(*Chenopodium album*).

- Lambs-quarters (*C. album*) is the best-known North American *Chenopodium.* British country folk observed that this species blooms on or around the first of August, or Lammas, the feast marking the beginning of the harvest quarter. (Lammas is a slurred form of "Loaf Mass," referring to the grain harvest.) In time, "Lammas Quarter's herb" became lambs-quarters. Lambs-quarters themselves are reason enough to celebrate, especially in late spring or early summer, when the young plants are a delicious and tender potherb.
- Good King Henry (*C. bonus-henricus*), a mealy, reddish European plant, was once as common as spinach in gardens. Good King Henry is on the lam now, thanks to changing eating habits, though it tastes just as good as ever. In fact, there is a movement afoot to reintroduce it as a perennial vegetable garden crop. Good King Henry is a little stouter than most *Chenopodiums,* and its succulent young stems are often steamed whole and served like asparagus. Incidentally, while some sources report that Good King Henry was named after England's Henry VII, this doesn't seem to be the case. Apparently, the Germans named a poisonous look-a-like "bad spirits," commandeering the word *heinrich* (elf) to represent the spirits. This was mistranslated into Latin as *Malus Henricus,* or Bad

Henry. By association the edible plant became Good Henry. Successive generations inserted "King" into the name, simply because it sounds like it ought to be there. And so it remains to this day.

· The striking, bright red fruits of strawberry blite (*Chenopodium capitatum*) look like big, juicy berries. In reality they are bland and uninspiring food, but the foliage of this species is quite as good as lambs-quarters or Good King Henry. This is good news for foragers in the Far North, as strawberry blite grows right to the margin of the tundra.

· The frilly, fragrant *Chenopodiums* are too strong-tasting to be eaten as a vegetable, and in any case they are potentially toxic in large amounts. Epazote (*C. ambrosioides*), also called wormseed or Mexican tea, is one of these. But its aromatic leaves contribute a sweet, sagelike savor to Mexican dishes, especially beans. Whether this is because epazote-seasoned beans taste good, or because epazote curbs flatulence, is a chicken-and-egg question. The narrow, feathery foliage of Jerusalem oak (*C. botrys*) is used in the same way.

Most *Chenopodiums* bear large quantities of seed that can be processed using the procedure outlined in "Grist for the Mill," page 144. *Chenopodium* seed is used in Appalachian baking in place of poppy seeds. It can also be boiled like oatmeal or bulgur wheat, or kneaded into bread.

Chenopodium foliage is rich in vitamins A and C, as well as B-complex vitamins and calcium. Quinoa is a favorite grain among people who are allergic to wheat. High in protein and calcium, quinoa is also easily digested, making it a useful treatment for those suffering from malnutrition and gastric problems. The only prerequisite for cooking quinoa grain is to rinse it thoroughly in a sieve under cold running water before cooking. This rinse is necessary to remove the bitter chemical known as saponin from the outside of the grains.

Like amaranth, *Chenopodium* plants absorb minerals and chemicals from the soil. Those growing on a polluted or nitrate-saturated site, such as a farmer's field or the ground over a septic tank, may be toxic and should be avoided. Some *Chenopodiums,* especially arid-zone species, only grow in very alkaline soils, and are not suitable for eating. Epazote is a famous and effective vermifuge, but it too must be used with caution, as too much can make the patient sicker than the worms would have. Oil of epazote, pressed from the plant's seeds and sold in health-food stores, is particularly dangerous if over-administered, especially to children, who are also the most vulnerable to parasitic infection. This effective natural remedy should be used only under professional supervision.

Cichorium

The cafés and diners of New Orleans serve up some of North America's most colorful fare, from blackened redfish to spicy gumbo and crayfish étouffé. After a copious meal, diners enjoy conversation or world-renowned jazz as chicory coffee prods their insides to undertake the daunting task of digestion.

Chicory (*Cichorium intybus*) has dandelion-like foliage and beautiful, lavender-colored flowers that bob as much as three feet above the ground on wiry stems. The daisylike blossoms reminded British children of the flat, wide-brimmed hats worn in Queen Victoria's navy, which gave rise to the alternate common name, "blue sailors."

Chicory (*Cichorim intybus*).

A characteristic weed of dry, gravelly soil, this European immigrant came to colonial gardens as a medicinal and culinary herb. It disappeared from mainstream North American diets in the late 1700s, until the 1980s, when manipulated European varieties became as trendy as endive and radicchio. Wild chicory is still a well-known herb in Appalachia, where its young leaves are eaten as a spring green, and of course its roasted roots are ground into coffee on the Mississippi Delta. Oddly, virtually all of the chicory that finds its way into Southern coffee is imported from Europe.

Chicory leaves bound for the pot must be picked very young, and even then they are apt to be bitter. The best are those still largely underground. Italian peasants dig down an inch or so and take the whole plant, with a stub of the taproot. The pale, tender newborn leaves are then separated out for salad, and the older leaves and root chopped for fried greens.

A perennial, chicory does not reseed aggressively. Therefore, care must be taken not to wipe out an entire colony when digging roots. Depending on local conditions, about a quarter of the plants can be taken from a healthy stand without endangering its survival. Digging should be modified to reflect the colony's health over succeeding years.

Chicory roots are peeled, sliced, boiled, and eaten as a vegetable in the Middle East. I have never tried this, though it sounds like a bitter dish indeed. Of

Some foragers cover chicory plants with a bucket or other lightproof container for a week or so, a procedure known as blanching. (Not to be confused with the brief boiling greens get before freezing, which is also called blanching.) The pale, blanched leaves are lower in nutrients, as the plant requires sunlight to produce them, but they are also less bitter. Chicory sprouts sold in stores as endive are also produced by forcing the roots in darkness.

course, they can also be roasted and ground as a coffee additive or substitute, using the procedure described below under *Taraxacum*.

Chicory is a traditional bitter herb of Passover. Like fellow spring greens it is packed with minerals, notably vitamin C. Also like them, it is believed to purify the blood. Folk healers prescribe this diuretic herb against kidney, liver, and spleen disorders, and to stimulate digestion.

Helianthus

In the 1600s, an exotic New World vegetable became tragically hip among Europe's smart set. The fad was so relentless, wrote one London sophisticate, that he hoped he'd never see another tuber as long as he lived.

It would take a lot of Jerusalem artichokes (*Helianthus tuberosus*) to bring me to that point. The crisp, lightly sweet tubers are one of the most delicious vegetables on earth. Developed by First Nations cultures, they are nothing like artichokes (the plant is actually a perennial sunflower) and have nothing to do with the Middle East. Jerusalem artichoke was fairly typical of North American diets until the steam-driven market shake-up of the late nineteenth century. The lumpy little tubers proved too susceptible to bruising and had too narrow a field-to-market window, particularly before refrigerated transport, to compete in the railroad-based market. Thus, they disappeared from our plates.

Today, the most reliable source of Jerusalem artichokes is the vacant lot. Jerusalem artichoke plants have classic sunflower morphology, with tough, raspy stalks and sharply toothed, lance-shaped leaves growing in opposite pairs. The stems can reach fifteen feet under ideal conditions, but typically attain one third that height. In late summer a vibrant orange-yellow blossom appears, with large sunflower petals but no seed-filled center disc. Instead, the center is the same color as the petals. In the ground beneath lie dozens of bumpy, beige, tan, red, or purple tubers. These are the famous "artichokes."

A number of theories attempt to explain how this vegetable, whose texture, shape, and flavor recall water chestnut, comes by its common name. "Jerusalem" may be a corruption of the Spanish *girasol,* or sunflower (the word literally means "turns toward the sun"), but I have yet to find a plausible explanation for "artichoke."

Jerusalem artichoke is common east of the Rockies, turning up anywhere dirt has been plowed up. It also appears sporadically in the Far West, though mostly in areas where it was intentionally introduced at some time in the past. Each tuber or part thereof is capable of generating a new plant, making Jerusalem artichoke famously hard to eradicate. Ironically, the variety most often encountered on vacant lots was developed in France for agricultural production. Imported to this continent as a garden vegetable, it escaped and recolonized regions where overharvesting and loss of habitat had eliminated the native variety. French tubers are the size and color of small potatoes, while the original sort are bumpier, reddish, and walnut-sized.

Jerusalem artichoke (*Helianthus tuberosum*).

Jerusalem artichokes may be harvested any time of year, but connoisseurs consider them best after a frost kills the plant's aerial parts. As long as the ground isn't frozen, the tubers can be pried up with a digging stick or potato fork. If the latter is used, it should be driven only about halfway into the soil to avoid uprooting the whole plant. Knock tubers from the clod with a tap of the tines, then slice them from the stems with a greens knife or pruning shears, and press the soil back down to preserve the root system and remaining tubers. Though harvested tubers do not keep well, they effectively store themselves in the ground and can be dug up periodically over the winter. They can also be sliced and rack-dried for later use or ground into flour.

Jerusalem artichokes' uneven surface can make cleaning them difficult. I've found that breaking large knobs off beforehand, then lightly scrubbing with a toothbrush under running water, works well. As the peel is tender and tasteless, there is no need to remove it.

It's a mystery why Jerusalem artichoke, so tasty, so nutritious, so versatile, is having such a tough time breaking back into North American kitchens. Any competent advertising agency ought to be able to provide consumers with the preparation instructions. The plant's effusive growth and natural resistance to North American pests enables tubers to be produced at an attractive price. Yet Jerusalem artichoke is still waiting for a comeback in its own homeland.

Foragers, on the other hand, can enjoy it right now. Jerusalem artichokes can be sliced and boiled or fried, baked whole, puréed, or pickled. Their clean, sweetish flavor even lends itself to wines. In pies and other sweet dishes Jerusalem artichokes behave something like apples, and are particularly agreeable in conjunction with tart fruits.

However, Jerusalem artichokes taste so good raw that they seldom last long enough to be cooked in my house. They're delicious sliced and served with a creamy dip, sprinkled with lemon, sumac, or marigold vinegar, or just munched like an apple. Jerusalem artichoke slices make a novel addition to a party tray or a salad. Fresh Jerusalem artichokes should be eaten as soon after harvest as possible, as they become faintly woody and lose some of their sweetness if stored in the refrigerator for more than a few days.

The pernicious fallacy that cooked Jerusalem artichokes taste like potatoes is probably due to their superficial resemblance to those tubers. The confusion may be partly responsible for Jerusalem artichokes' failure in the marketplace. Neither mealy nor starchy, Jerusalem artichokes are nothing like potatoes. Overboiled, they disintegrate into mush. Mashed, they are translucent and watery, something like mashed *new* potatoes, but not at all like mashed white potatoes. Baked, they have the pulpy consistency of squash. Nor do they deep-fry well. Properly prepared Jerusalem artichokes seldom disappoint, but while some sources exhort cooks to "substitute Jerusalem artichokes for potatoes in your favorite dish," in my experience this is a recipe for disaster.

In place of potatoes' starch, Jerusalem artichokes contain inulin, a polysaccharide proven beneficial to diabetics and others who must avoid starch for medical reasons. Jerusalem artichokes are also extremely high in iron, which is especially good news for women. Very low in fat, yet high in natural sugars, Jerusalem artichoke is also popular with dieters.

In the 1980s, speculating crop brokers convinced farmers across North America to plant Jerusalem artichokes. According to the theory, the tubers' diet and health food potential, coupled with their prolific growth, would make this ancient First Nations crop the toast of North America, just as it was in Europe three centuries ago. They even changed the name, ostensibly to make the product "sexier." "Sunchokes" appeared in supermarkets across the continent, pre-packaged in shrink-wrapped, plastic trays. Sadly, consumer education lagged behind distribution, while retail prices remained too high to tempt fussy shoppers. (One might also ponder whether a brand name with "choke" in it is the best choice for overcoming consumer hesitation.) Jerusalem artichoke farmers ended up taking a crushing financial hit at a time when many were already literally losing the farm. Rough break for a deserving tuber, to say nothing of North America's shrinking agricultural sector. Jerusalem artichokes still appear from time to time in gourmet sections of supermarket produce departments, always overpriced. Until that situation changes, Jerusalem artichokes will remain largely the province of foragers.

Lactuca and Sonchus

To foragers, wild lettuce (genus *Lactuca*) and sow thistle (genus *Sonchus*) are a single resource. Edible for only a short period, hard to gather in quantity, and with a flavor that ranges from bland to bad, these genera are not among the top five wild greens. But insofar as they frequently occur alongside others that are, such as dandelion and dock, they are worth knowing.

Wild lettuce and sow thistle are closely related, bear similar descriptions, and are used the same way. Each has milky white sap and erratically lobed or pointed leaves that may be bor-

Wild lettuce (*Lactuca* sp.).

dered with flexible bristles that are inoffensive when young. Wild lettuce flowers resemble tiny blue, lavender, or yellow dandelions; sow thistle blossoms are always yellow.

Though wild lettuce is the ancestor of the garden variety (*L. sativa*), you have to look closely to spot the family resemblance. Wild species set sparse, floppy leaves of pale green, reddish, or blue-green that clasp a hollow stalk. Gardeners may detect a faint resemblance to bolted leaf lettuce in some species. Sow thistle has a coarser, somewhat rubbery appearance, with dirty-looking, olive-drab leaves grasping a fibrous green stalk. The leaves are deeply and irregularly toothed and lined with tiny spines, giving the general impression of a dandelion with an attitude. Older leaves of both plants are tough and bitter, but brand new ones can be quite as good as garden lettuce during their brief early-spring season. Those too bitter for salad may be better cooked, especially with milder-flavored greens such as dock or nettles. A pernicious weed in Britain, persuasive if circumstantial evidence suggests that sow thistle was unknown there until the Roman occupation. The Romans had a documented fondness for sow thistle salad, and the prevalence of this coarse wild green around their ruined forts suggests it first appeared in imperial officers' mess gardens.

Wild lettuce is a well-known sedative, and infusions of it are used to that purpose in lands as diverse as China, the Middle East, and Haiti; it was also an important herb in colonial North America. *Lactuca*'s use in opiate addiction therapy suggests it is fairly strong as herbal sedatives go. The white sap of wild lettuce is also a topical wart remedy in most of the cultures that use it as a sedative.

Sow thistle is a sedative as well, also used to soften opium withdrawal and as a wart remover, though it is not mentioned nearly as often as wild lettuce in either of these capacities. *Sonchus* has laxative properties, and so should be eaten in moderation. Like most bitter greens, sow thistle is high in vitamins and trace elements.

> **Sow thistle and wild lettuce concentrate nitrates and pollutants from the ground, and so should only be gathered from clean, unfertilized soil.**

Matricaria

Identifying pineapple weed (*Matricaria matricarioides*) is a snap. Nothing else looks like it. More importantly, nothing else smells like it. Pineapple weed is a scrubby little plant whose leaves are so narrow they look like the feathery veins left after some insect has gnawed the tender parts away. Its flowers are pineapple-shaped cones without obvious petals. Their fluorescent avocado color, made famous by a million sofas in the 1970s, stands out against the equally unnatural sea green of the alleged foliage. Whether the common name comes from these groovy flowers or from the fact that the plant smells like pineapple when crushed is a matter for debate. In any case, pineapple weed's overall appearance is more that of an aquatic than a terrestrial plant.

Pineapple weed
(*Matricaria matricarioides*).

Pineapple weed is common, and sometimes a plague, across the northern two-thirds of the continent. It loves compacted clay, so is often the only plant sticking out of otherwise bare ground. Pineapple weed can take an incredible amount of abuse, with dirty, ragged specimens poking gamely from cracks in parking lots and along curbs.

Pineapple weed has only one culinary use, but it's a good one. The foliage, when bruised and covered with boiling water, makes a sweet tea that rivals anything sold in stores. Some liken the flavor to pineapple juice, others to chamomile. At any rate, it's so pleasant, and the plant so widespread, that it deserves a prominent place in any tea mixer's repertoire.

Matricaria, whose name means "mothering," actually won passage from Europe on the strength of its healing properties. Several compounds in *Matricaria*'s volatile oils have proven antibacterial, antiviral, and antifungal properties. These constituents explain why mashed *Matricaria* has been applied to cold sores, eczema, and athlete's foot, as well as to broken skin, since at least Roman times. They also vindicate traditional healers' use of *Matricaria* infusions against gastric ulcers and infections of the mouth and throat.

> Wild chamomile's (*M. chamomilla*), flowers are similar to pineapple weed's but rather more cucumber- than pineapple-shaped. Its medicinal properties are similar to pineapple weed.

Mentha

The neighborhood without a mint patch somewhere is rare indeed. Mint (genus *Mentha*) is ideally suited to the suburban environment, combining rapacious growth, forgiving environmental demands, and strongly aromatic chemistry that turns away predators while inspiring a certain tolerance from human inhabitants. As a result, foragers who keep an eye out for mint are seldom disappointed.

Most wild mints in North America today were introduced from the Old World. Typical species include spearmint (*M. spicata*), peppermint (*M.* x *piperita*), pennyroyal (*M. pulegium*), water mint (*M. aquatica*), orange mint (*M. citrata*), and tiny Corsican mint (*M. requienii*), as well as native field mint (*M. arvensis*).

All mints have square stems and toothed, coarsely veined leaves in opposite pairs. Some are narrow and very pointed, like those of spearmint, or oblong with virtually no point at all, like those of water mint. Spearmint leaves are crinkly, while peppermint's are hairy and pennyroyal's are smooth and somewhat shiny. Most mints are erect plants, some reaching three feet in height, especially in the American South. Exceptions include creeping pennyroyal varieties and Corsican mint, a mosslike ground cover best identified by its powerful, lemony mint odor.

Given mint's penchant for pollen swapping, to the point that several species will blend into a single hybrid if planted too close, telling them apart can be difficult. Fortunately, all are pleasant-tasting and easily identified by their similar morphology and powerful aroma. As their flavor varies widely, finding a new clump of mint is always an adventure.

Mint prefers moist conditions and is most often found along ditches and streams, and in wet fields. This aggressive, runner-propagating invader carves small monocultures from any compatible habitat unless actively contained. Mint's tendency to "run" means it frequently slips under fences and over curbs to establish itself in public areas. One summer, my wife and I picked three kinds at various points along a single alley. Each had busted out of a fenced yard and colonized the shoulder. By pooling our pickings, we were able to accumulate enough for a batch of mint jelly.

Mint is strongest when fresh, but the leaves dry readily for off-season use. The most efficient way to dry mint is to hang it upside down until the leaves and stems are completely dry. A brief stint in an oven prewarmed at the lowest setting ("brief" is the operative word here, since mint's aromatic oils are extremely volatile) crisps the leaves so they can be removed from the stem by pulling it between thumb and forefinger. Dried mint keeps for about a year in an airtight container. After that, it begins to lose its flavor.

Spearmint (*Mentha spicata*).

For a plant that can't anchor a dish by itself, mint is remarkably useful. Herbal teas benefit from a hefty shot of mint, and it even renders odious medicinals such as willow tea drinkable. Given a sufficient supply, mint tea readily replaces purchased coffee or black tea in the daily regimen. Though Western cultures mostly use mint to flavor beverages, such as the famous Southern mint julep, and sweet foods such as ice cream and candy, the Arabs use it in salads, spicy dishes, and meat sauces. After a satisfying meal in North African and Middle Eastern restaurants, diners enjoy the digestive effects of scalding mint tea that skilled waiters pour into tumblers from a height of three feet.

After-dinner mints and mint-flavored antacids recall the days when mint beverages played a similar role in the West. Traditional healers still recommend this benign, effective herb for morning sickness associated with pregnancy. Mint's effectiveness against gall bladder and kidney problems is supported by scientific studies, and antiviral constituents in mint tea may help cold, flu, and herpes sufferers. Some herbalists recommend mint poultices or ointments for cold sores, whether they appear on the lips or the genitals. Other external uses include rubbing mint decoctions, tinctures, or infusions into cramped muscles, arthritic joints, and freshly shaved skin.

A few mints have specific medicinal applications. Peppermint is particularly indicated for a host of complaints, including headache and emphysema, while pennyroyal, whose species name means "flea," is a recognized insect repellent. Pennyroyal tea is also a common treatment for menstrual difficulties, though abuse of essential oil of pennyroyal has endangered lives. Women who wish to try pennyroyal should do so in consultation with a competent professional.

The Mustards

The botanical family Brassicaceae (formerly known as Cruciferae) includes a legion of edible plants, both wild and domestic. Its members, called "crucifers" for their four-petalled, cross-shaped flowers, include cole crops such as cabbage, cauliflower, and broccoli, as well as radishes and Asian crops that have *choy* in their names, including bok choy and suey choy. Wild plants called mustard or cress (a corruption of crucifer) are also members of the Brassicaceae. For convenience's sake, I call this family "the mustards."

Mint has many look-alikes. Some are toxic, most taste bad, and all should be avoided. All *Mentha* species smell and taste strongly of mint, which makes identification easy. One exception is false pennyroyal (*Hedeoma pulegioides*), doubly dangerous because it is often simply called "pennyroyal." *Hedeoma* has the pleasant smell of the real thing, and a few of the same medicinal applications, but it poses real danger to pregnant women and those who mistakenly take it for menstrual problems. While spearmint and peppermint have a long-established reputation in traditional obstetrics, pregnant women should consult their doctor before treating themselves with this or any other foraged plant.

The mustards comprise several genera, most introduced to North America, and all edible in some capacity. Some even show up from time to time in supermarket produce sections. Though they vary widely in size and shape, all bear long, skinny seedpods that resemble snap beans. No crucifer has milky sap, an important identifying feature. The following list includes some of the most widespread and best-tasting species.

· Field mustard (*Brassica campestris*) bears hand-sized, asymmetrical, dusty green, slightly fuzzy leaves that pop up in well-drained, recently turned soil. Field mustard is one of the best wild greens, with sharp, slightly musty-flavored young leaves that unfurl in midsummer, long after other greens have become bitter and inedible. Field mustard is also an excellent fried green and an important foodstuff in the hill cultures of the American South.

· Black mustard (*Brassica nigra*) has smaller, rounder leaves than field mustard, but bears copious quantities of seed that can be ground with

Wild mustard (*Brassica* sp.).

cold water to make a powerful condiment. (See "Grist for the Mill," page 144, for details.)

·   Shepherd's purse and peppergrass (see *Capsella* entry, page 147).

·   Horseradish (*Armoracia rusticana*) is a perennial garden crop that often goes feral. Horseradish has large, wavy, translucent leaves that resemble dock. They have finely serrated edges and coarse white veins, and release a faintly mustardy scent when crushed. The aroma doesn't seem to deter snails, though; where I live, horseradish leaves are inevitably Swiss-cheesed long before I find them. Very young horseradish leaves may be eaten raw. After that they can be cooked with milder greens, though they are too strong to be eaten alone, and eventually become too bitter even for this. Horseradish root is a well-known condiment, though the wild sort tends to be tougher and is sometimes bitter. Best gathered in fall, winter, or spring, horseradish is famously potent, sending searing vapors into the sinuses of incautious diners. The fresh-grated root is significantly hotter and tastier than the jarred version sold in stores. Horseradish is also added to the ground seeds of other mustards to make a more aggressive condiment.

·   Garlic mustard (genus *Alliaria*) is also called jack-by-the-hedge. Newcomers to this genus will scarcely be surprised to learn that its dark, irregularly toothed, spade- or lilypad-shaped leaves smell and taste like garlicky mustard greens. With their deeply veined leaves, they bear a strong resemblance to nettle (see *Urtica,* page 184), except of course that they don't sting. Young garlic mustard can be eaten in salads, but the older leaves must be cooked. They should be gathered only in the cold months, as they are bitter in spring and summer. Some foragers grate the taproot for use like horseradish.

If caught quite young, mustard greens can be tossed sparingly in salads. After that, but before the plant blossoms, they are good fried, simmered with well-herbed Italian dishes such as spaghetti or lasagna, and in spicy Southern cuisine. I find them wonderfully zesty, sometimes a tad bitter, but always delicious. Less enthusiastic diners (my wife likens the pungent zip of field mustard greens to dirty socks) use them conservatively to give depth to chili, soups, or blander greens.

In deciding whether to take whole plants, or just snip leaves and leave the rootstock, consider what kind of mustard you are gathering and how much of it there is. Field mustard aggressively invades building sites and fallow fields, forming a solid patch. Under such circumstances, you can pull up and bag whole plants. Otherwise, cut off plants at ground level, leaving the root to grow again. When collecting horseradish, make a clean slice with a fiddling shovel to cut the long white root off a few inches below ground, leaving the rest to produce again. Besides, few foragers can use two feet of horseradish root: a little goes a long way.

If enough seeds are available, some foragers might like to try their hand at homemade mustard. Mustard seed is generally ground with cold water, then aged in a nonreactive container for a week or so to develop full flavor. Other spices can be mixed in at this time, but vinegar may inhibit the aging process, so it should be added afterward. (For seed processing techniques, see "Grist For the Mill," page 144.)

Folk healers reserve special respect for strong-flavored plants, and the mustards are no exception. All of them are considered cleansing herbs, stimulating the liver and digestive system to expel accumulated toxins. Recent scientific studies suggest that mustard greens may combat certain kinds of cancer. They are also high in minerals, particularly calcium, potassium, and vitamin C. Oil pressed from mustard seeds is a powerful antiseptic, used since at least the time of the ancient Greeks to combat fungal infections. All mustards, especially the stronger ones, are eaten to expel intestinal parasites.

Horseradish root is an antiseptic, and anyone who has experienced this intense condiment will have no trouble believing that few microbes can survive in it. *Armoracia* is also an aggressive antimucus agent. Some sources claim its penetrating, eye-watering vapors clear stuffed-up sinuses, though it appears to have the opposite effect on me. Mashed horseradish is mixed with milk to bring color to the skin, particularly the face, but such poultices, made too strong or left on too long, can cause painful chemical burns.

> **Wintercress (*Barbarea vulgaris*) is** almost identical to watercress (*Nasturtium officinale;* see Foraging Advisory, page 188) except that it grows on dry land. Its thick, rubbery foliage and greenish heads recall broccoli, only smaller. Wintercress is one of the few wild edibles that can be gathered in winter. In fact, it's inedible in other seasons due to its intense bitterness. I don't find wintercress terribly appealing in any season, but I haven't yet tried blanching it, which some foragers claim turns it into a vegetable resembling kale. (For instructions on blanching, see the *Cichorium* entry, page 151).

Opuntia

Many a barefoot child has waded into long grass or weeds, only to receive a footful of spines from a hidden, ground-level attacker. To those of us who have been there, prickly pear (genus *Opuntia*) remains etched in memory. Revenge, however, is at hand.

Opuntia is easily identified in non-desert areas, simply because it is usually the only cactus that grows there. In fact, prickly pear turns up in some startling places. My childhood run-in (or run-out, as the case may be) occurred in Kentucky. In the late eighteenth century, Royal Navy surgeon and naturalist Archibald Menzies was astonished to encounter *Opuntia*'s oblong, leathery, wickedly spiny beaver tails on the coast of British Columbia. And though no cactus occurs naturally outside the Americas, I once came upon a Provençal hillside thickly covered with explosively healthy *Opuntia*. Further enquiry revealed that cacti were a nineteenth century landscaping fad in the south of France, and this riotous thicket was a feral remnant of that period. *Opuntia* has even come to figure in many Mediterranean peasant cuisines. In Hawaii it's called *panini* and is a respected "leeward" crop, cultivated on the dry side of mountainous tropical islands.

Opuntia's spiny oval pads distinguish it from other cacti. These sprout from the ground itself and lean every which way in chaotic fashion, often covering the ground with a thick, invulnerable mat. When conditions are right, new pads may sprout out of existing ones, sometimes forming long chains that climb several feet into the air. (Some species also have a round, stubby base.) *Opuntia* blossoms are quite beautiful, generally bright yellow, soft, and fragile, in stark contrast to the vicious thorns that surround them.

O. ficus-indica and *O. megacantha*, called nopal cactus, play an important role in cuisines of Mexico and the southwestern United States. Called Indian pear and Indian fig because of their large, sweet fruit, they bear edible pads as well. Native to many arid areas, nopal cacti are popular ornamentals, and foragers who live within their range are particularly fortunate. Beyond the desert, smaller, thinner *Opuntias* that have more spines per ounce of edible flesh are the rule. It's up to the individual to decide if processing the local variety is worth the trouble.

For all its nonedible appearance, prickly pear offers two tasty treats. Most famous is the fruit, which on the best species is large, round, spiny (of course), and green, red, pink, yellow, or orange. These are the "pears" from which the plant draws its name. Skinning them with a knife and fork eliminates the spines quickly and easily. Slice off the ends, slit the fruit down the middle, and work the skin off with the utensils.

Prickly pear is often compared to watermelon in smell and taste. It can be eaten raw, or seeded and simmered into fluorescent sauces, or whirled in a blender to make sweet, frothy cold drinks. In Mexico and the Southwest, the pulp is fermented into alcoholic beverages. Prickly pears can be picked when not quite ripe and stored in a paper bag until they become soft. Particularly tart varieties are sweetened with sugar before eating.

The other edible part—the pads—should be taken young, and can even be crunched raw when very young. Raw prickly pear pads have something of the coolness and mildness of cucumber, with a hint of lima bean and bell pepper. They are mucilaginous, and may ooze a bit. Some find this repulsive,

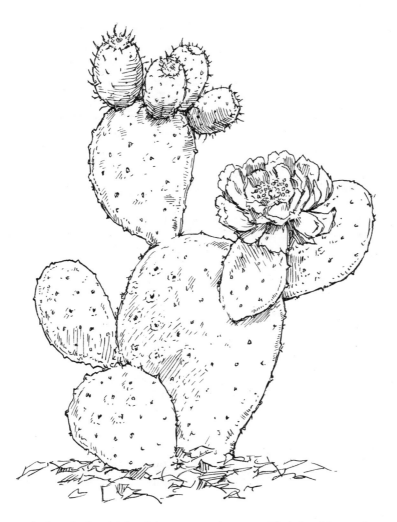

Nopal cactus, or Indian fig
(*Opuntia ficus-indica*).

but it comes in handy for thickening soups and sauces. Slightly older pads can be sliced for stir-fries and barbecue, or wrapped in foil with a few drops of water and baked at 375°F for thirty minutes to an hour. Some fans even bread and fry the strips, or use them in tempura. They also pickle nicely using cucumber pickling recipes.

The watchword for *Opuntia* is safety. Prickly pear is armed not just with large, visible spines, but also with thousands of hair-fine, almost invisible ones. These are the most dangerous, since they break off in the skin and create a painful, longer-term problem than the jabs of their larger kin. Heavy leather gloves are obligatory for handling prickly pear. Even with gloves it must be handled gingerly, as the large spines will pierce leather if the opportunity arises.

Slice prickly pear pads and fruits away from the plant with a long blade, such as a butcher knife. This is one instance where sharp is safer than dull, as a sharp knife keeps sawing to a minimum, reducing the chances that hands and fingers will come into contact with the spines. Carry pads and fruits in a bucket, as they quickly reduce plastic shopping bags to shreds. In any case, a bagful of *Opuntia* represents a considerable threat to unsuspecting individuals who might brush, or worse (and this even hurts to write), sit on it.

Despining the pads is a challenge, and no two foragers have the same approach. Most begin by tearing out the larger spines with pliers, or nipping them off with pruning shears or nail clippers. Next, every last one of the tiny spines must be removed before the pad comes anywhere near a human mouth. Some aficionados rub them off with canvas or a damp towel. Desert First Nations people burn the spines off over a fire, or just roast the pads in the coals as is, after which the blistered skin can be pulled off. Echoing this approach, an acquaintance of mine despines his pads with a blowtorch. Once the spines are gone, a potato peeler makes short work of the bumps, called "eyes," from which they grew. Slicing these off definitively renders the pads safe for human consumption.

> Some cultivated *Opuntias* have few or no spines, and *O. compressa*, a wild species of the eastern part of the continent, is said to be naturally spineless. The fruits of purple cactus (*Mammillaria vivipara*), found across the Great Plains into Alberta and Saskatchewan, are also reputed to be edible. I have never met this species, but it is said to be excellent. Other cacti are edible as well, though most are highly regional. Many are protected by law due to poachers, who dig up whole stands to sell to the ornamental market. Readers who live in cactus country should inform themselves on local laws before collecting cacti or their fruits.

Prickly pear fruits are high in vitamin C, potassium, and calcium. Highly colored ones may turn the urine bright red, a feature that greatly entertains boys and college students. The pads are a rich source of protein, iron, and vitamins A and C. Like the fruits, they are also high in calcium.

Plantago

I doubt there is a suburbanite anywhere on the continent who doesn't know plantain (genus *Plantago*), though many don't know its name. Plantain's wiry flower stems routinely survive lawn care, and I well remember cursing the pellet-shaped flowers, with their Saturn ring of orbiting white petals, that bobbed over lawns I had just mowed when I was a boy. Tough, deeply ribbed plantain leaves also sprout in driveway cracks and along building foundations, and on any stretch of untended ground.

A few dozen *Plantago* species grow in North America, the most common ones introduced from Europe as herbs. All have salient, parallel ribs in the leaves and unlikely looking blossoms. The major distinctions among species are leaf width and shape. Common plantain (*P. major*) has rounded leaves with bowed ribs like the meridians on a globe. Buckthorn plantain (*P. lanceolata*) has long, narrow leaves that can reach a foot in length under ideal conditions, but are usually half that. Other plantains turn up in various parts of the continent, most bearing the ribbed leaves and odd flowers typical of the genus.

Plantain is often recommended as a vegetable, and it does in fact make a nice cooked green if taken very young. The window of opportunity is narrow, though, as the leaves become tough almost the instant they unfold. Neverthe-less, plantain seldom becomes intensely bitter, so it can be simmered into a nutritious vege-tarian stock or infused for medi-cinal tea long after the leaves have become tough.

Common plantain (*Plantago major*).

Even new plantain leaves offer more texture than flavor. Fortunately, they nearly always grow near dandelion, dock, and other greens. Cooked with flavorful leaves such as these, plantain is quite palatable. Some foragers apparently toss it in salads, but I find even very young plantain too tough to be an attractive salad green unless chopped small and used sparingly.

Plantain seeds are the plant's chief value to suburban foragers. Plantain seed is easily threshed, and has long been ground for use as flour. Today, a more likely approach is to add whole seeds to baked goods, like wheat germ, or to sprinkle them over muffins and breads like poppy seeds. Boiled with hot breakfast cereals, they assume a slightly gelatinous quality. Care should be taken not to go overboard on plantain seed, however, as it is an effective laxative.

In fact, as commercially refined psyllium, plantain seed is the main ingre-dient of Metamucil and other commercial laxatives. Soak foraged plantain seed in hot water to make a laxative tea or broth, and swallow the softened seeds while drinking it. The seed works by absorbing moisture in the intestines, which is why small doses combat diarrhea. Large doses create the illusion of bulk, triggering the body's eliminating reflex. Plantain seed has been used as a folk remedy for amoebic dysentery, evidently because it absorbs moisture the parasites need to survive, and it also soaks up excess stomach acid, making it an effective antacid.

Cut plantain stems as the seedheads ripen, then dry thoroughly as described in "Grist for the Mill," page 144. The seeds can then be stripped into a container by pulling the stems between the thumb and forefinger. Large quantities of plantain seed can thus be threshed in little time.

Plantain leaves are an important medicinal in their own right. Poultices of mashed plantain are especially renowned for treating skin conditions involving inflammation, including insect bites, boils, hemorrhoids, sore eyes, and infections of the mouth. Taken as a tea, they treat catarrh and cough, and soothe ulcers. While plantain leaves are a bit of a nutritional disappointment compared with other wild greens, they do offer respectable quantities of protein, fiber, and potassium. On the other hand, they also contain more than ten times the fat of other greens.

> **Saxon children once picked** plantain flower stems, wrapped the base several times around the part just behind the flower, then "shot" the flower off by pushing the coiled stem against it. Naturally, this was most fun with another child as the target, so pitched plantain battles were likely to erupt anywhere children found the plants in abundance. To this day in some parts of England plantain is called "kemps," from the Saxon word for warrior.

Polygonum

When I was seven, my family moved into town. Our house was on the edge of a large gully entirely occupied by Himalayan blackberry. The sole exception was a patch of something my friends and I called "bamboo," which grew along one side of our yard. There the six-foot canes formed a monoculture of their own, from which redoubt they rebuffed the imperialistic brambles year after year. Their broad, heart-shaped leaves dropped in winter, leaving barren, jointed stems that rattled in the wind below my bedroom window. In April, fat red and green sprouts punched through the dead leaves, looking exceedingly edible. But I knew better than to taste them on that basis alone. Besides, at seven I was no fan of vegetables. Knotweed (genus *Polygonum*) would have to wait another twenty years to become my favorite wild herb.

Japanese knotweed (*Polygonum cuspidatum*) and giant knotweed (*P. sachalinense*), both immigrants from northeast Asia, occur across Canada and the United States. Their hollow, chambered stems have earned them the common name "Mexican bamboo" in some locales. Knotweed prefers moist, humus-rich soil, where it handily outcompetes most other plants. Sprays of minuscule, highly fragrant white or yellow flowers come on in midsummer, to the delight of honeybees, butterflies, and other nectar-sipping insects that flock to the site.

Size is the only substantial difference between Japanese and giant knotweed, the largest *Polygonum* species. (*Polygonum* is a huge genus, encompassing a full spectrum of mostly low-growing plants such as smartweed and bistort, but no others approach the size of the great knotweeds.) Japanese knotweed canes reach about six feet, with six- to eight-inch leaves. Giant knotweed is noticeably bigger. One clump that I encountered in a Washington State alder grove had canes easily two inches in diameter and ten or more feet high, and huge, two-foot leaves. The overall effect was of a cluster of young banana trees, weirdly surrealistic in that boreal setting. Giant knotweed rarely gets *that*

Japanese knotweed (*Polygonum cuspidatum*).

giant, however. The two species also seem to crosspollinate readily, as individual patches often look too large for one, too small for the other.

Gardeners imported knotweed to the New World at the beginning of the twentieth century for use as a screen, and for its beautiful flowers and foliage. In the intervening years it has lost favor as an ornamental and is practically never intentionally planted today. As is so often the case, we can no longer admire knotweed aloud for fear of ridicule. Knotweed does in fact displace native species and is the target of government eradication campaigns across the continent, but beauty is beauty, whether it is friendly to our interests or not.

Actually, knotweed is friendly to foragers' interests, insofar as its thick shoots are an excellent vegetable. They resemble fat asparagus spears, which is presumably why many sources say they taste like asparagus. Unfortunately for asparagus fans, they only faintly suggest that vegetable. Rather, knotweed shoots have a tangy, earthy, rhubarblike quality, equally at home in sweet or savory dishes. Young knotweed shoots can be simmered in water, stock, or wine with garlic and onion, and served hot, or chilled and served on toast with a cream sauce or salad dressing. They also make an outstanding velouté (see Recipes, page 192). Young knotweed leaves can be cooked like other edible greens. They are mild and tender, a good starter green for those unused to robust wild flavors and textures. Though uncooked sprouts and leaves are edible, they are chewy, extremely mucilaginous, and, quite frankly, disgusting.

Knotweed fairly leaps out of the ground in early spring, growing several inches per day. A stand at peak production is virtually impossible to overharvest. This, coupled with knotweed's outlaw status, means that landowners seldom refuse collecting privileges. It is also one of the easiest wild herbs to locate off-season, since the dead, jointed brown canes persist through the winter. Foragers have only to watch the ground beginning around late March to catch the shoots in season. Within weeks, brick red, fingertip-sized nubs appear at the base of the canes. They soon grow an inch or two and turn white. They are mildly toxic at this stage, but the change signals the imminent harvest. A day or two later they shoot up to six inches, doubling in diameter and turning green with red highlights, with sticky, papery collars at the joints. The light-colored shoots are easily spotted against the dark canes and leaf litter, which, together with the absence of underbrush, makes them especially easy to gather.

Overripe knotweed is toxic, though the canes are bitter and twine-tough and few foragers would be tempted to eat them. Knotweed rhizomes (the underground portion of the stem) are poisonous as well. While some sources list them as edible or medicinal, subterranean knotweed parts are not good candidates for foraging or self-treatment by amateurs, and should be avoided. Some individuals report mild photosensitivity after eating knotweed.

A shopping bag's worth of shoots can be cut in minutes when sprouting is in full swing. A greens knife is useful for gathering knotweed sprouts, which may be crushed if snapped off. Once collected, the sprouts need not be peeled or sliced. A good rinse, and they're ready for action.

When the shoots left behind reach one to two feet, with a few small leaves, well-developed joints, and a stringy, fibrous sheath, they become too tough and strong-tasting to be cooked as a vegetable. At this point, peel away the tough skin by carefully stripping it down from the sprout's cut end or scraping with a knife or potato peeler, and slice the peeled stalk into translucent, bright green rings. These can be used in rhubarb recipes. When the sprouts become bitter and so fibrous that cooking no longer makes them tender—generally at about two feet in height—the collecting season is over.

The only thing standing between knotweed and mainstream diets seems to be the name. I tell fussy eaters it is "Japanese asparagus," and everyone's happy. My marketing strategy was most effective in the 1980s, when things Japanese were trendy and politicians used the term "disinformation" with a straight face, but it continues to answer the call today. Later, when serving knotweed sauce, pie, or jam, I have only to finesse this fiction to squeeze more mileage out of it. "Japanese rhubarb" sounds quite palatable, and since it *is* quite palatable, no one need be the wiser.

The slime that renders raw knotweed repulsive is eliminated in cooking, so, unlike other mucilaginous vegetables, it is not very useful as a thickener. Knotweed also varies in flavor from locale to locale, particularly in tartness, so it's a good idea to gather from as many patches as possible to find the ones that taste best. Knotweed shoots keep about a week in the refrigerator. The spears don't freeze well, and so are a once-yearly delicacy. I have successfully frozen *velouté d'asperges japonaises,* though with some loss of flavor. Sauces and jams can be canned like other preserves. I like to rent a video during Japanese rhubarb season and peel and slice a whole heap of rings while I watch. Then I pop them in the refrigerator. In the following days, I bake my annual Japanese rhubarb pie, using a recipe for standard rhubarb pie with a pinch of nutmeg added, and put up a year's worth of sauce (see Recipes, page 192). Japanese rhubarb actually kicks off the canning season in my house.

Knotweed is high in vitamin C and other nutrients that creatures coming out of hibernation crave. Like other *Polygonums,* it is a traditional remedy for gastrointestinal problems, especially diarrhea. Scientific studies suggest that chemicals in knotweed may also be effective against stomach cancer.

Portulaca

Most neighborhoods have at least one sunbeaten, gravelly wasteland. Whether an impromptu parking lot, a little-used corner of the schoolyard, or a vacant lot from which the topsoil has been scraped away, such areas seem to be part and parcel with suburban development. By happy coincidence, they are also perfect habitats for one of the most widely appreciated suburban wild edibles.

With its succulent, prone stems, purslane (*Portulaca oleracea*) is one of suburbia's most readily identifiable wild plants. Purslane looks like a prostrate jade plant, with whorls of glossy, jade green leaves and reddish mucilaginous stems up to three quarters of an inch thick. The leaves are much thinner than those of the popular potted ornamental, however. Tiny yellow blossoms appear in

Purslane (*Portulaca oleracea*).

midsummer, ceding to small, pointed seed capsules. These pop open in late summer, spilling tiny, glossy black seeds that reestablish the colony year after year. (Purslane is an annual.) Though rare in some localities and rampant in others, purslane turns up on dry soil in every subarctic region of the continent.

Purslane's central root cluster sends leafy, trailing feelers in every direction, eventually throwing a netlike carpet over entire acres if left undisturbed. Also a yard and garden weed, in some places purslane is an inveterate pest. Yet these days it is actually being invited into some gardens. After all, this rather attractive plant makes a fine ground cover for sterile areas that would otherwise remain bare, and it seldom declines an invitation. As a result, purslane cultivars sometimes even show up in garden centers nowadays. One of the most popular has brassy yellow stems and is probably related to the variety cultivated as a potherb in the Old World.

> **Purslane is high in omega-3 fatty** acids, believed to encourage the body to flush cholesterol from the blood.

Called *pourpier* in France and *verdolaga* in Mexico, purslane is a sought-after vegetable everywhere in its nearly global range—except here. A conventional salad green in the Middle East (see Recipes, page 198), the Arabs introduced *Portulaca* to Europe in the eighth century when they invaded Spain. European colonists later brought it to the Americas. Purslane has a tart, crisp quality, with a hint of the copper flavor associated with green beans. Originally imported as human food, purslane's exuberant growth, nutritional content, and monocultural habits have earned it recognition as the third of the three "pigweeds," along with *Amaranthus* and *Chenopodium*.

Nothing could be simpler than collecting and preparing purslane. The plant is cut and washed, then chopped and eaten raw or cooked. The stems can be cut to jar length and pickled. In this capacity, the very fattest ones, which can be as thick as an adult's thumb, are preferred, if only because they reduce processing time. Young purslane is the most tender and has the least brassy aftertaste, but the plant remains palatable throughout its life. If a lot of purslane is at hand (and in many regions it grows so fast it can't be overharvested), gather young sprigs in quantity to blanch and freeze for later use.

Raw purslane leaves are a traditional accompaniment for tomatoes, cucumbers, and other popular high-summer salad vegetables. They are excellent in spicy sandwiches such as tacos and pita pockets. The leaves and stems can be cooked with potatoes, eggs, or pork, simmered in soup and pasta sauces, or simply steamed—leaves and stems together—as a side dish. A mucilaginous plant, purslane is often used to thicken soups and stews.

Purslane is high in vitamins A and C and is a traditional cure for scurvy. Somewhat astringent, with a measure of tannin, purslane treats hemorrhoids and wrinkles when mashed into a mucilaginous poultice, and the raw leaves are eaten to counter diarrhea. Antibacterial properties in purslane have prompted folk healers across its range to use purslane poultices as a balm for wounds.

Rumex

Genus *Rumex* includes two of the world's most common and most highly esteemed wild herbs. Why these remarkably different plants have been stuffed into one genus is a question best left to taxonomists, but whereas foragers consider *Amaranthus* and *Chenopodium,* or *Lactuca* and *Sonchus,* a single resource, *Rumex* must be split in two. I call these hypothetical subgenera "*Rumex*-D" (for dock) and "*Rumex*-S" (for sorrel).

Yellow dock (*Rumex persicaroides*), during spring runoff.

Dock

Everyone knows the *Rumex*-D species, though many don't notice them. Their dark, crepelike leaves are positively omnipresent, poking through chinks in sidewalks and parking lots and drooping over playgrounds, fields, and vacant lots. Curly (*R. crispus*), red (*R. sanguineus*), yellow (*R. persicarioides*), and patience dock (*R. patientia*) are but four of the many varieties. The leaves of most are narrow or oval and dark green, with a bumpy, orange-peel texture. The foliage arcs over the surrounding ground like fluttering banners. The stems of some common varieties are red. Later, a central stem bolts up to three feet, with a long, branched seed spike at the top that turns rusty red and persists through the winter. Fully mature leaves may reach a foot or more in length, usually with red or yellow spots. Only new leaves are mild and tender enough for the table. "Scrolls"—leaves that haven't completely unrolled yet—are the tastiest and most tender. Most North American *Rumex*-D's are immigrants, though First Nations cultures have used native species since well before European contact.

Steamed dock looks and tastes like strong, slightly chewy chard, and can be eaten accordingly, dressed with lemon or sumac

Sheep sorrel (*Rumex acetosella*).

juice or vinegar. A pinch of dill fancies it up a bit. Dock is also one of the most practical wild greens (see "Cooking with Greens," page 186) and is superb fried. More elegant fare includes crêpes stuffed with steamed dock and ham (see Recipes, page 194).

A close relative of buckwheat, dock is frequently mentioned as a source of seeds for flour. I once tried to sprout a fistful of them for salad, but found the heavy brown hulls, which make up two-thirds of each seed's overall mass, unpalatable. Given the large ratio of this inert material to the kernels, I wonder how nutritious dock seed flour really is. At any rate, it must be high in fiber.

Dock is rich in iron and vitamins, and is a traditional cure for scurvy. Dock root is a famous and well-respected medicinal herb, one of the top folk remedies for feminine troubles. It stimulates bile production, in effect flushing out the machinery that filters the blood. Dock is therefore indicated for anemia and other blood-related difficulties, as well as liver problems such as those caused by past alcoholism. Herbalists recommend dock, taken internally and applied externally, for psoriasis, acne, and other skin problems. The greens are also effective against gastrointestinal problems such as diarrhea, constipation, and gas.

Sorrel

Though the species of *Rumex*-S are as widespread and readily recognized as dock, they are an entirely different herb.

Sorrels bear spearhead-shaped leaves with a smooth, slightly grainy surface. Direct sunlight gives sorrel a subtle, three-dimensional sheen. It has none of the orange-peel texture of dock leaves, doesn't grow as big, isn't as tough, and has an entirely different shape from the more or less oval dock leaves.

Where dock prefers rich, moist soil, sorrel requires a sandy, well-drained, infertile medium. It does send up a reddish seed spike, which is something like dock's, but much smaller. Sorrel leaves are intensely sour, becoming somewhat chewy with age but seldom bitter like dock.

Sheep sorrel (*R. acetosella*) is the most common *Rumex*-S, present in yards, vacant lots, and anywhere else it finds sandy soil. Its rubbery stems are sometimes reddish, and its normally sparse, spade-shaped leaves have "horns" at the base. Sheep sorrel leaves ordinarily reach a maximum of two inches in length. Introduced by the first wave of Europeans, sheep sorrel is the "sourgrass" so dear to North American children. As such, it is one of the most widely recognized wild edibles in suburbia.

Later settlers introduced garden sorrel (*R. acetosa*), whose larger leaves were judged more desirable. Garden sorrel leaves can reach five inches in length, are wavy and thinner than sheep sorrel's, and have less pronounced horns at the stem end. They are generally more tender, and have more lemony bite, than sheep sorrel. Garden sorrel is seldom cultivated in North America today, though it never lost favor in Europe. While it has recently made a modest comeback on this side of the Atlantic, foragers are still more likely to encounter "garden" sorrel as a weed.

Sorrel varies widely according to local conditions, a feature typical of herbs that prefer nutrient-poor soil. I was forcefully reminded of this when my landlord tore out my tiny backyard with a backhoe to service a septic tank. When the dust settled, dust was all I had left. The once thickly vegetated area between my house and the road was a mound of sterile glacial till. Fortunately this was well before the growing season. As summer approached, a lush growth of the most beautiful sorrel I've ever seen carpeted the slag heap. Evidently, phenomenal drainage, coupled with serendipitous regulation of sunlight by surrounding trees, and perhaps even a few trace elements from the original plumbing problem, provided the perfect sorrel habitat. Though only sheep sorrel, its stems were jammed with four-inch leaves. Tender and tangy, they were more than acceptable compensation for other losses. I have never seen the like again, even in cultivated sorrels.

Sorrel has been a central ingredient of relishes and sauces since early times. A common medieval meat sauce was made by moistening finely chopped sorrel leaves with vinegar and thickening the mixture with a little sugar. Thickened with butter instead, the same mixture makes a fine condiment for fish and potatoes. Chopped sorrel is a tasty stuffing for whole fish, and makes a quick and pleasing dip mixed with yogurt or sour cream.

In Europe, sorrel is the taste of summer. Cream of sorrel soup (see "Cooking with Greens," page 186) is a French luncheon standard, served hot or cold. Sorrel also brings tang to salads, sandwiches, and fried greens. People in Mediterranean countries use sorrel and other greens to build a hearty farmer's omelette that is a meal in itself. (See Recipes, page 193.) Infusions of chopped sorrel are similarly connected with the easy days of summer, as they make a respectable substitute for lemonade when iced and sweetened to taste.

Sorrel's sour nature is a dead giveaway for its extremely high vitamin C content, and it has been on the short list of scurvy treatments since the dawn of medicine. It also has a stimulating effect on the kidneys and urinary system, and is an antiseptic, no doubt due to its high oxalic acid content. Sorrel poultices are a traditional response to acne and other skin problems, a practice that betrays its relationship with *Rumex*-D species. As a mouthwash, sorrel infusions are said to speed the healing of canker sores, though the effect must be something like swishing around a mouthful of orange juice.

Sorrel owes its tartness to oxalic acid. This chemical, present in smaller quantities in knotweed and other tangy greens, can cause diarrhea and other gastric problems if ingested in large amounts. Sorrel should therefore always be consumed in conjunction with other foods, and should never anchor a meal by itself. Whereas a few sorrel leaves in a salad are harmless, a salad of nothing *but* sorrel might cause stomach upset. (And anyway, diners would wince at the sourness.) Finally, oxalic acid exacerbates existing joint and kidney problems, so arthritis and gout sufferers and those with a history of kidney stones should avoid it. On the bright side, a good silver cleaner can be made by mashing sorrel and fine salt into a paste. The oxalic acid loosens tarnish, and the salt scours it away. Sorrel juice is also an effective bleach for certain tenacious stains such as mildew and rust.

Solidago

Mention goldenrod (genus *Solidago*) and people frown. This North America native is widely believed to cause hay fever, the eye-watering, nose-running plague of millions. Scientists aren't sure goldenrod is the actual culprit. (Ragweed, a nondescript plant often found growing near goldenrod, is now the prime suspect.) What is certain is that goldenrod has a long, auspicious history as a medicinal and beverage herb.

Goldenrod grows in dense banks along roadsides just about everywhere in North America, with the exception of the Pacific slope of the U.S. Though some are low-growing wildflowers, the thin, fairly woody stems of the herbal goldenrods reach six feet, with narrow, grasslike leaves and no branches. But by far

Sweet goldenrod
(*Solidago odora*).

the most telling feature is the dense head of tiny yellow blossoms that turn each stem into a flaming torch in late summer. These flowering tops, which can gild roadsides for miles on end, are prized by herbalists.

Though most goldenrods can be used as tea stock, sweet goldenrod (*S. odora*) is the most highly flavored. Readily identified by its anise-like odor, sweet goldenrod was a tea mixing staple for pioneer societies within its largely eastern range. The flowering tops were gathered, chopped, and dried in quantity, then infused as needed, often with other ingredients such as mint, rose hips, or orange peel. In this fashion, goldenrod tea brought a touch of summer to cold winter days.

> **Goldenrod contains vast quantities of pollen. Individuals who are allergic to pollen should approach tinctures or infusions of goldenrod with caution.**

Where sweet goldenrod is unavailable, the less aromatic flowering tops of other tall species can be used. Canada goldenrod (*S. canadensis*), western goldenrod (*S. occidentalis*), smooth goldenrod (*S. gigantea*), tall goldenrod (*S. altissima*), or fragrant, white-flowering silverrod (*S. nemoralis*) can all be infused. Few have sweet goldenrod's flavor, however, so they are more useful for medicinal than beverage tea.

Goldenrods occur in Asia and Europe as well as the New World, and are important herbal medicines everywhere they appear. Ironically, tincture of goldenrod has recently received much attention as an antiallergen, taken to combat the very symptoms that so many believe goldenrod causes. This tincture is made by infusing chopped goldenrod flowering tops in strong liquor for four to six weeks, then straining out the plant materials. The tincture is said to be good for the watery eyes, sore throat, and sinus trouble associated with hay fever.

An effective diuretic, goldenrod tea is a traditional remedy for urinary disorders and kidney or bladder stones. Goldenrod leaves were crushed and applied to wounds as an antiseptic in medieval Europe, and modern herbalists still recommend infusions of the plant's aerial parts as a douche against candida and yeast infections. Goldenrod infusions are also taken for thrush, canker sores, and ulcers.

Stellaria

Novice foragers who wish to have chickweed (genus *Stellaria*) pointed out to them have only to seek out the nearest gardener. A lush, ground-hugging annual that thrives in soft, rich, well-watered soil, chickweed was literally designed to invade gardens. Its thick, tangled mats spread across flower beds and vegetable plots almost overnight. Any gardener can spot chickweed at thirty paces, and most let foragers take it all, free of charge.

Chickweed was one of the most valued herbs in early colonial times, painstakingly cultivated in the very gardens it must crash today. A beneficial food and medicinal, chickweed's prolific growth and nearly year-round availability established it as an essential in traditional healing. While the common name reflects the plant's popularity with chickens and other birds, chickweed is also a favorite rabbit fodder and a standard dietary supplement for ailing stock of all kinds. The widespread use as animal feed suggests that chickweed is unusually high in nutrients, which is indeed the case.

Most *Stellaria* species are called chickweed or starwort in layman's terms.

Common chickweed
(*Stellaria media*).

Those answering the general description of common chickweed (*Stellaria media*), a European species and the most widespread in North America today, are interchangeable in herbal applications. Chickweed has small tongue-shaped leaves, reaching three-quarters of an inch in length, in opposite pairs. The bright little white flowers that twinkle here and there among the matted foliage gave the genus its name, from the Latin for "star." The branches are weak and trail along the ground, bending sunward at the end to give the false impression of several individually rooted plants. In fact, the luxurious carpet is anchored to the earth by a single tender stem, making the entire mass very easy to uproot.

If chickweed is to be removed completely, as when a gardener wishes to obliterate it, gathering is straightforward. No tools are required, though the collector should be careful to nip off the small root ball that comes up with the rest of the plant. This can soil the greens if not removed immediately, and washing the grit out of the voluptuous tangle is difficult.

Chickweed grows year-round in my wife's deck garden. She actually planted one box in chickweed when we first moved in, using seeds I collected the previous year, to ensure an opulent supply. We snip off handfuls of leafy tips all winter long to add welcome greenery to our off-season fare. Over time the chickweed has managed to colonize most of the other boxes, so when planting time rolls around and the chickweed booms, we chop and dry all but one mat. (I also like to fry a handful of fresh chopped chickweed with other greens during

The Eatin' o' the Greens

Like diets of yore, mine is governed by the seasons. I can therefore attest to the fact that a glass of elderflower champagne or a crisp Jerusalem artichoke brings me the sort of joy that others must spend a lot more money to achieve, simply because these foods are unavailable much of the year. That's why after a long winter of squash and root vegetables, I observe the Eatin' o' the Greens with tremendous gusto.

Rural cultures in all of the world's hard-winter zones observe this ancient rite. The basics are the same everywhere: The cabin-fever victim spots tender green shoots poking through the mud. He or she rushes out and rips up great basketfuls between rain squalls. Then the weak-eyed creature scurries back inside, where the plunder is immediately prepared and wolfed down.

Most cultures defend this gluttony on medical grounds. English-speaking ones call spring greens "tonics," and claim inhaling them by the bushel flushes "winter impurities" from the body. Science is less convinced of this. What is certain is that spring greens contain vast quantities of nutrients missing from winter fare, suggesting that the urge to binge on them may indeed be biological.

Whatever the pretext, wild greens are delicious and available only a few weeks a year. That's why I enjoy knotweed soup, dandelion crown salad, and dock-stuffed crêpes nearly every day in spring. I celebrate the return of the good life by collecting a large bag of dock, dandelion, and other greens, frying them up (see Recipes), and savoring a heaping plateful. (Apparently, my system doesn't require a yearly break-in period for greens. Others might react differently. First-timers should observe regular first-try protocol.) Spiced with fresh air, the rich smell of earth, and the drum of rain on the roof, these lunches are among my happiest memories. I don't know if they flush anything out of my body, but they sure sweep winter cobwebs from my mind.

the Eatin' o' the Greens.) We use the dried chickweed like parsley, then snip fresh tips from the remaining mat for salads and sandwiches.

Chickweed's dainty stems are surprisingly elastic, even after cooking, so the plant is best chopped before use. It has fairly strong flavor but is not in the least bitter, tasting of moist earth, with a subtle mineral-water aftertaste that must originate in its high mineral content. Some dislike eating chickweed straight, but use it as an alfalfa or bean sprout substitute in sandwiches and stir-fries. Chopped chickweed also makes a rich cream soup, and a tablespoon of fresh, chopped leaves are a welcome garnish in other soups. Chopped chickweed also brings color and flavor to sauces and stuffings.

When dried, chickweed has an earthy, alfalfa-like scent similar to parsley but more pronounced. Sealed in an airtight container, it keeps indefinitely and is

> **Mouse-ear chickweed (Cerastium** *vulgatum*) is not a *Stellaria* species. Like other *Cerastiums,* many of which are also called chickweed, mouse-ear chickweed is edible, but has little to offer in the way of medicinal or nutritional benefits. Furthermore, its woolly leaves irritate the throat if eaten raw.

a good parsley substitute for those who appreciate its stronger flavor. The dried herb is also handy for making nutritious or medicinal broth and teas, particularly in the months when chickweed is unavailable or under snow.

Topical uses alone might have earned chickweed a place on the crowded sailing ships that first brought European settlers to this continent. A poultice of simmered and mashed chickweed was the universal treatment for nearly every skin disorder, including cuts, scrapes, swellings, hemorrhoids, sties, rashes, and boils. The pulp was bound into wounds, then the water poured over the bandages. Patients then ate chickweed or drank chickweed tea, attacking infection on two fronts. Modern herbalists echo these traditions by beating dried, powdered chickweed into creams and ointments.

Chickweed also enjoyed a colonial reputation as a treatment for colds, scurvy, and constipation. High in potassium, vitamin C, and other nutrients, yet easy on the stomach, steamed chickweed was used to restore victims of famine or malnutrition. Today it enjoys some celebrity as a weight loss aid. (Unfortunately, it is only effective if eaten instead of, rather than as well as, more fattening foods.) Chewing a few tips of chickweed sweetens an acid stomach, and chickweed tea or broth gently strengthens the weak stomach that lingers after a flu or other illness.

Taraxacum

Of all the herb-to-weed stories, dandelion's (genus *Taraxacum*) is by far the most dramatic. This remarkable herb, one variety of which even bears the prestigious *officinale* species name, was considered a necessity of life until recently. As a food, beverage stock, medicine, and dietary supplement, *Taraxacum* is unrivalled in the plant kingdom. Indeed, no other genus has stepped forward to fill the vacuum in the century and a half since dandelion's fall. Thriving in all but the most extreme climates, with versatile reproductive capabilities that ensure survival, dandelion is everything humanity could wish for in a crop. Its modest yellow blossoms and whimsical heads of parachute seeds belie dandelion's prestigious place in human history.

With the Industrial Revolution, and attendant urbanization and centralization of resources, dandelion was summarily demoted from the most respected herb to the most despised. From healer of the sick and feeder of the hungry, *Taraxacum* has been reduced to that blackest of suburban blackguards, an invader of lawns.

True to form, even in disgrace dandelion is an overachiever. In fact, it has become the godfather of the entire outlaw-herb mob. A quick sweep of the herbicide aisle in any garden supply center inevitably nets a buggy-load of jars, cans, and boxes, all bearing the image of the hated dandelion. Clearly, *Taraxacum* is Public Enemy Number One. But it doesn't have to stay that way, if suburban foragers ply their ancient, iconoclastic craft.

Though several *Taraxacums* are native to North America, the two most common species are refugees from colonial gardens. Common dandelion (*T. officinale*) and red-seeded dandelion (*T. erythrospermum*) both have the classic yellow flowers, round, fragile seedheads, and the familiar shock of deeply toothed leaves popularly associated with dandelion. (The word "dandelion," from the Norman *dents de lyon,* or lion's teeth, reflects the fanglike leaf indentations.) The longer

Common dandelion (*Taraxacum officinale*).

flower stems of pure *T. officinale* specimens are pale green, almost white. Its leaves are larger and lighter than those of *T. erythrospermum,* with fewer, blunter teeth, a blunt lance-headed tip, and a slightly mat or grainy surface. Its fat taproots are dirty white. There is very little red in a true *T. officinale.*

Pure *T. erythrospermum* specimens are smaller than their more famous counterparts. Their red flower stems are shorter, narrower, and more rubbery, their leaves darker and finer, with sharp, rakelike teeth that go all the way to the end, forming a shallow arrowhead at the tip. *T. erythrospermum* foliage is smooth and dark green, and often forms a dense, convex hummock, as opposed to *T. officinale*'s bowl-shaped foliage. Its taproots are reddish tan, pencil-thin, and often forked. As both the common and species names imply (*erythrospermum* means "red-seeded" in Greek), this species bears red seeds.

That said, both dandelions exuberantly crosspollinate, passing genes back and forth from species to species and hybrid to hybrid with such abandon that a single yard may host a dozen variations. Fortunately, all are largely interchangeable for herbal purposes.

Every part of the dandelion except the flower stem is edible in some capacity, and when collected in season and properly prepared, all are excellent. Beginning at the top, dandelion blossoms make a delicious appetizer when fried or sautéed (see Recipes, page 199). Some foragers even throw a few raw ones in salads. They have a sweet, mild flavor without a hint of bitterness, as long as the stem and most of the green parts are removed.

Dandelion blossoms also yield the world's most famous flower wine. A mellow, somewhat tangy golden elixir, poets craft metaphors such as "distilled sunshine" or "spring in a jug" to describe this once-common delicacy. Dandelion wine's aging requirements are such that the annual batch is tapped just as the longest winter nights roll around. Dandelion wine is therefore a traditional Christmas treat in rural Europe. As with other classic farmer wines, the fermenting process can be as simple or as complex as the maker desires. Some recipes are extremely straightforward, while others challenge the most accomplished winemaker. Most home winemaking guides include at least one dandelion wine recipe. Some include several, spanning various levels of difficulty. Dandelions have also been brewed with beer. Dandelion blossoms and roots were fermented with other wild herbs such as dock and nettle to make fizzy soft drinks that were sold at public events from the Middle Ages up until the nineteenth century. These concoctions are the ancestors of North America's root beer, as well as a modern British soda pop called dandelion and burdock.

The tightly clenched, pellet-like flower buds clasped at the plant's center just before the stems shoot skyward are an uncommon treat. The approximate size, shape, and color of green peas, they can be added to the skillet while frying greens, steamed alone, or sautéed in butter or olive oil and served as a side dish.

Young dandelion greens are the quintessential spring tonic, bursting with nutrients, with a bitter-tart zip that relegates bland winter fare to memory. While the commercial dandelion greens sold by some specialty greengrocers have been engineered to remain palatable for several weeks, the wild variety must be cut very early. This is particularly important if the leaves are to be eaten raw. As the most well-known wild green, dandelion is the first, and often the last, wild vegetable many would-be foragers attempt, because they don't know that dandelion leaves become extremely bitter once the plant flowers. Dandelion has this in common with many cultivated vegetables, but, unlike them, the plant seldom attracts attention before it blossoms.

Picked in season, dandelion greens make a sublime salad, and are perhaps the best fried greens there are. I find red-seeded dandelion, or hybrids with a lot of *Taraxacum erythrospermum* characteristics, more palatable than *T. officinale,* especially raw. Those who make their own pasta will find that dandelion greens produce highly flavored and colored noodles if substituted for spinach in noodle recipes.

Dandelion leaf crowns are a rare treat, available only in early spring. The crown is that part of the leaf rosette between the ground and the point where the broad, thin, green part of the leaves begins, roughly one to two inches of white stem. These must be collected before the plant flowers. Slice off the plant at ground level, then remove the leaves and set them aside to be cooked separately or reunited with the crowns in a salad. Thoroughly wash the crowns, which at this point resemble a stiff, round brush, taking care to remove any foreign matter nestled between the stem bases. Tossed with a salad and served with vinaigrette dressing, they add a crunch and slightly nutty flavor not entirely different from artichoke. In a salad of store-bought ingredients, crisp white dandelion crowns keep guests guessing. Some foragers steam or sauté young dandelion crowns as a side dish. Though I find them so delightful raw that cooking seems almost criminal, I confess to having once substituted dandelion crowns for artichokes in a Spanish paella recipe, adding them at the very end to preserve their crispness, with very satisfactory results.

Having eaten the plant to the ground, we are left with the taproot. Some foragers peel this with a potato peeler and parboil it as a vegetable. I find the small, red, hard-to-peel roots of red-seeded dandelion edible when prepared this way, but far too labor-intensive and not especially interesting. Common dandelion's carrot-sized white taproots are easier to collect and prepare, but are so bitter as to be inedible. Evidently they require multiple boilings, which I generally avoid. In any case, dandelion roots destined to be eaten as a vegetable must be dug before the plant flowers.

Making coffee-like beverages is where dandelion taproots really excel. As a tea drinker I find that dandelion coffee tastes just as bad as the real thing, but my wife likes coffee, so with her cooperation I've put dandelion coffee through rigorous trials. Nathalie has pronounced the results acceptable, even tempting. In her opinion, there is little difference between coffee made from red-seeded and common dandelion roots; therefore I collect the larger ones. While some authorities impose a number of qualifications on acceptable roots, such as how old they must be or in what season they must be dug, Nathalie has not noticed enough difference between them to warrant so much fuss. I fiddle up a few roots while I'm collecting other things, mostly in the spring but in other seasons as well, and dry them until I get enough to warrant roasting and grinding.

As a general rule, the size of a dandelion root is comparable to the diameter of its flower stems. (Leaf size and stem length don't seem to have any relation to root size.) Occasionally a dandelion with a huge, misshapen flower stem turns up, and these inevitably have the biggest roots of all. Soil composition has everything to do with how efficiently dandelion roots may be gathered and how large they get. Sandy or loamy ground is best. Very rocky ground or soil that contains a lot of clay produces small roots that are hard to fiddle up.

To make coffee, I briefly scrub the taproots clean with a toothbrush under running water, then split them down the middle. Very fat ones are quartered. (At this point they can be air-dried for later processing if necessary.) I spread the pieces in a single layer on a baking sheet or pie tin and roast at 250°F until they are dry and snap smartly. Then I turn the heat up to 350°F and roast the roots until they are deep brown throughout, with a savory, smoky, coffee-like aroma. The entire house fills with a most delicious odor during this process. The roasted roots are then ground with a coffee grinder, grain mill, or mortar and pestle, and sealed in an airtight container. Dandelion taproots roast down to nothing, so it takes a good bucketful of fresh ones to make an appreciable amount of coffee. Fortunately, dandelions are everywhere, and landowners don't mind giving them away.

Ground roasted dandelion taproots can be percolated alone, added to real coffee, or mixed with other herbal coffee substitutes such as juniper berries and chicory. Nathalie uses a glass-knobbed percolator, the old-fashioned kind that gurgles and sighs. She feels it

> **Whole books could be written** about dandelion and its uses. As a matter of fact, one already has been. For an in-depth examination of this multipurpose herb, see Peter Gail's *The Dandelion Celebration,* listed in Further Reading.

does a better job than newfangled drip coffee machines on dandelion coffee.

Dandelion's medicinal honor roll is long and illustrious. It is best known as a diuretic, as the modern French name *pissenlit* and archaic English equivalent "piss-the-bed" attest. Dandelion greens contain significant quantities of vitamins A and C as well as potassium, calcium, and iron, and have been a respected liver tonic since the advent of medicine. Science affirms their salutary effect, giving dandelion the nod for such liver-related conditions as jaundice, hepatitis, high blood pressure, gallstones, and even radiation poisoning. Dandelion taproots also contain large amounts of inulin, a starch substitute of value to diabetics. (See *Helianthus,* page 152.)

Dandelion's alkaline nature makes it handy for treating heartburn and other pH imbalances, and it helps build and maintain healthy skin, teeth, and bones. Dandelion wine is an ancient anodyne, in case anyone needs an excuse to drink it. Tea brewed from fresh or dried leaves has the same reputation, though it is not as pleasant a regimen. European and North American country folk have squeezed dandelion's milky sap onto warts. Reliable accounts suggest that this treatment, faithfully pursued over a period of weeks, kills warts as effectively as commercial salicylic acid preparations, though some suggest that only the sap of older plants is effective.

Trifolium

North Americans generally leave clover (genus *Trifolium*) to the bees and cows, but in the past this unlikely herb supported First Nations and European cultures. Limited practicality keeps clover out of the top ten most useful herbs, but its sheer ubiquity makes it worth knowing.

Clovers occur virtually everywhere in subarctic North America. Red clover (*T. pratense*) is raised commercially for fodder and to nourish honeybees. It is a sparse, leggy plant, reaching a foot or two above the ground, with large oval leaves occurring in groups of three at the ends of the branches. Red clover seldom turns up in lawns and gardens, but is extremely common on unmanaged or marginally managed land such as vacant lots, parks, and neglected corners of yards.

Japanese clover (*T. repens*) is the most widespread white-flowering species. An alternate common name, Dutch clover, suggests some confusion about the origins of this clover. *T. repens* is a familiar lawn pest, its dense, tender foliage creating lush islands in unmowed grass. Red clovers are the ones most used for herbal applications, apparently because they are bigger and cultures that used clover had no other. But white clover can be used in the same ways, and its leaves

Japanese or Dutch white clover (*Trifolium repens*).

may even be superior to its red clover counterparts for taste and texture.

Before the time of European contact, Pacific Northwest tribes harvested tremendous quantities of red clover roots from coastal prairies in the spring and fall. After washing the dirt from the roots, they dried them in sun or smoke, then tied the dried roots into bundles and stored them for later use. When needed, the roots were steamed or boiled, dipped in fish oil, and devoured with great appetite. First Nations peoples still use clover rhizomes to thicken soups.

Because processing significant quantities of clover root is tedious and requires digging up a lot of ground, using it as the First Nations do isn't feasible for most suburban foragers. However, rural European societies relish clover greens, usually sautéed in butter. They taste like hay to me, but I do enjoy them mixed with other greens or used to add texture and flavor to bland foods such as mashed potatoes and polenta. Sautéed clover greens can also serve as a bed for steamed fish or shellfish. Raw clover leaves are

Trifolium is a member of the botanical family Fabaceae along with beans and peanuts. Those who are allergic to these or other legumes should steer clear of clover. Even those who are not allergic should proceed with caution, as our comparatively primitive digestive system doesn't do as good a job in breaking down clover greens as a cow's four-chambered, three-stage model. For this reason, a bellyful of clover, particularly raw clover, may lead to extreme gastric discomfort in humans. Finally, only true clovers, those belonging to genus *Trifolium*, should be eaten. Sweet clover (genus *Melilotus*) can be very dangerous if not processed and administered correctly.

sometimes tossed in salads, but foragers should exercise restraint, as gastric upset could result if too many are eaten at once.

Clover blossoms are of greater interest, at least to me. Dry clover blossoms using the paper-bag method, and then pull the petals from the domelike green base with your fingers. Clover petals make a fragrant tea by themselves, and blend readily with mint, goldenrod, and other tea-mixing herbs. They may also be stirred into muffins and sweet breads to add texture, sweetness, and fiber, or kneaded into butter and served with hot scones or muffins.

Clover greens are high in protein, calcium, and vitamin C. Thanks to their fiber content, they are an effective laxative if used sparingly. Practitioners of holistic medicine recommend clover flower tea as a blood purifier and to relieve bronchial spasms.

Urtica

Nettle (genus *Urtica*) is in a league with dandelion for usefulness, and is just as underexploited today. At least two great cultures were founded on this productive plant. Medieval European monks and nuns, the greatest scholars of their time, depended on it. The monastic diet was based on nettle broth, tea, and boiled greens. Nettle root soup was virtually the only dish served in the severest orders. Yet the standard of health among monks and nuns remained higher than that of people outside the walls. More permissive houses brewed nettle beer, or used the leaves to curdle milk for cheese. Monastics wore habits woven from nettle fibers, sowed nettles in fallow ground as a green manure, boiled the plant whole to make liquid fertilizer and organic pesticide, and whipped their bare backs with bundles of fresh nettles to strengthen their spiritual discipline. Nettle also figured highly in monastic medicine. A regimen of nettle broth was often imposed on patients automatically, pending diagnosis. Today, banks of nettle veil monastery ruins all over Europe, an ever-faithful servant shielding the bones of the once-great monastic system from the mocking view of the profane.

On the other side of the planet, North Pacific coastal tribes slurped steamed nettle shoots and nettle root soup while building their own highly advanced culture. Nettle was used to mortify the flesh and concentrate the mind in North Coast religious rituals, while the harpooneer—central figure of the whale hunt and an important religious figure—plunged his hand into a bag of nettles to prevent his thoughts from wandering as he searched the misty ocean. North Coast First Nations used fibers from pounded nettle stems to spin cordage so strong that a line of just three- or four-fiber weight could bring a ten-foot halibut canoe-side. Nettle fiber nets made industrial-scale salmon fishing a reality, which in turn formed the basis of the entire North Coast economy. It is not an exaggeration to say that North Coast history would have been dramatically different had nettle not been available, and had indigenous peoples not had the ingenuity to exploit it.

Suburban foragers have little call for reef nets or homespun fabric, but nettle's food value, both in nutritional and aesthetic terms, propels it to the forefront of wild greens. Redundantly named stinging nettle (*U. dioica*), a native species with a dozen or more regional subspecies, is the most common nettle in North America. Introduced species also crop up from time to time. All have heart- or spade-shaped leaves with sharply toothed edges, covered with stinging hairs. On nettle's square stems these hairs become fine spines. The young leaves are purplish, especially underneath, while cascades of grainy yellow flowers droop from the leaf junctions from late spring to mid-summer, then ripen into seeds. Nettle looks like a hairy, oversized mint, to which it is a close cousin. It prefers shade and moist, rich soil, and usually gets about waist high, though it can reach six feet under optimum conditions.

Stinging nettle (*Urtica dioica*).

Nettles appear in March or April in most regions. Shoots to about eight inches are edible. They should be cut rather than plucked, to avoid ripping up roots and rhizomes and disrupting the colony's ability to recover. For the same reason, I avoid collecting subterranean parts, although they too are edible. If a neighbor were eradicating a nettle patch, however, I might ask permission to gather roots for soup.

Scissors or pruning shears are good choices for collecting nettle greens. Where young shoots form a thick carpet, lawn-trimming shears are most efficient. Slice off several shoots at each pass by sliding the blades along the ground and closing them. When a sufficient number have been "mown," simply scoop them into a sack.

As it happens, I enjoyed a pot of nettle soup (see "Cooking with Greens," page 186) for lunch before I sat down to write this section. While I was washing the shoots, a single spine pierced the flimsy latex surgical glove I was wearing. That was four hours ago, and my thumb still burns as if it just happened. The

Cooking with Greens

A resourceful cook can do many things with wild greens besides frying them. Here are just a few tempting techniques:

· Tender young leaves make good salad greens. Those too strong to eat alone can be torn up and added to store-bought or garden greens to create healthier, more interesting salads.

· For a thick, creamy soup, steam wild greens in stock until tender, add an equal amount of milk or cream, and whirl in a blender until smooth.

· Steamed greens simmered in a cream sauce or partly diluted condensed cream soup, such as mushroom or chicken, make a delicious side dish. Creamed greens can also be served on a "shingle" (a slice of toast), diner-fashion. This is a particularly good way to use strong-tasting greens.

· Steamed greens dress up a grilled cheese sandwich. Place a slice of ham or some soft-cooked bacon on a slice of bread, then layer the greens on top. Add sliced cheese last, then grill the sandwich as usual. The result is tasty beyond description. Dandelion greens are especially good this way.

· For a rich sauce base, simmer greens and seasonings in plain tomato sauce, then run greens and sauce through a blender until smooth. Meat and vegetables can then be added to make pasta or pizza sauce.

· Fresh whole leaves can be layered into lasagna, pizza, calzones, or Wild Greens Rockefeller (see Recipes, page 197).

· Pepper tames bitter greens. Very strong greens (or roots) are often palatable in chili or other spicy dishes. Other approaches involve soaking the leaves in an acid solution (a tablespoon of vinegar, lemon, or sumac juice per quart of water) before cooking, or adding a pinch of baking soda to the cooking water. Foragers who don't mind the extra work and lost food value can fall back on the old standby, multiple boilings.

moral is: Nettles demand respect. Leather gloves must be worn for collecting, and heavy rubber or vinyl ones, such as those made for dishwashing, for processing.

Fresh nettle greens have a complex bouquet, mingling faint mint overtones with a hint of the seashore. Boiled shoots make a good bed for steamed or baked salmon, and fresh ones can form a bed for steamed clams, then be eaten as a side dish. I call the blue-green water left over from steaming the shoots "nettle nectar" because it tastes something like clam nectar and can be used similarly. Mix nettle nectar with tomato juice for a refreshing, super-nutritious drink. Eggs poached in nettle nectar, with perhaps a dash of red wine, and served on toast make a sublime lunch or late supper. To prepare nettle broth, boil shoots in enough water to cover until they are completely soft, then run the shoots and water through a blender and strain through wet muslin. This broth can be eaten alone or used as a protein-rich vegetarian soup stock. Non-vegetarians will appreciate the added richness of nettle broth made with chicken or lamb stock.

Nettles are delectable fried, though their slight fuzziness puts some people off. An easy and delicious way to camouflage nettle greens' novel texture is to cook them into an omelette. For one omelette, crack three eggs into a cup and beat slightly with a quarter cup of milk. Prepare fried nettles (see Fried Greens in the recipe section), but omit the bread crumbs. When the nettles are almost done, pour the egg mixture into the pan, turn with a fork to blend evenly, cover the frying pan, and reduce heat to medium. Cook until the eggs are completely set. Remove the pan from the heat and carefully fold the omelette with a spatula. Serve with tangy red seafood cocktail sauce. I like to eat this the way God intended, straight from my cast iron frying pan.

Nettle shoots are only available a few weeks a year, but they freeze well if blanched first. Dried and powdered, they can be used as a dehydrated stock base or seasoning. The easiest way to dry nettle shoots is to wash them well, then hang them upside down in a dry place until they are completely brittle. The dried shoots powder more readily if they are popped for a minute or so into an oven prewarmed at the lowest setting.

Few vegetables, wild or domestic, approach nettle for nutritional value. Protein-wise, it outperforms beans, without causing their infamous side effects. Nettle shoots pack a significant wallop of iron, vitamins A and C, calcium, magnesium, and a long list of other nutrients. Young leaves and seeds are dried for use in a medicinal tea for joint pain. It seems the monks of old Europe were right to put patients on nettle broth, since in addition to being a nourishing, easily digested liquid diet, nettle broth is hypoallergenic. Even the sting is a respected folk remedy. Intentionally inflicting nettle rash, a procedure known as "urtication," has long been prescribed for gout, rheumatism, and depression, a practice that actually appears to have some basis in fact. Scientists attribute nettle's effects to the release of endorphins and enriched blood flow to afflicted areas, both occasioned by intense pain. Also, psychologists believe some depression is rooted in guilt, which punishment of a sort may dispel. Traditional cultures have known this for ages, as monastic and North Coast societies, nettles in hand, confirm.

> **Each little hair or spine on a nettle plant is really a hollow tube containing a minuscule amount of formic acid (the same substance that puts the fire in fire ants). When brushed, the hairs stab into the skin, break, and deliver their payload. Thus, nettle's fiery dermatitis is really a multitude of microscopic chemical burns. Thorough cooking or drying disarms this defensive system, so boiling in several changes of water, as some sources advise, is unnecessary. Nettles become toxic when they flower, so medicinal infusions should not be made from over-ripe nettles. And they make a lousy salad at any stage.**

Dyers' Notes

The flowering tops of St. John's wort (*Hypericum perforatum*) give a yellow dye on alum-mordanted fibers, or red with tin and a little vinegar.

Plantain yields yellow-green when chopped, infused, and paired with an alum mordant. Dock can be used the same way. If the root alone is used, it gives a brighter yellow.

Poke berries are often listed as dyestuffs, but experts say they aren't worth the trouble because their shades aren't colorfast.

Goldenrod, a major dyestuff in times past, produces a very colorfast yellowish tan with alum, gold with chrome, and green with iron mordants. Only the flowering tops are used, and must be infused fresh because the dried product gives disappointing results.

Tansy's aerial parts give a grass green color with a tin mordant, pale yellow with alum.

Dandelion counts dye source among its other accolades. The whole plant is chopped to render greyish purple on iron-mordanted wool, purplish red with alum, and a buttery yellow with no mordant at all.

Aside from producing fiber for weaving, nettle yields greenish yellow on alum-treated stock when aerial parts of young plants are infused.

 Foraging Advisory

Experienced foragers may wonder why poke (genus *Phytolacca*) and milkweed (genus *Asclepias*), both traditional wild edibles, are not included in these pages. The short answer is that both require multiple boilings, which conflicts with the limited-fuss theme of this book. Both (especially poke) are also dangerous if not processed correctly. Interested readers will find detailed processing information about both plants in Euell Gibbons' *Stalking the Wild Asparagus* and Steve Brill's *Identifying and Harvesting Edible and Medicinal Plants in Wild (and Not So Wild) Places* (see Further Reading).

St. John's wort (*Hypericum perforatum*) has become a trendy medicinal herb. While a body of scientific evidence supports its use as an antidepressant, just as much evidence indicates that St. John's wort slows down the heart, and may stop it completely in severe cases. It also heightens photosensitivity in some individuals. Therefore, I can't recommend St. John's wort as a good candidate for self-treatment by amateur herbalists.

The nightshades, an informal group of genera whose poisonous nature has been celebrated since the invention of drama, are common weeds in many neighborhoods. Every year, poison centers treat children lured in by their bright, translucent fruits, many of which bear a remarkable resemblance to jelly beans. There are too many nightshades to list them all here, but one of the most common is climbing nightshade (*Solanum dulcamara*), which shares a genus with eggplant and potato. Also called European bittersweet, this viny perennial bears tough, heart-shaped leaves; tiny, drooping, neon blue flowers; and berries that ripen jewel red, looking like tiny Roma tomatoes, another close relative. Climbing nightshade fruits are middling toxic, its foliage virulently so. Fellow *Solanum* black night-shade (*S. nigrum*) is bushier, with black stems and leaf highlights, white flowers, and round, pea-sized berries that ripen into black glass beads. Deadly nightshade (*Atropa belladonna*) has rather unattractive, vase-shaped, brownish red flowers and lustrous black fruits embedded in a heavy green calyx. Although some nightshades actually bear edible fruit, none of them are worth the risk.

Though the seeds of Queen Anne's lace (genus *Daucus*) are sometimes used as a caraway-like spice, they are not included in this chapter because I don't find them flavorful enough to risk accidentally harvesting seeds from other, poisonous members of the family Apiaceae (formerly listed as Umbelliferae), many of which are easily confused with *Daucus*. Horrifically dangerous examples are poison hemlock (*Conium maculatum*), found in the same poor, dry soil favored by *Daucus*, and water hemlock (genus *Cicuta*), which grows along ditches and streams. Before harvesting *Daucus*, foragers must be certain they can identify these and other poisonous local look-alikes.

Iris (genus *Iris*) rhizomes look something like Jerusalem artichokes, but they are poisonous. Unlike their edible look-alikes, iris rhizomes grow on top of the soil or partially buried, and their light-colored skin is rough and thick, with visible growth rings. Iris foliage doesn't look anything like that of *Helianthus*. The flower stalk is smooth and wiry, and the leaves, which grow straight out of the rhizomes, look like giant blades of grass.

Tansy (*Tanacetum vulgare*) is a traditional culinary and medicinal herb in Europe. I used to use it like sage to season chili and other highly flavored dishes, until I uncovered reliable research suggesting that this could be dangerous. Tansy is a tall, feathery weed that is rife in some areas. In summer it sets broad umbels of vibrant, mustard yellow, button-shaped flowers that have no petals. But the most telling feature is the powerful, savory-sweet odor tansy releases when crushed. This odor is caused by thujone, the same chemical found in cedar and other aromatic (and toxic) lacy-scaly evergreens. The problem is, tansy's thujone levels vary widely from place to place and even season to season. I might enjoy tansy-enhanced chili for years without experiencing any side effects, and then one day a bowl of it could kill me. I no longer use tansy as food or medicine, though I still hang bunches indoors to freshen rooms with its pleasant, insect-repelling aroma.

Though tansy ragwort (*Senecio jacobaea*) is called "tansy" in many locales, it is unrelated to real tansy. Tansy ragwort sets clustered yellow flowers that recall the real thing but have petals and daisy-like morphology. It also has a vague, musty odor, entirely different from *Tanacetum's* pungent, fairly pleasant smell. Like other members of its vast genus, tansy ragwort is poisonous to stock. It doesn't do people any favors, either.

The loss of watercress (*Nasturtium officinale*) is as dramatic an indicator of environmental degradation as northern spotted owl or snail darter populations, but there is unfortunately no watercress lobby, so the chances of recovering this priceless resource are nil. To be sure, riotous underwater mats of the pale green vines with fine white roots still choke streams and ditches across the continent, their classic broccoli-leaf-shaped mustard foliage and tiny white flowers reaching a few inches above the surface. Sadly, none of it is edible; water pollution and biological contamination have poisoned all the wild watercress in North America. Some foragers simply can't live without cool, crisp, piquant watercress, so luscious in salads, soup, and sandwiches, so they soak locally foraged cress in water treated with water purification tablets purchased at camping supply stores. This eliminates amoebas, *Giardia lamblia, Escherichia coli,* and other pathogens, but it can't do anything about polychlorinated biphenyls (PCBs), petroleum, pesticides, and all the other toxins present in suburban wetlands. The loss of watercress is as tragic as the disappearance of American chestnut. It may even be worse; at least the chestnuts aren't still around, mocking us with bumper crops of delicious but poisonous nuts year after year. Nevertheless, foragers should steer clear of the wild watercress they encounter in streams and ditches, no matter where they are.

Cattail (*Typha latifolia*) is comparable to nettle and dandelion for versatility and food value. It is also surprisingly well represented in urbanized areas, its characteristic reedlike leaves and corn-dog flowers appearing anywhere the soil remains saturated year-round. Unfortunately, suburban foragers have far less access to this resource than do their rural counterparts. To begin with, cattails play an important role in purifying water and stabilizing erosion, major concerns in residential areas. Not only must suburban cattail tubers and rootstocks, perhaps the plant's most valuable edibles, remain undisturbed to preserve viability, but nestled as they are in toxic mud, they represent a health threat. The same goes for shoots, pith, and green flower spikes, all valuable edibles. Depredation would weaken the colony's ability to perform its environmental services. What's more, all the pollutants cattails filter out have to go somewhere. My guess is they're in the plant's tissues.

The only cattail resource suburban foragers can reasonably exploit is pollen. This heavy golden powder thickly coats cattail's cylindrical flowers in midsummer. It doesn't harm the colony to take some, and suburban foragers are unlikely to find enough of it to endanger their health with any trace elements that might be present. Harvest cattail pollen by pulling a plastic bread wrapper over the top of the flower and shaking the flower stem vigorously. A dusting of yellow powder will collect in the bottom of the bag. By repeating the process with other flowers, a usable quantity can be obtained. Added to baked goods such as bread, muffins, and pancakes, cattail pollen enhances color, flavor, texture, and protein content.

Recipes

Chinese Colcannon

SERVES 6.

Chinese peasants make an amaranth and potato stew powerfully reminiscent of colcannon, a potato and cabbage dish popular with Scottish common folk. As a fan of both colcannon and amaranth, I blend the two recipes.

4 large potatoes, or 6 medium ones, peeled and quartered
About $1/4$ cup buttermilk
2 pounds tender young amaranth shoots, washed (a bundle about 6 inches in diameter)
1 clove garlic, pressed or minced
1 medium onion, chopped
2 tablespoons fresh chickweed or parsley, chopped (or 1 tablespoon dried)
1 tablespoon corn or peanut oil
1 tablespoon soy sauce
Freshly ground black pepper to taste

Place the potatoes in a large saucepan with enough water to cover. Cover the pan and bring it to a boil. Reduce the heat to medium-high and boil the potatoes for 20 minutes, or until tender.

Drain off the water, return the pan to the heat and shake it vigorously to dry the potatoes, about 30 seconds. Remove the pan from the heat.

Mash the potatoes thoroughly with a potato masher or electric mixer. Beat in just enough buttermilk to make the mashed potatoes smooth and fluffy.

Cover the potatoes and keep them warm until the amaranth is ready.

Coarsely chop the amaranth shoots and place them in a small dish. Place the minced garlic and chopped onion together in a second dish, and place both dishes near the stove.

Heat a wok or heavy frying pan over high heat, swirl in the oil and wait 30 seconds.

Add the garlic and onion and toss for 30 seconds.

Add the chickweed or parsley and amaranth, and toss until bright green (or red), about 1 minute.

Add the soy sauce and toss the vegetables until coated.

Remove the wok or frying pan from the heat and fold the amaranth mixture gently into the mashed potatoes.

Serve hot, with a generous grinding of black pepper.

Velouté d'Asperges Japonaises
(Creamy Knotweed Soup)

SERVES 6.

Velouté literally means "velvety," a fitting description for this tangy soup. *Asperges japonaises* is French for "Japanese asparagus." The white lie and French name fool many a picky eater into liking this elegant dish.

> 1 pound knotweed shoots (about sixteen 6-inch shoots,
> 3/4-inch thick at the base) · 1 large clove garlic
> 4 cups chicken stock · 1/2 teaspoon dill or caraway seeds
> 1/2 cup chopped onion · Salt and pepper to taste
> Butter and chives, if desired

Place all ingredients except the butter and chives in a large pot and bring it to a boil. Lower the heat and simmer until the shoots are soft, about 10 minutes.

Pour the vegetables and broth into a blender. To avoid a potentially dangerous mess, fill the pitcher no more than half-full, then place a folded dishtowel on top and hold the lid down firmly while turning on the blades. Blend until the soup is smooth, repeating with the rest if necessary.

Return the soup to the pot and reheat. The velouté should be a bit thinner than split pea soup, a bit thicker than a cream soup. If it is too thick, add water while reheating.

Serve hot, with a pat of butter in the middle and a sprinkling of chives if desired.

Japanese Rhubarb Sauce

MAKES 2 PINTS.

Knotweed can be a "fruit" or a vegetable, as the situation warrants. This chunky sauce is made from 1- to 2-foot shoots and resembles a syrupy jam. It's delicious on pancakes and toast or in filled cookies.

> 4 cups 1/4-inch knotweed rings
> 1 cup sugar
> 1/2 teaspoon nutmeg

Place all ingredients in a large saucepan and stir until the sugar absorbs liquid from the knotweed and becomes syrupy.

Place the pan over low heat and stir until the sugar dissolves completely. Bring the mixture briefly to a boil, then lower the heat and simmer until the rings are completely soft. "Japanese rhubarb" sauce may be served immediately, refrigerated for two or three weeks, or canned like jam for later use.

Tortilla Campesina

MAKES ONE LARGE OMELETTE.

Sorrel and mint enliven this *tortilla,* or omelette, from rural Spain. Unlike traditional North American omelettes, this one isn't folded. Rather, it is flipped like a pancake, browned on the upper side, and served "in the round." Measuring the greens is a subjective art, since the amount depends on the type and character of greens available.

1 handful each of two wild greens, such as dock, dandelion, or nettle
1 tablespoon butter or olive oil
1 small red onion, chopped
Half a handful of sorrel leaves
$1/2$ teaspoon fresh mint, minced
2 anchovies, minced, or $1/2$ teaspoon anchovy paste
1 tablespoon chopped parsley or chickweed
4 eggs, slightly beaten
Salt and pepper to taste

Wash the greens and sorrel. Tear them up separately, then place the greens in a saucepan and steam them in just the water left from washing. Remove from heat and drain.

Melt the butter or heat the olive oil over medium heat and sauté the onion in it. Add the steamed greens, sorrel, mint, anchovies, and parsley or chickweed, and sauté until the fresh greens are tender and bright green.

Pour in the eggs and turn to mix evenly with the greens mixture. Cook until browned on the bottom.

Loosen the tortilla with a pancake turner, then carefully flip it all the way over (don't fold). Brown it on the upper side and serve.

RECIPES

Sourdough Crêpes Stuffed with Ham and Dock

MAKES 12 CRÊPES.

There's no two ways about it: this is posh nosh. Ordinary crêpes can be substituted, though they haven't got sourdough's rich flavor. Other wild greens or steamed knotweed spears can be substituted for the dock.

SAUCE:

1 can condensed cream of mushroom soup
1/2 cup onion, chopped
1 clove garlic, crushed
1 tablespoon cooking sherry
1/4 cup water
1/2 teaspoon soy sauce
Freshly ground black pepper to taste

CREPES:

2 cups sourdough starter, the sourer (hungrier) the better
2 tablespoons sugar
4 tablespoons salad oil
2 eggs
1 teaspoon baking soda, divided
4 tablespoons lukewarm water, divided

FILLING:

8 cups fresh young dock leaves, tightly packed
12 thin slices of ham

Mix the sauce ingredients together in a saucepan and simmer them until the onions are tender. If the sauce is too thick, thin it with water. Move it to a back burner and keep it warm.

Beat all the crêpe ingredients together except for the soda and water. Divide the batter in half. Dissolve 1/2 teaspoon of the soda in 2 tablespoons of lukewarm water.

Heat a sautéing pan, frying pan, or griddle to medium-high. (Cast iron implements work best.) When ready to begin frying, grease the cooking surface, then drop the dissolved soda into one half of the batter and stir briefly. The batter will immediately begin to rise, eventually reaching as much as twice its former level.

Begin frying. The faster the crêpes are made after the soda has been added, the better. (Contrary to usual crêpe protocol, I brown sourdough crêpes on both sides, like pancakes.) Keep the first batch of crêpes warm while repeating the process with the second half of the batter, then keep all of them warm while preparing the filling and sauce.

Wash the dock leaves and place them in a saucepan with no more than the water left from rinsing. Steam the leaves over medium-high heat until they are limp. Drain and turn them onto a warm plate.

Place crêpes, sauce, dock, and ham slices side by side on a counter or table with an empty dinner plate and a warm serving platter. Lay the crêpes one at a time on the plate, place a slice of ham on top, spoon cooked greens over it and ladle on a little sauce. Roll up the crêpe and place it on the serving platter. Repeat until all the crêpes are stuffed and lying side by side on the platter. Pour the remaining sauce over the top and serve immediately.

Stir-fried Chickweed

SERVES 6.

A simple vegetarian dish that makes a quick lunch or side dish.

1 tablespoon corn or peanut oil
1 small onion, chopped
2 tablespoons peanuts or cashews, chopped
5 cups fresh chickweed, chopped
1 teaspoon fresh ginger, finely chopped
1 tablespoon soy sauce
Steamed rice

Heat a wok over high heat and swirl in the oil.

Add onions and stir-fry for 30 seconds.

Add nuts and toss for 20 seconds.

Add chickweed and ginger and toss to coat. Sprinkle soy sauce over the greens and toss them just until they become bright green, generally about 30 seconds.

Remove the wok from the heat, spoon the chickweed over steamed rice, and serve.

Fried Greens

Convincing people to try their first helping of fried wild greens can be a challenge, but the second requires no salesmanship at all. This traditional Southern and Mediterranean dish is down-home cooking at its finest. Eligible greens include young knotweed leaves, dandelion, dock, plantain, chicory, sorrel, chickweed, nettles, and mustard leaves, or any mixture thereof. After washing, tear the leaves into pieces, then steam them briefly in just the water left on the leaves. When they wilt and turn bright green, typically a matter of minutes, turn them into a colander or sieve to drain. The greens are then ready for frying. Like spinach, wild greens shrink to about a fifth of their raw volume when cooked. Foragers should therefore gather about five times more than the desired final quantity.

Fried greens make a fine lunch in and of themselves, or a nice side dish for fried or broiled fish. For a hearty twist, stir fried greens into hot tomato soup.

Here are only two of many possible variations.

Southern-Style Greens

Serves 6 as a side dish, 2 as a main dish.

2 strips bacon
1/4 cup chopped onions
1 clove garlic, sliced thin
1/3 cup dry bread crumbs
1/4 teaspoon each sage and thyme
1 hard-boiled egg, chopped
3 cups steamed wild greens
1 teaspoon cider vinegar
Freshly ground black pepper to taste

Fry the bacon in a heavy frying pan. Spread the fried strips on paper towels to drain. Briefly pour off the grease. (Do not allow the pan to drip completely, as a thin layer of grease is needed for the next step.)

Reheat the pan over medium-high heat, or until a piece of onion actively sizzles. Sauté the onion and garlic in the residual bacon drippings until the pieces begin to soften. Add the bread crumbs, sage, and thyme, and toss with a spatula until the crumbs are browned. Scoop the mixture into a bowl, shred the bacon on top of it, and add the chopped hard-boiled egg. Set aside.

Return the frying pan to the heat. When it is sizzling hot, dump in the greens and fry for a minute or so, keeping them moving with the spatula.

Return the crumb mixture to the pan and toss briefly to mix. Sprinkle the greens with vinegar and pepper, remove from the heat, and serve piping hot.

Mediterranean-Style Greens

SERVES 6 AS A SIDE DISH, 2 AS A MAIN DISH.

1 tablespoon olive oil
1 clove garlic, pressed
$1/4$ cup chopped onion
$1/4$ cup chopped pepperoni
$1/4$ cup dry French bread crumbs
2 tablespoons freshly grated Parmesan cheese
$1/4$ teaspoon each rosemary and thyme
Ground cayenne pepper to taste
3 cups steamed wild greens
1 teaspoon red wine vinegar

Swirl the olive oil into a heavy frying pan, and sauté the garlic, onion, and pepperoni over medium-high heat until the garlic and onion are translucent.

Add the bread crumbs, Parmesan cheese, and seasonings, and brown. (The Parmesan cheese will "pop" in the heat. Tossing with a spatula while browning minimizes the disorder.) Remove the crumb mixture to a bowl and set aside.

Add the greens to the pan and fry for a minute or so, keeping them moving with the spatula. Add the crumb mixture and toss briefly to mix.

Sprinkle the greens with vinegar, remove the pan from the heat, and serve piping hot.

Wild Greens Rockefeller

SERVES 6.

This dish is reminiscent of the Oysters Rockefeller served in chic restaurants. I'm not sure Old Man Rockefeller would approve of his name being associated with such a proletarian dish, but it amuses me to no end.

2 cups soft bread crumbs
$1/4$ teaspoon each sage, marjoram, thyme, and dill
1 tablespoon parsley or chickweed
Salt and pepper to taste
$1/4$ cup grated cheddar cheese
16 large knotweed sprouts, cooked, or 2 cups wild greens, steamed
2 hard-boiled eggs, sliced
$1/2$ can condensed cream of mushroom soup
$1 1/2$ cups milk

Toss the bread crumbs, seasonings, and cheese together in a bowl. Line an 8-inch baking pan with half of the crumb mixture.

Gently lay the sprouts or greens on top of the crumb layer, lay the sliced hard-boiled eggs over them, and cover them with the rest of the crumb mixture.

Thoroughly blend the milk and mushroom soup and pour over the top.

Bake at 400°F until bubbly, about 25 minutes. Let casserole stand 5 minutes before serving.

Fattoush (Lebanese Salad)

SERVES 6.

Purslane adds cool, tangy crunch to this classic Lebanese dish, perfect for summer picnics and potlucks. Chickweed, sumac, and mint join in to make this salad a showcase of the forager's art.

DRESSING:

1/2 cup olive oil
6 tablespoons sumac or lemon juice
1 large clove garlic, crushed
Salt and pepper to taste

SALAD:

2 stale pita breads
1 head romaine or 2 heads Bibb lettuce, shredded
1 cucumber, diced
3 large tomatoes, diced
4 green onions, chopped (include some of the green part)
1/4 cup chopped fresh chickweed or parsley
3 tablespoons chopped fresh mint
1 green pepper, chopped
1 1/2 cups chopped fresh purslane

Mix the dressing and set it aside to let the flavors infuse.

Toast the pita at 375°F until crisp and lightly browned, about 15 minutes. Cool and break into 1-inch pieces.

Toss the vegetables and fresh herbs together. Add the toasted pita and dressing and toss again. Serve immediately.

Dandelion Appetizers

A heaping plate of either of these recipes, served with toothpicks or just eaten with the fingers, is a real crowd-pleaser. The blossoms should be as fresh as possible, with all traces of the bitter, milk-oozing stem removed. (The green calyx is less problematic and holds the flower together.) Rinse the flowers just before cooking and shake off the excess water.

Sautéed Dandelions

MAKES ABOUT TWO DOZEN.

1 cup flour
$1/4$ teaspoon black pepper
$1/2$ teaspoon each thyme, marjoram, sage, and paprika
Salt to taste
24 dandelion blossoms
3 tablespoons oil

Thoroughly blend the dry ingredients and spread the mixture on a dinner plate. Place the plate and the blossoms near the stove.

Swirl the oil into a frying pan and heat over medium heat, until a pinch of flour sizzles and browns.

Use a fork to roll five or six dandelion blossoms in the flour mixture. (They should be dewy from rinsing, but not wet.) Then drop them into the hot oil. Sauté lightly until golden, generally a minute or so.

Turn the fried blossoms onto newspapers or paper towels and pop them into a warm oven.

Repeat with the rest of the blossoms, replenishing the oil as necessary. Serve hot.

Southwestern-Style Dandelion Poppers

MAKES ABOUT TWO DOZEN.

$1/2$ cup cornmeal
$1/4$ cup flour
3 tablespoons grated Parmesan cheese
$1/4$ teaspoon each ground cayenne pepper and chili powder
Salt to taste
1 egg, beaten
24 dandelion blossoms
3 tablespoons oil • Lime juice

Mix the dry ingredients thoroughly and spread the mixture on a dinner plate. Place the beaten egg in a shallow bowl, then place the egg, the plate with the cornmeal mixture, and the blossoms near the stove.

Swirl the oil into a frying pan and heat over medium heat, until a pinch of flour sizzles and browns.

Use a fork to roll five or six dandelion blossoms in the egg, then in the cornmeal mixture, and drop them into the hot oil. Fry the blossoms until crisp and golden, generally a minute or so.

Turn the fried blossoms onto newspapers or paper towels and pop them into a warm oven.

Repeat with the rest of the blossoms, replenishing the oil as necessary.

Sprinkle lime juice over the fried blossoms and serve hot.

TABLE 1: Principal Uses of Plants Listed in the Text

	Air freshener	Baking	Beverages	Candied blossoms	Chewing gum	Coffee substitute	Condiment	Fresh fruit	Fresh vegetable	Grain	Lemon juice substitute
Acer											
Agave			x								
Amaranthus										x	
Auracaria											
Arbutus											
Arctium											
Armoracia							x				
Bamboo									x		
Berberis											
Betula			x								
Calendula											
Capsella							x				
Carya											
Chenopodium										x	
Chrysanthemum											
Cichorium						x					
Conifers	x										
Cornus			x					x			
Crataegus			x								
Dianthus		x	x								
Elaeagnus											
Eschscholzia											
Eucalyptus	x										
Fagus			x			x					
Ginkgo											
Gleditsia			x								
Helianthus		x							x		
Hemerocallis											
Juglans											
Juniperus			x			x					
Lactuca/Sonchus											
Magnolia											
Mahonia			x								
Malus		x	x					x			
Matricaria			x								
Mentha			x								

Principal Uses of Plants Listed in the Text

	Medicinal Tea	Nuts	Pectin	Pickles	Pollen	Potherb	Preserves	Salads and Sandwiches	Seasoning/Flavoring	Sweetener	Yeast
Acer								x			
Agave											
Amaranthus						x					
Auracaria		x									
Arbutus							x				
Arctium						x					
Armoracia						x		x			
Bamboo						x		x			
Berberis			x				x				x
Betula											
Calendula						x		x	x		
Capsella						x		x	x		
Carya		x									
Chenopodium						x			x		
Chrysanthemum						x		x			
Cichorium						x		x			
Conifers									x		
Cornus							x				
Crataegus	x						x				
Dianthus							x		x		
Elaeagnus							x				
Eschscholzia	x										
Eucalyptus											
Fagus		x									
Ginkgo		x									
Gleditsia										x	
Helianthus						x		x			
Hemerocallis						x		x			
Juglans		x		x							
Juniperus									x		
Lactuca/Sonchus	x					x		x			
Magnolia								x	x		
Mahonia			x			x	x	x			x
Malus			x				x				
Matricaria											
Mentha								x	x		

Principal Uses of Plants Listed in the Text

	Air freshener	Baking	Beverages	Candied blossoms	Chewing gum	Coffee substitute	Condiment	Fresh fruit	Fresh vegetable	Grain	Lemon juice substitute
Morus		x	x					x			
Mustard seeds							x				
Mustards											
Oenothera											
Opuntia			x					x	x		
Picea			x		x						
Pinus											
Plantago										x	
Polygonum		x									
Portulaca											
Primula			x	x							
Prunus		x	x					x			
Rhamnus											
Rhus			x								x
Ribes		x	x					x			
Rosa		x	x	x							
Rubus		x	x					x			
Rumex-D										x	
Rumex-S			x				x				x
Salix											
Sambucus		x	x								
Solidago			x								
Sorbus			x								
Stellaria											
Tagetes											
Taraxacum			x			x			x		
Tilia			x								
Trifolium			x								
Tropaeolum											
Typha											
Urtica			x								
Viburnum		x									
Viola			x	x							
Yucca											

Principal Uses of Plants Listed in the Text

	Medicinal Tea	Nuts	Pectin	Pickles	Pollen	Potherb	Preserves	Salads and Sandwiches	Seasoning/Flavoring	Sweetener	Yeast
Morus						x	x			x	
Mustard seeds											
Mustards						x		x	x		
Oenothera						x		x			
Opuntia				x		x					
Picea									x		
Pinus		x									
Plantago	x					x		x			
Polygonum						x	x				
Portulaca				x		x		x			
Primula	x					x	x	x			
Prunus							x				x
Rhamnus	x										
Rhus						x			x		
Ribes			x				x		x		
Rosa							x		x		
Rubus			x			x	x		x		
Rumex-D						x					
Rumex-S						x		x			
Salix	x										
Sambucus							x		x		x
Solidago	x										
Sorbus							x				
Stellaria	x					x		x	x		
Tagetes									x		
Taraxacum	x					x		x			
Tilia											
Trifolium						x		x	x		
Tropaeolum				x				x	x		
Typha					x						
Urtica	x					x					
Viburnum							x				
Viola						x	x	x			
Yucca						x		x			

TABLE 2: Seasonal Availability of Plants Listed in the Text

This information is generalized. Exact seasons may vary in some regions.

	Spring			Summer			Autumn			Winter		
	Early	Mid	Late	Early	Mid	Late	Early	Mid	Late	Early	Mid	Late
ACER												
New leaves	▓											
AGAVE												
Leaf juice and pulp	▓	▓	▓	▓	▓	▓	▓	▓	▓	▓	▓	▓
AMARANTHUS												
Young greens				▓								
Seeds						▓	▓					
ARAUCARIA												
Nuts						▓						
ARBUTUS												
Fruits							▓	▓	▓			
ARCTIUM												
Leaf stems	▓											
Young flower stalks				▓								
Roots	▓	▓	▓	▓	▓	▓	▓	▓	▓	▓	▓	▓
ARMORACIA												
Leaves	▓	▓										
Roots	▓	▓	▓	▓	▓	▓	▓	▓	▓	▓	▓	▓
BAMBOO	Depends on species											
BARBAREA												
Foliage										▓	▓	▓
BETULA												
Bark	▓	▓	▓	▓	▓	▓	▓	▓	▓	▓	▓	▓
CALENDULA												
Leaves				▓	▓	▓	▓					
Flowers						▓	▓					
CAPSELLA												
Leaves	▓											
Green seed pods		▓	▓	▓	▓	▓						
Ripe seed pods			▓	▓	▓	▓	▓					
CARYA												
Nuts							▓					
CHENOPODIUM												
Young greens				▓								
Seeds						▓	▓					

Seasonal Availability of Plants Listed in the Text

	Spring			Summer			Autumn			Winter		
	Early	Mid	Late	Early	Mid	Late	Early	Mid	Late	Early	Mid	Late
CHRYSANTHEMUM												
Leaves			▓	▓								
Flowers				▓	▓							
CICHORIUM												
Leaves	▓											
Roots to eat	▓											
Roots for coffee	▓	▓	▓	▓	▓	▓	▓	▓	▓	▓	▓	▓
CORNUS												
Cornelian cherries							▓	▓				
Kousa balls							▓					
CRATAEGUS												
Flowering tops			▓	▓								
Fruits						▓	▓	▓	▓	▓		
DIANTHUS												
Blossoms				▓	▓	▓						
ELAEAGNUS												
Fruits (varies by species)						▓	▓	▓	▓	▓	▓	
ESCHSCHOLZIA												
Flowers			▓	▓								
Foliage		▓	▓	▓	▓							
EUCALYPTUS												
Nuts				▓	▓							
FAGUS												
Nuts							▓	▓				
GINKGO												
Nuts							▓					
GLEDITSIA												
Pods					▓	▓						
HELIANTHUS												
Tubers	▓	▓	▓	▓	▓	▓	▓	▓	▓	▓	▓	▓
HEMEROCALLIS												
Shoots	▓											
Flowers				▓	▓	▓						
Pods					▓	▓						
Tubers	▓	▓	▓	▓	▓	▓	▓	▓	▓	▓	▓	▓

Seasonal Availability of Plants Listed in the Text

	Spring			Summer			Autumn			Winter		
	Early	Mid	Late	Early	Mid	Late	Early	Mid	Late	Early	Mid	Late
JUGLANS												
Green nuts			▓	▓								
Ripe nuts								▓	▓			
JUNIPERUS												
Young foliage		▓										
Berries	▓	▓	▓	▓	▓	▓	▓	▓	▓	▓	▓	▓
LACTUCA/SONCHUS												
Leaves	▓											
MAGNOLIA												
Flower buds	▓				▓	▓						
MAHONIA/BERBERIS												
Young leaves	▓											
Fruits				▓	▓	▓	▓					
MALUS												
Apples				▓	▓	▓	▓	▓	▓			
MATRICARIA												
Foliage and flowers			▓	▓	▓	▓	▓	▓				
MENTHA												
Leaves				▓	▓	▓	▓	▓				
MORUS												
Young shoots	▓	▓	▓									
Fruits				▓	▓	▓						
MUSTARDS												
Greens	▓	▓	▓	▓	▓							
Seeds				▓	▓	▓						
OENOTHERA												
Leaves	▓	▓										
Roots	▓	▓	▓	▓	▓	▓	▓	▓				
OPUNTIA												
Pads	▓	▓	▓	▓	▓	▓	▓	▓	▓	▓	▓	▓
Fruits				▓	▓	▓	▓	▓				
PICEA and other conifers												
Buds	▓	▓										
Spruce gum	▓	▓	▓	▓	▓	▓	▓	▓	▓	▓	▓	▓
PINUS												
Nuts					▓	▓						

Seasonal Availability of Plants Listed in the Text

	Spring			Summer			Autumn			Winter		
	Early	Mid	Late	Early	Mid	Late	Early	Mid	Late	Early	Mid	Late
PLANTAGO												
Young leaves	▓											
Old leaves	▓	▓	▓	▓	▓	▓	▓	▓	▓	▓	▓	▓
Seeds						▓	▓					
POLYGONUM												
Young shoots "Japanese Asparagus"	▓	▓										
Older shoots "Japanese Rhubarb"		▓	▓									
PORTULACA												
Foliage & young stems		▓	▓	▓	▓							
Large stems for pickling				▓	▓	▓	▓					
PRIMULA												
Leaves	▓	▓										
PRUNUS												
Cherries			▓	▓	▓	▓	▓	▓				
Plums						▓	▓					
RHAMNUS												
Bark	▓	▓	▓	▓	▓	▓	▓	▓	▓	▓	▓	▓
RHUS												
Fruits				▓	▓	▓	▓	▓				
RIBES												
Fruits (varies by species)				▓	▓	▓	▓	▓				
ROSA												
Leaves	▓	▓	▓	▓	▓	▓	▓	▓	▓			
Blossoms			▓	▓	▓	▓						
Hips				▓	▓	▓	▓	▓	▓	▓		
RUBUS												
Raspberries			▓	▓	▓							
Blackberries					▓	▓	▓	▓				
Thimbleberries					▓	▓						
Salmonberries					▓	▓						
RUMEX												
Dock	▓	▓	▓	▓								
Sorrel	▓	▓	▓	▓	▓	▓	▓	▓	▓			
SALIX												
Bark	▓	▓	▓	▓	▓	▓	▓	▓	▓	▓	▓	▓

Seasonal Availability of Plants Listed in the Text

	Spring			Summer			Autumn			Winter		
	Early	Mid	Late	Early	Mid	Late	Early	Mid	Late	Early	Mid	Late
SAMBUCUS												
Flowers	X	X			X							
Red, blue & black fruit			X (red fruit)	X		X (blue & black fruit)	X	X				
SEMPERVIVUM												
Leaves	X	X	X	X	X	X	X	X	X	X		
SOLIDAGO												
Flowering tops					X	X	X	X	X			
SORBUS												
Fruits					X	X	X	X	X			
STELLARIA												
Foliage in most areas	X	X	X	X	X	X	X	X	X	X	X	X
TAGETES												
Foliage	X	X	X	X								
Flowers					X	X	X	X	X			
TARAXACUM												
Greens	X											
Roots for eating	X											
Flower buds	X											
Leaf crowns	X											
Roots for coffee	X	X	X	X	X	X	X	X	X	X	X	X
Flowers	X	X	X	X	X	X						
TILIA												
Flowers				X	X	X	X					
TRIFOLIUM												
Foliage	X	X	X	X	X	X	X	X				
Blossoms				X	X	X	X	X	X			
Rhizomes	X	X	X	X	X	X	X	X	X	X	X	X
TROPAEOLUM												
Leaves			X	X	X	X	X	X				
Flowers					X	X	X					
Seed pods					X	X	X					
URTICA												
Shoots	X											
Roots	X	X	X	X	X	X	X	X	X	X	X	X
VIBURNUM												
Fruit (varies by species)				X	X	X	X	X	X	X		

Seasonal Availability of Plants Listed in the Text

	Spring			Summer			Autumn			Winter		
	Early	Mid	Late	Early	Mid	Late	Early	Mid	Late	Early	Mid	Late
VIOLA												
Leaves	▓	▓	▓	▓								
Flowers	▓	▓	▓	▓	▓	▓	▓					
YUCCA												
Fruits									▓			

GLOSSARY

abortifacient	A substance that induces miscarriage.
aerial parts	The parts of a plant that grow above the ground, as opposed to the root system.
aggregate	Said of fruits such as mulberries that are made up of many tiny fruits growing close together.
alum	An aluminum salt used as a mordant to fix color in the dyeing of cloth.
amygdalin	A toxic substance found in the pits of many tree fruits.
annual	A plant that flowers and fruits in its first growing season, then dies.
anodyne	A substance that relieves pain.
antiallergen	An herb or medicine that reduces allergic reactions.
antidepressant	An herb or medicine used in the treatment of clinical depression.
antibiotic	An herb or medicine that inhibits the growth of bacteria.
antiscorbutic	An herb or medicine that prevents or cures scurvy.
antiseptic	A substance that combats or prevents infection.
antispasmodic	An herb or medicine that eases muscle spasms and cramps.
antiviral	An herb or medicine that inhibits the growth of viruses.
aromatic	Containing volatile oils; aromatic plants have a strong odor.
astringent	A substance that causes tissues to tighten or contract.
berry hook	A stick with a hook on one end, used to pull branches within reach while harvesting wild edibles.
biennial	A plant that flowers and fruits in its second growing season, then dies.
biodiversity	The number of species found in a given area.
bud	The unopened precursor of a leaf or flower.
calyx	The leafy green "holder" to which a flower's petals are attached.
carcinogen	A substance that causes cancer.

cambium   The moist, smooth, pale inner bark found on the underside of a tree's dark, dry, rough outer bark.

cellar   To store an infused or fermented liquid in a cool, dark place to allow it to come to full flavor.

chaff   Leaves, bits of stem, husks, and other foreign material that remain in grain after threshing or harvesting.

chrome   A chromium compound used as a mordant in the dyeing of cloth.

constipation   Difficulty defecating.

contact dermatitis Skin irritation caused by contact with certain chemicals.

crown   The leaf stem portions of a young plant, usually pale green or white, found between the top of the taproot and the point where the flat, green, leafy structures begin; also called a *leaf crown.*

culm   The jointed stem of a grass or sedge, but especially used for the tall woody cane typical of bamboos.

cultivar   A plant variety produced by human intervention.

cyanide   A toxic substance found in the pits, bark, and other parts of many trees and shrubs.

cyanogenic glycocides Toxic substances chemically related to cyanide.

decoction   A concentrated infusion made by simmering herbs in water.

demulcent   An herb or medicine that soothes the skin.

diuretic   An herb or medicine that promotes urine production.

digestive   An herb or medicine that promotes digestion.

double blossom   A flower having two rows of petals, often crowded together to give the blossom a "cabbage" effect.

drupe   Small, berry-like fruits, usually hanging from the branch on long stems.

dry hives   Nausea spasms that produce no vomit.

emetic   A substance that causes vomiting.

emollient   An herb or medicine that moisturizes the skin.

exotic   Any species that is not native.

expectorant   An herb or medicine that loosens phlegm.

family	The level above genus in biological taxonomy, uniting genera that have certain characteristics in common.
feral	Said of exotic species that establish themselves in the wild after having been introduced as domesticated crops.
folk healer	One who practices folk medicine.
folk medicine	The body of medical knowledge, generally unverified by science, collected by trial and error through the generations.
foraging	The art and practice of gathering food and medicine from the wild.
gastric upset	Painful disruption of the digestive system.
gastrointestinal	Having to do with the stomach or intestines.
genus (plural: *genera*)	The second level of biological taxonomy, uniting a "household" of closely related plants, like the common surname of a human family.
heirloom	A historical or original plant variety that has since been manipulated into new varieties that have become more common.
herbalism	The study of herbs and their uses.
herbalist	One who studies herbs and their uses.
jam	A jelled preserve made from the pulp, juice, and often the seeds of a fruit or plant.
jelly	A jelled preserve made of juice or other liquid.
laxative	An herb or medicine that provokes defecation.
lobed	Said of leaves that have rounded "fingers" or projections.
monoculture	A habitat completely occupied by a single species, such as a cornfield or stand of knotweed.
mordant	Any of several chemicals used to treat cloth to make dyes colorfast.
morphology	The general shape and texture of a plant or part of a plant.
mucilaginous	Said of plants that ooze a clear, slimy substance when cut.
muslin	Common cotton cloth such as bedsheets are made of.
nonreactive	Said of plastic, glass, porcelain, stainless steel, and other materials that do not react to corrosive substances such as salt and acid.

obstetrics	The branch of medicine that deals with pregnancy and childbirth.
officinal	Any of about sixty herbs recognized by botanists as among the most useful to humanity, identified by the species name *officinalis*.
panacea	An herb or medicine thought to cure all diseases.
perennial	A plant that lives for several years.
peripheral	A plant normally used to demarcate boundaries, as in borders, hedges, or as greenery in a landscaping scheme.
persistent	Said of wild plants that remain after a habitat has been altered by human activity.
photosensitivity	A condition in which skin burns more readily than normal when exposed to sunlight and eyes may be extremely sun sensitive.
pickling salt	Pure salt without additives, used in canning.
pigweed	Plants of genera *Amaranthus, Chenopodium,* and *Portulaca,* traditionally harvested as stock feed because they form dense monocultures like sown crops, are easily harvested in bulk, and provide a range of vitamins and minerals.
potherb	Any plant cooked as a vegetable.
poultice	Chopped or mashed vegetable matter applied to the skin for medicinal reasons.
purgative	An herb or medicine that tends to cleanse, especially by inducing evacuation of the bowels.
rehydrate	To replace fluids in patients suffering from dehydration, or to restore dried foods to a semblance of their natural appearance by soaking them in water.
rhizome	A subterranean member, usually of greater diameter than the roots, by which plants propagate.
salicylates	Substances that chemically resemble aspirin, originally identified in willow but present in many other plants as well.
saponins	Chemicals that lather when rubbed and are often used as soap, but are harmful if ingested in large quantities.
self-seeding	The practice by which some annuals drop winterproof seed, thereby producing a new generation without human intervention.

serrated	Sawtoothed.
single blossom	A flower having just one row of petals.
species	The first and most precise level of biological taxonomy; the second word in a plant's botanical name.
spoon test	The practice of dipping a cold spoon into boiling preserves, cooling the liquid, and allowing it to drip off, thereby giving the cook an indication of how firmly the product will jell when cool.
stomachic	An herb or medicine that eases stomach problems such as indigestion and heartburn.
symbiotic	Said of two organisms that live together without harming one another, and sometimes with mutual benefit.
systemic	Said of pesticides designed to be taken up by a plant's roots, to become part of the plant itself.
tannin	An astringent used in tanning, dyeing, and winemaking, present in many plants, and toxic in large quantities.
taproot	A single thick, vertical root, such as dandelions have.
taxonomist	A scientist who assigns organisms their place in the biological taxonomy.
taxonomy	The classification system by which all life forms are assigned a kingdom, phylum, class, order, family, genus, and species.
thresh	To knock grain or seeds from their stems or husks.
thujone	An aromatic toxin common in cedar trees and other fragrant plants.
tincture	Alcohol in which herbs have been infused.
tonic	Said of certain herbs believed to purify the blood.
topical	Refers to the outside of the body, particularly the skin.
tuber	A swelling at the end of a root, by which a plant propagates.
umbel	An umbrella-like spray of blossoms, such as those of elder.
urogenital	Having to do with the urinary tract or reproductive system.
urticaria	A rash or swelling caused by friction or contact with an irritating chemical.

varicose	Said of swollen veins visible under the skin.
variegated	Flecked or streaked with many colors in no specific pattern.
vermifuge	An herb or medicine that causes parasites to be expelled from the digestive tract.
winnow	To remove chaff from grain or other harvested material.

Angier, Bradford. *Field Guide to Medicinal Wild Plants*. Harrisburg, Pa.: Stackpole Books, 1978.

Barash, Cathy Wilkinson. *Edible Flowers from Garden to Palate*. Golden, Colo.: Fulcrum Publishers, 1993.

Bremness, Lesley. *Herbs*. London: Dorling Kindersley Ltd, 1994.

Brill, Steve, and Evelyn Dean. *Identifying and Harvesting Edible and Medicinal Plants in Wild (And Not So Wild) Places*. New York: Hearst Books, 1994.

Buchanan, Rita. *A Weaver's Garden*. Loveland, Colo.: Interweave Press, 1987.

Byler, Emma. *Plain and Happy Living*. Cleveland: Goosefoot Acres Press, 1991.

Castle, Coralie. *Cooking from the Gourmet's Garden: Edible Ornamentals, Herbs, and Flowers*. Santa Rosa, Calif.: Cole Group, 1994.

Chevallier, Andrew. *The Encyclopedia of Medicinal Plants*. Montréal: The Reader's Digest Association (Canada) Ltd, 1996

Coffey, Timothy. *The History and Folklore of North American Wildflowers*. New York: Facts on File, 1993.

Costenbader, Carol W. *The Big Book of Preserving the Harvest*. Pownal, Vt.: Storey Communications, 1997.

Creasy, Rosalind. *The Complete Book of Edible Landscaping*. San Francisco: Sierra Club Books, 1982.

Duke, James A. *The Green Pharmacy*. Emmaus, Pa.: Rodale Press, 1997.

Farrar, John Laird. *Trees of the Northern United States and Canada*. Ames: Iowa State University Press, 1995.

Freitus, Joe. *Wild Preserves*. Washington, D.C.: Stone Wall Press, 1977.

Gail, Peter. *The Dandelion Celebration*. Cleveland: Goosefoot Acres Press, 1994.

———. *The Delightfully Delicious Daylily*. Cleveland: Goosefoot Acres Press, 1995.

Garret, Blanche Pownall. *Canadian Country Preserves and Wines*. Toronto: James Lewis & Samuel, Publishers, 1974.

Gibbons, Euell. *Stalking the Healthful Herbs*. New York: D. McKay Company, 1966.

———. *Stalking the Wild Asparagus*. New York: D. McKay Company, 1962.

George, Jean Craighead. *Acorn Pancakes, Dandelion Salad, and 38 Other Wild Recipes*. New York: Harper Collins, 1995.

Krause, Steven A. *Wine from the Wilds*. Harrisburg, Pa.: Stackpole Books, 1982.

Lathrop-Smit, Hermine. *Natural Dyes*. Toronto: James Lorimer & Company, Publishers, 1978.

Lesem, Jeanne. *Preserving in Today's Kitchen*. New York: Henry Holt, 1997.

Levinson, Leonard Louis. *The Complete Book of Pickles and Relishes*. New York: Hawthorn Books, 1965.

Lyle, Katie Letcher. *The Wild Berry Book*. Minocqua, Wis.: North Word Press, 1994.

McGrath, Judy Waldner. *Dyes from Lichens and Plants*. Toronto: Van Nostrand Reinhold Ltd, 1977.

McIntyre, Anne. *The Medicinal Garden*. New York: Henry Holt, 1997.

Moore, Michael. *Medicinal Plants of the Pacific West*. Santa Fe: Red Crane, 1993.

Morse, Kitty. *Edible Flowers: A Kitchen Companion*. Berkeley, Calif.: Ten Speed Press, 1995.

Murray, Michael T. *The Healing Power of Herbs*. Rocklin, Calif.: Prima Publishing, 1995.

Onstad, Dianne. *Whole Foods Companion*. White River Junction, Vt.: Chelsea Green Publishing Company, 1996.

Peterson, Lee. *A Field Guide to Edible Wild Plants of Eastern and Central North America*. Boston: Houghton Mifflin, 1977.

Phillips, Roger, and Martyn Rix. *The Random House Book of Shrubs*. New York: Random House, 1989.

Robertson, Seonaid. *Dyes from Plants*. Toronto: Van Nostrand Reinhold Ltd, 1973.

Stewart, Hilary. *Wild Teas, Coffees and Cordials*. Vancouver: Douglas & McIntyre, 1981.

Szczawinski, Adam F., and Nancy J. Turner. *Common Poisonous Plants and Mushrooms of North America*. Portland, Oreg.: Timber Press, 1991.

————. *Edible Garden Weeds of Canada*. Ottawa: National Museums of Canada, 1978.

————. *Edible Wild Fruits and Nuts of Canada*. Ottawa: National Museums of Canada, 1979.

————. *Wild Coffee and Tea Substitutes of Canada*. Ottawa: National Museums of Canada, 1978.

————. *Wild Green Vegetables of Canada*. Ottawa: National Museums of Canada, 1980.

Vargas, Pattie, and Rich Gulling. *Country Wines*. Pownal, Vt.: Storey Communications, 1992.

Wigginton, Eliot, editor. *Foxfire* (series). Garden City, N.Y.: Anchor. Volumes 2 (1973) and 3 (1975) contain the most foraging information. Volume 3 contains the index for Volumes 1–3, inclusive.

Willard, Terry. *Edible and Medicinal Plants of the Rocky Mountains and Neighbouring Territories*. Calgary: Wild Rose College, 1992.

INDEX

CHELSEA GREEN

Sustainable living has many facets. Chelsea Green's celebration of the sustainable arts has led us to publish trend-setting books about organic gardening, solar electricity and renewable energy, innovative building techniques, regenerative forestry, local and bioregional democracy, and whole foods. The company's published works, while intensely practical, are also entertaining and inspirational, demonstrating that an ecological approach to life is consistent with producing beautiful, eloquent, and useful books, videos, and audio cassettes.

For more information about Chelsea Green, or to request a free catalog, call toll-free (800) 639-4099, or write to us at P.O. Box 428, White River Junction, Vermont 05001. Visit our Web site at www.chelseagreen.com.

Chelsea Green's titles include:

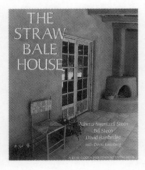

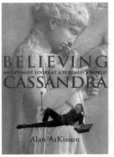

The Straw Bale House
The New Independent Home
Independent Builder:
   Designing & Building a
   House Your Own Way
The Rammed Earth House
The Passive Solar House
The Sauna
Wind Power for Home &
   Business
Wind Energy Basics
The Solar Living Sourcebook
A Shelter Sketchbook
Mortgage-Free!
Hammer. Nail. Wood.
Stone Circles
Toil: Building Yourself
The Bread Builders

Four-Season Harvest
The Apple Grower
The Flower Farmer
Passport to Gardening:
   A Sourcebook for the
   21st-Century
The New Organic Grower
Four-Season Harvest
Solar Gardening
Sharing the Harvest
Straight-Ahead Organic
The Contrary Farmer
The Contrary Farmer's
   Invitation to Gardening
Whole Foods Companion
Simple Food for the Good Life
Keeping Food Fresh
Good Spirits

Believing Cassandra
Gaviotas: A Village to Reinvent
   the World
Who Owns the Sun?
Global Spin: The Corporate
   Assault on Environmentalism
Hemp Horizons
Beyond the Limits
The Man Who Planted Trees
The Northern Forest
Loving and Leaving the
   Good Life
Scott Nearing: The Making of a
   Homesteader
Simple Food for the Good Life
Seeing Nature
Genetic Engineering, Food, and
   Our Environment